The Campus History Series

Arizona State University

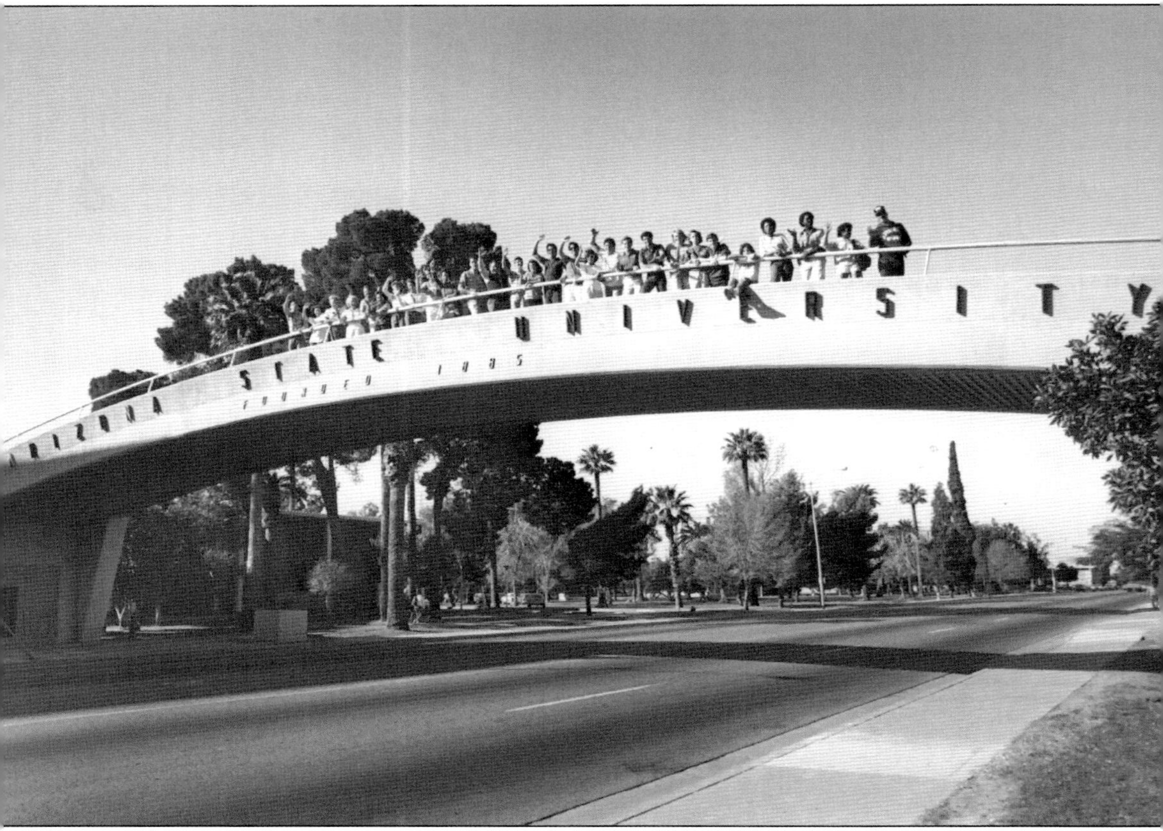

The University Drive Bridge is one of the many iconic structures on campus. It functions as a pedestrian overpass, also concealing lines for power, telecommunication, steam, and water. (Courtesy of University Archives, Arizona State University Libraries.)

On the Cover: The first library, a shelf with a dictionary and a globe in the Arizona Territorial Normal School, grew to a 700-volume library on the second floor of Old Main, where these students are studying in 1907. (Courtesy of University Archives, Arizona State University Libraries.)

Cover Background: Aesthetically located between two buttes, Sun Devil Stadium was built in 1958 with 30,000 seats. The first season's end zone left the last letter blank (AS_) until the results came in on a statewide ballot measure to change the name from "College" to "University." (Courtesy of Neil Miller.)

The Campus History Series

ARIZONA STATE UNIVERSITY

STEPHANIE R. DELUSÉ, PHD, AND DENISE E. BATES, PHD

ARCADIA
PUBLISHING

ISBN 978-0-7385-9545-0

Published by Arcadia Publishing
Charleston, South Carolina

Printed in the United States of America

Library of Congress Catalog Card Number: 2012941060

For all general information, please contact Arcadia Publishing:
Telephone 843-853-2070
Fax 843-853-0044
E-mail sales@arcadiapublishing.com
For customer service and orders:
Toll-Free 1-888-313-2665

Visit us on the Internet at www.arcadiapublishing.com

To all those who made ASU's past and future possible, we thank you and are humbled by your ingenuity and service.

Contents

Acknowledgments		6
Introduction		7
1.	A School of Many Names	9
2.	Academic Glimpses	37
3.	Moments in Athletics	67
4	Snapshots of Student Life	91
5.	Behind the Scenes	115

ACKNOWLEDGMENTS

This project would not have been possible without the support of countless people who shared photographs, offered us guidance, or extended a level of hospitality that we will never forget. Since space precludes thanking everyone for their support, please check the Web site at www.asuhistory.com for an extended list of acknowledgments as well as a bibliography. Naturally, however, some people are acknowledged alongside the photographs they contributed. Thus, here, we mention very few names and ask the understanding of those who we could not mention.

We thank Susan Drescher-Mulzet and Mark Mulzet for their generosity. We also appreciate Kevin Bates and Stanley Parkinson for all manner of assistance, book-related and not. And we thank our families and friends for their support.

We extend gratitude to Robert Spindler, Neil Millican, Kathy Krzys, Christine Marin, and Joyce Martin of the University Archives, Arizona State University Libraries (UAASUL). We are also thankful for photographs from special collections that are indicated in the text, the most common of which are Charles R. Conley (CC, UAASUL) and Jack A. Thompson (JT, UAASUL).

Finally, we give heartfelt thanks to Joshua Roffler and Dan Thompson of the Tempe History Museum (THM); Mark Jacobs, Peggy Nelson, and Ted Humphrey at Barrett, the Honors College; Virgil Renzulli of ASU Public Affairs; Christine Kajikawa Wilkinson of the ASU Alumni Association; Len Gordon and Richard Jacob of the Emeritus College; Linda Van Scoy and Dave Scheatzle of the ASU Retirees Association; the Murphy's Girls; Jason Manning and Kim Moore at the *State Press*; Joe Nucci of the Tempe Historic Preservation Office; Jeff Kidda and Nikki Kimbel at *Arizona Highways*, Wendi Goen of the Arizona State Archives, Nate Meyers at the Chandler Museum, and Ashley Smith of the Arizona Historical Society. Your assistance on this project was invaluable.

INTRODUCTION

There are two motivations that inspired this book: the personal and the academic. One of us has spent her adult life at this institution, discovering gems of people and pockets of research that can only serve to humble and inspire. The other came to ASU five years ago as a historian with a strong interest in understanding the institution's unique and varied past. Together, we share an appreciation for the history that surrounds us as we walk by John S. Armstrong Hall, along Cady Mall, or by any of the malls and buildings named for key people or important events from the past. We also jointly acknowledge the history that is being made as we pass faculty who may have just made a great stride in curing a dreaded disease or in engineering sustainability, a graduate student who is developing a program to solve a social problem, an undergraduate who could be our future president, or staff members who support and innovate to make all the rest of it possible. It is easy to walk along and just see throngs of people, but each one has a reason, a goal, a dream . . . something that coming to ASU helps make possible. Our remembering that makes every day on campus even more exciting.

We dug into books, archives, dusty photograph albums, and people's memories. In some ways, we feel that we only scratched the surface, yet we learned so much about the deep, broad, and more recent history that still needs to be written, as there is much to revise and update since *The Arizona State University Story*, by Ernest J. Hopkins and Alfred Thomas Jr., was published in 1960. We are grateful to them and authors like them, including Dean Smith, Nina Murphy, and Bob Eger, who chronicled various parts of the university's history. In the end, we learned more than can fit in this book, which means we had to make some tough decisions. We lament the fabulous events, people, and programs that we could not include. Many stressful and sad moments occurred as we had to make deeper and deeper cuts to our original plans, knowing we were leaving out someone else's contribution or legacy.

Yet, by far, this was a joyful and fascinating process that introduced us to many people who we were grateful and honored to meet. Yes, we may write more about ASU one day. Indeed, we hope you will contact us with your photographs and stories for potential future endeavors. A positive side effect of our reaching out to the community is how many people or campus units were reminded to dig through memories and files for history and write it down before time and circumstances make that impossible.

While other types of papers or books could be written about Arizona State University, we chose to start with this photographic narrative to help make the history more accessible and, importantly, to put some faces to a few of the names that helped make ASU what it is today.

And what it is today is pretty amazing. From one faculty member, it has grown to over 2,800 faculty and 9,300 staff, from 33 students to over 72,000, and from 20 acres to over 600 in Tempe, plus the West campus (278 acres), Downtown Phoenix campus (20 acres), and Polytechnic campus (594 acres), not to mention other facilities and the cyberspace that ASU Online occupies, growing from the early days of correspondence courses and, later, the College of Extended Education. ASU also has top-flight numbers in research expenditures, economic impact, and community impact from over 1,000 outreach opportunities.

Long before ASU's 16th president, Michael M. Crow, arrived to highlight the eight design aspirations he espouses—promoting that the university leverage its place, transform society, value entrepreneurship, conduct use-inspired research, enable student success, fuse intellectual disciplines, be socially embedded, and engage globally—the Arizona Territorial Normal School, named for the standard or "normal" curriculum in its noble endeavor of training teachers, already demonstrated many of these attributes. Founder John S. Armstrong, an educator, businessman, and legislator, leveraged place by establishing an institution of higher learning in the isolated but growing town of Tempe, founded by Charles Trumbull Hayden. This involved building the mutually beneficial relationships within the community that exemplify the social embeddedness that ASU still values at the local and now global level. Once established, the school's first focus was enabling student success, which it effectively did class after class. Those early commitments to education remain ASU's focus on access and excellence. Sometimes, that balance is challenging to manage, but it does well in embracing the educational needs of the entire community while continually attracting National Merit Scholars in the triple digits.

The efforts to transform society went beyond schooling educators who, in turn, educated others in the community. From early on and over the years, the school-turned-college-turned-university personified value entrepreneurship and conducting use-inspired research, responsive to the community's needs at the same time that it helped set the agendas. Whether it was adding new programs in agriculture or artists performing for the public, the institution flexed to partner with the citizens, offering and receiving support, ideas, and facilities. All of this continued to be mutually beneficial. The institution grew, as did individual students and citizens in professional spheres. This enhanced the economic situation of people and areas first in Tempe and then in the valley and state. Now ASU affects the nation and the globe.

Indeed, this institution went from being an underdog in a few ways to major player in many, many ways. ASU has been ranked fourth (of 70 schools) by *US News and World Report* as one to watch, and it is often held out as an example of an institution that does not just survive but innovates when many others are struggling. Not that ASU has not struggled (this book reminds us of some early struggles), and challenges remain in meeting growth while maintaining morale and quality, especially in times when some traditional forms of support have waned. But if any institution can meet the challenges before us, whether locally or globally, it is this one.

To undertake the task of capturing a university's history in 229 photographs and captions is, to state the obvious, improbable. Here, we offer primarily pre-1980 glimpses of ASU to show how the past touched the future, demonstrating how early subjects became vibrant, world-class programs, and how a normal school became a research university of international status. We can imagine an offering that expands on the fine leadership of later presidents like John Schwada, Russell Nelson, and Lattie Coor Jr., not to mention that of President Crow, who boldly leads ASU toward a vision of the "New American University."

One

A School of Many Names

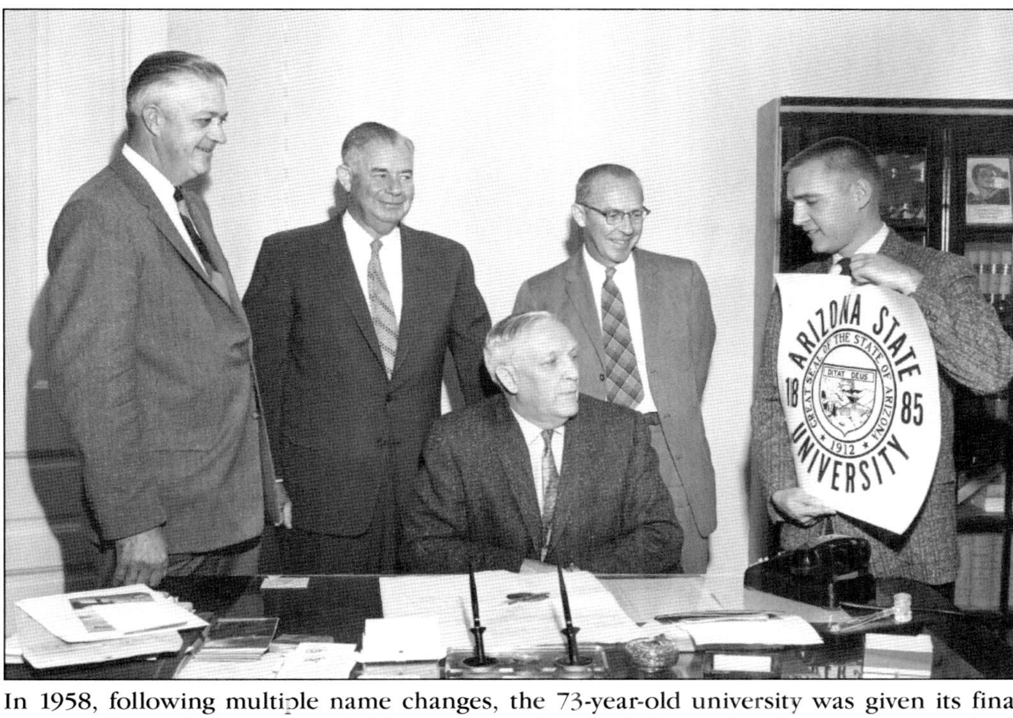

In 1958, following multiple name changes, the 73-year-old university was given its final name and unveiled its new seal. There was much to look forward to; however, it was also a time for reflection. Although the school bore a new name, its identity remained connected to its rich history dating back to the Arizona Territory. (Courtesy of THM.)

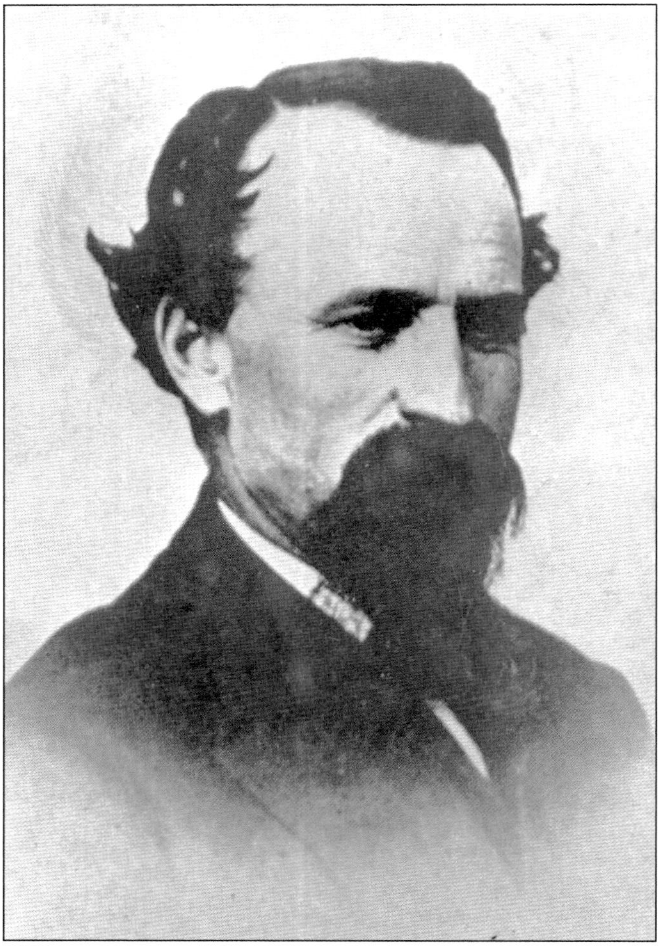

This story begins in 1869, when Anson P.K. Safford arrived in Arizona Territory by stagecoach with a box of textbooks and a desire to take the reigns as the third territorial governor. He crusaded to bring public education to the desert frontier by building schools and bringing in teachers. By 1877, a total of 28 elementary schools had been established. As the territory's population grew, the demand for teachers reached a critical point. "Let Arizona train its own teachers!" demanded local newspapers. Safford's dream was in jeopardy, and it took the efforts of Charles Trumbull Hayden and John Samuel Armstrong to put things back on course. Hayden, a former county judge and businessman, founded Hayden's Ferry (later known as Tempe) in 1872 at the base of a butte, where he operated a cable ferry to cross the Salt River. (Left, courtesy of UAASUL; below, THM.)

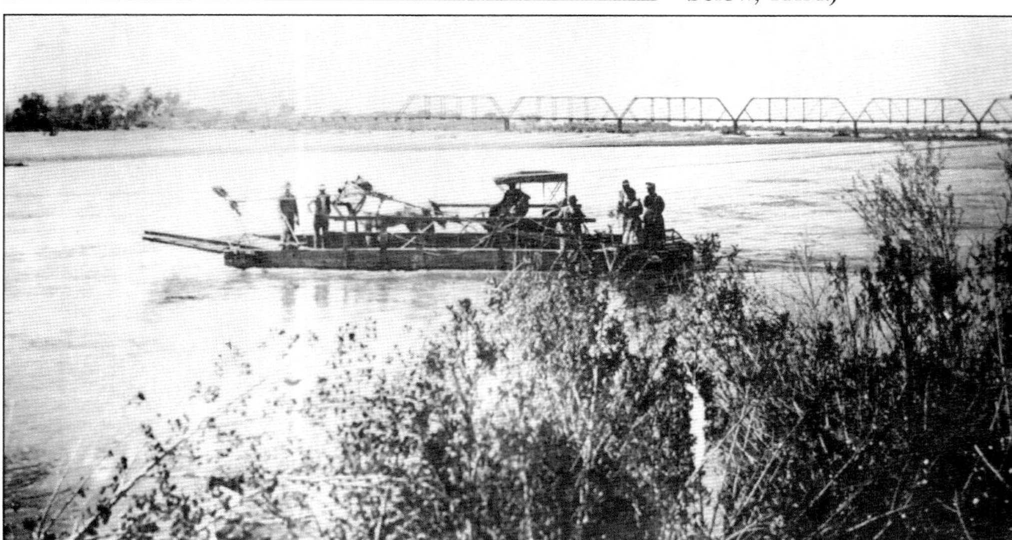

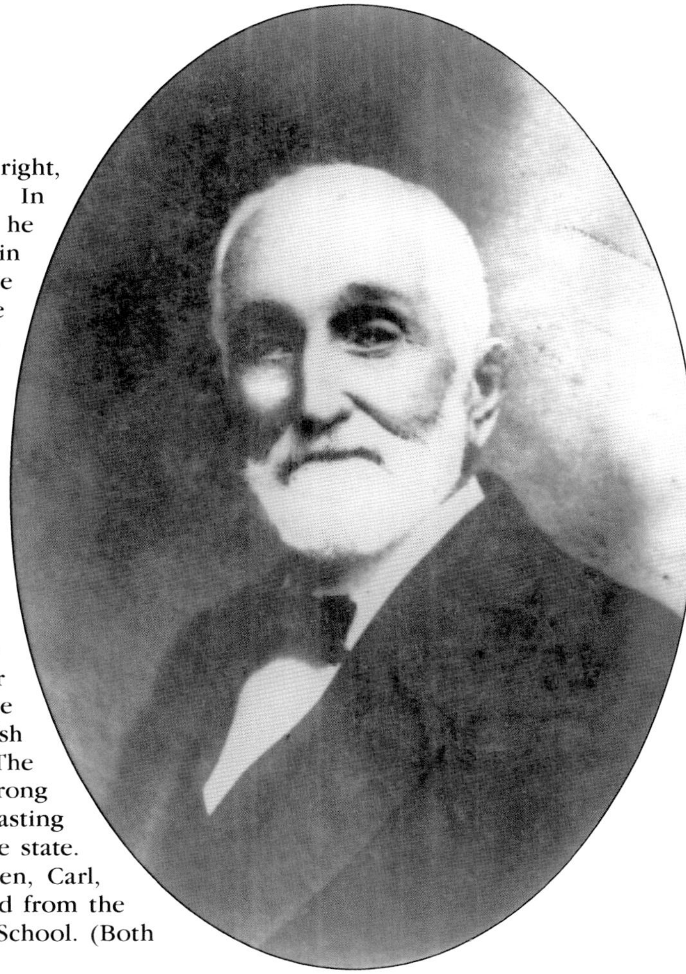

Charles Trumbull Hayden, right, was an ambitious man. In addition to the cable ferry, he also opened a store and grain mill. The main road from the ferry crossing inland became Mill Street, as pictured below in 1900, and it was not long before others joined Hayden in making Tempe their home. In 1882, a 25-year-old John Samuel Armstrong and his wife, Sarah, purchased an adobe house and settled in the town to raise their growing family. Both former teachers, the Armstrongs were aware of the territory-wide teacher shortage and identified Tempe as an ideal place to establish a teacher-training school. The contributions that Armstrong would go on to make had a lasting impact on the people of the state. Even Hayden's three children, Carl, Sallie, and Mapes, graduated from the Arizona Territorial Normal School. (Both courtesy of THM.)

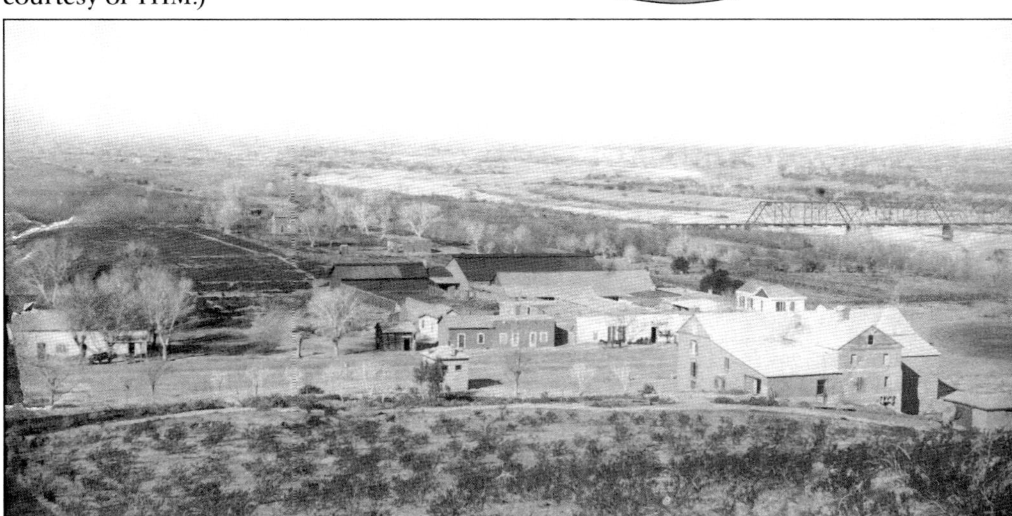

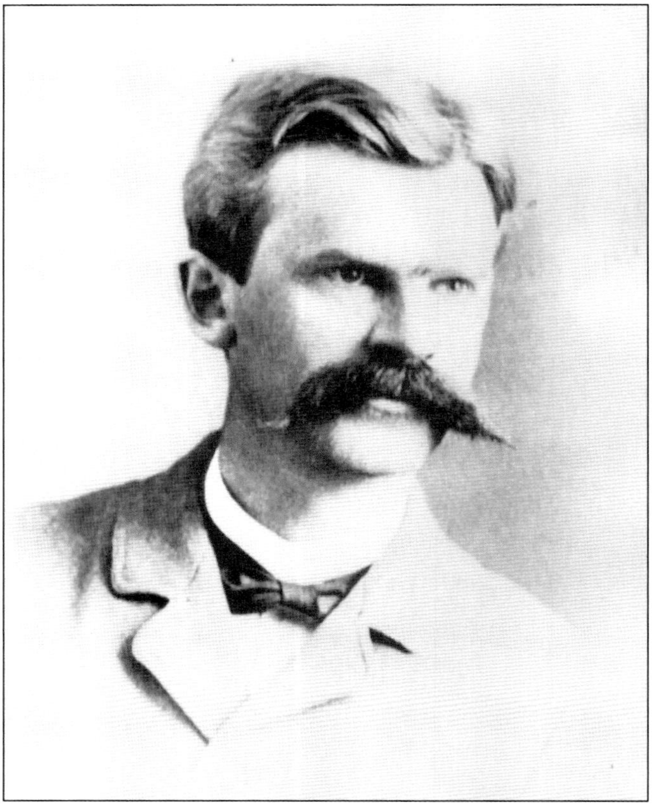

Elected to the 13th Territorial Assembly in 1885, John Samuel Armstrong displayed political savvy when he pushed for a teacher-training school in Tempe. Despite being the youngest member of the assembly, he commanded respect and was made chairman of the House Committee on Education. Among other achievements for the area, he successfully maneuvered the Territorial Normal School Bill through the legislature just a few hours before the creation of the university in Tucson. (Courtesy of John Samuel Armstrong III.)

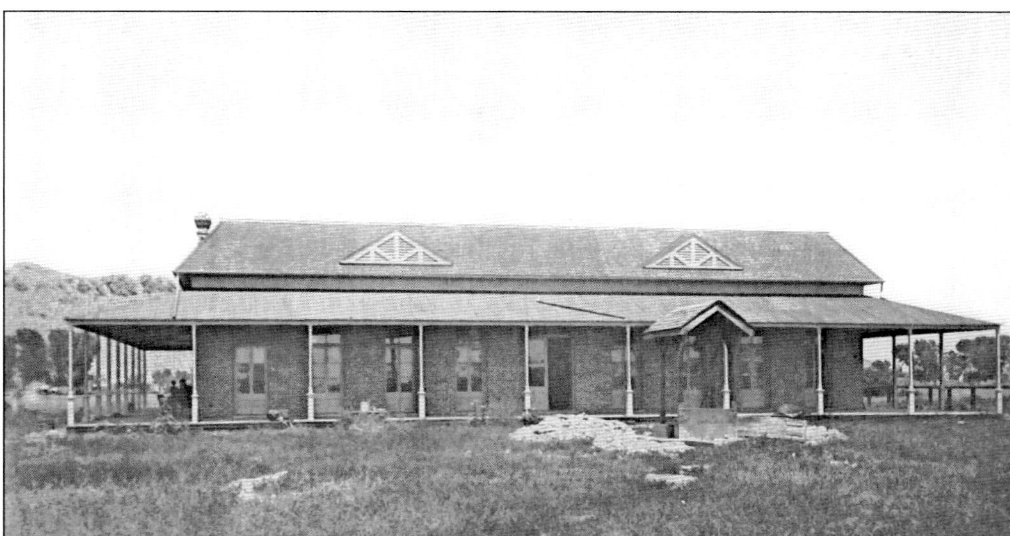

While Armstrong worked to secure the legislation, the people of Tempe rallied to find a location. George Wilson, the town butcher, offered five acres of pastureland for $500 plus a 15-acre endowment for the school site. On February 8, 1886, the modest four-classroom brick school, equipped with a well and outhouses, welcomed its first students. Wilson was the groundskeeper until his death in 1916. (Courtesy of THM.)

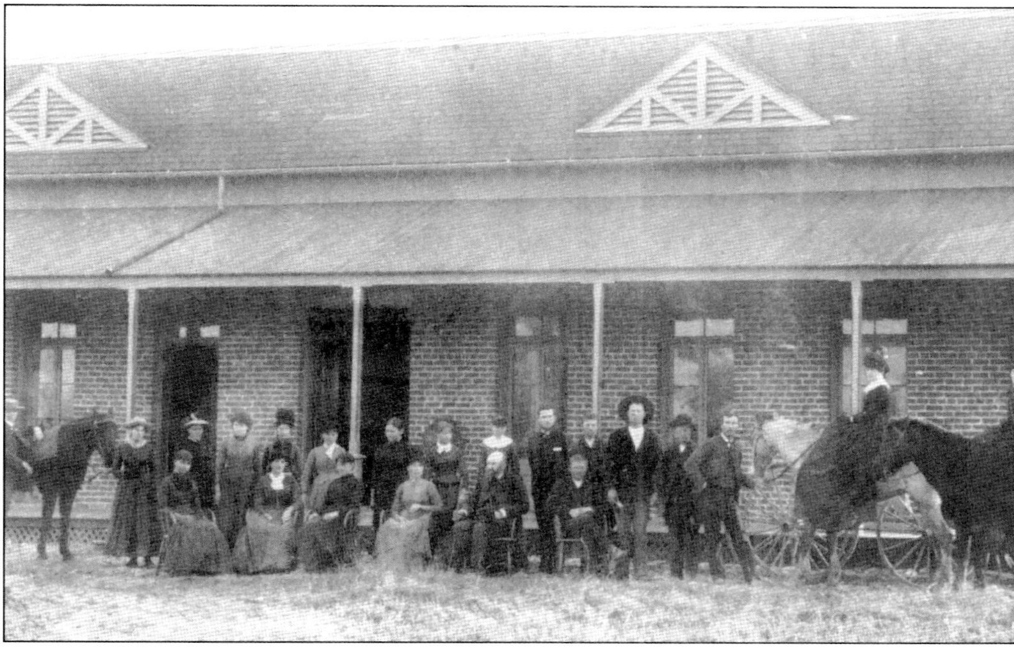

Schoolmaster Hiram Bradford Farmer, seated at center with his students in 1886, was both principal and instructor to the first 33 students. With a monthly salary of $230, Farmer established a two-year curriculum to train teachers and prepare them for examinations. His home served as the first unofficial dormitory at $20 a month. Students had their own horses, which they watched graze while sitting in class. (Courtesy of THM.)

From the beginning, many normal school students displayed a loyalty to the institution that would prevail through their lifetimes. Garfield Goodwin (second step), an alumnus who played on the first informally organized football team in 1896, served on the board of education, as did his wife, and he became president of the alumni association from 1932 to 1933. Goodwin's son Kemper was an architect who designed many of the campus buildings. (Courtesy of THM.)

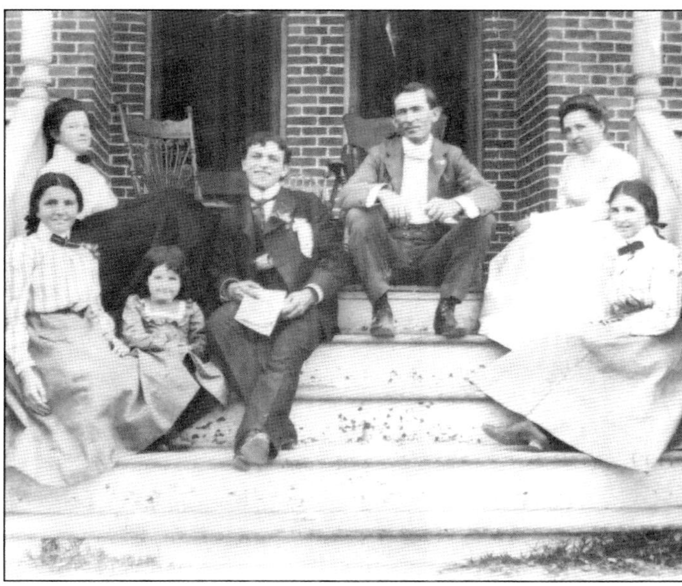

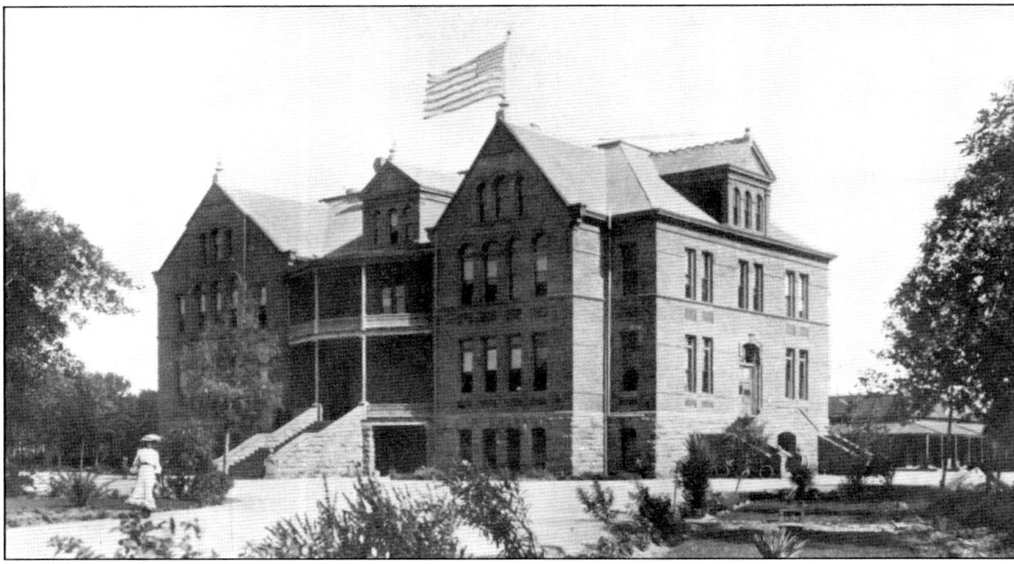

Remarkable things were achieved in the first several years of the normal school's existence. A series of principals took the reins following Hiram Farmer, who left after 18 months, helping the school grow its enrollment, diversify offerings, and improve the school's physical appearance. One of the most notable accomplishments was the completion of the Main Building, later called Old Main, in 1898. Principal Edgar Storment drew out the original sketches in 1893 and even took a pay cut to help fund the construction. Old Main was built 60 feet to the north of the original school building, as seen in these images of the facade and rear. Rocks were used from Tempe Butte for part of the three-story structure at a cost of $44,071.34. It was the largest building in the valley for decades and the first in Tempe to be wired for electrical lighting. (Both courtesy of UAASUL.)

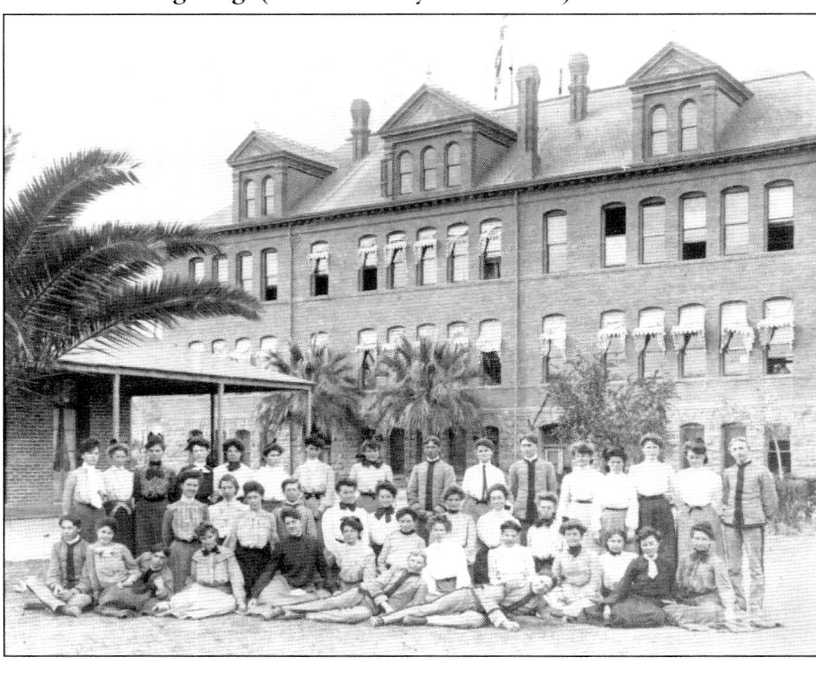

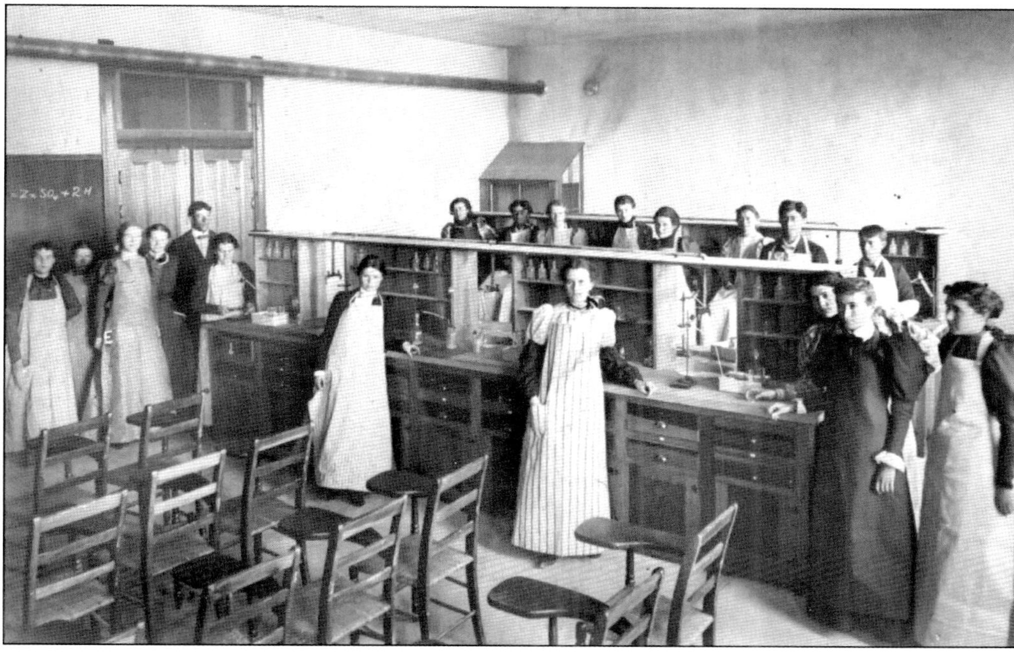

Old Main was completed during James McNaughton's tenure as principal (1895–1899), during which time enrollment reached 101, plus 34 training school pupils. Under his administration, the curriculum was extended to three years and the number of faculty grew from four to seven, including Frederick M. Irish in 1896, who, among many other roles he took on, developed a more rigorous program in the sciences. Pictured above is Irish's chemistry class inside a lab in Old Main. Old Main also contained a library (as seen on the cover) and rooms dedicated to geography, music, and drawing. There was an auditorium on the upper floor, pictured below. Old Main was a symbol of progress, and following its completion, alumni lobbied to increase admissions standards to the growing institution. (Both courtesy of UAASUL.)

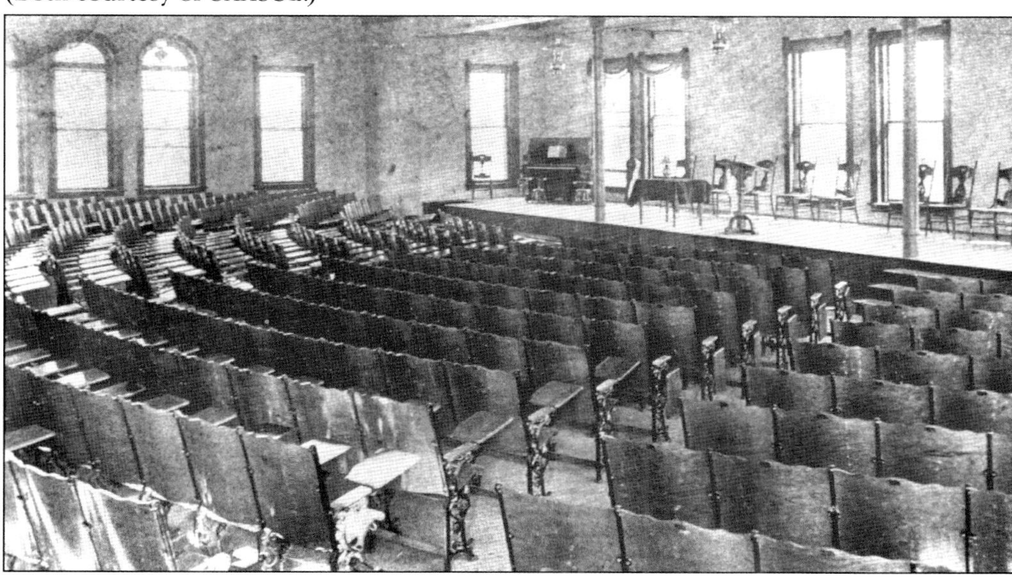

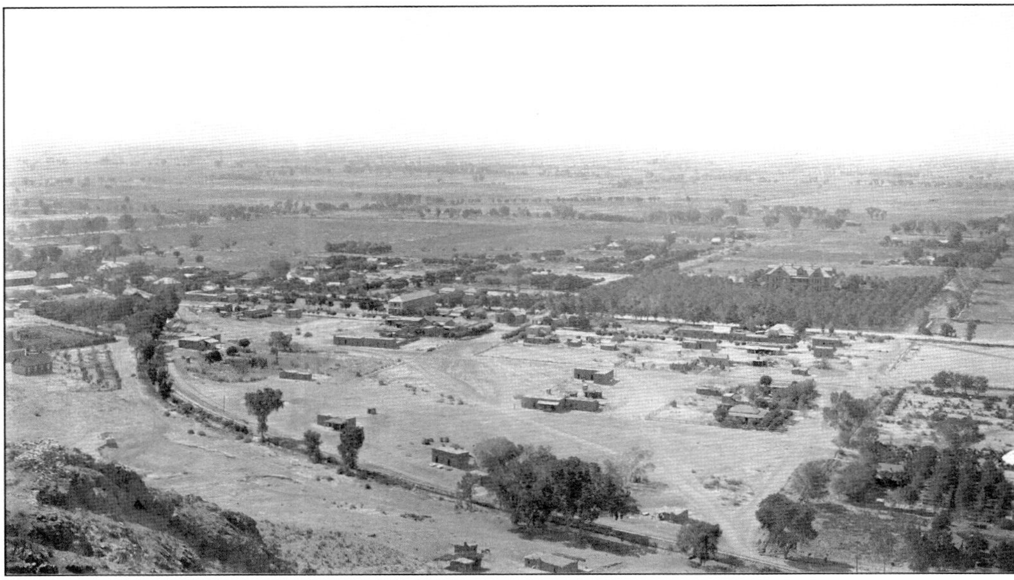

Old Main, right of center in the photograph above, became a landmark that neighbored the San Pablo Barrio, located at the foot of Tempe Butte, from which this photograph was taken in 1900. Indian and Mexican pioneers, integral to the development of Tempe, first settled San Pablo. St. Mary's Catholic Church, located on College Avenue and University Drive, adjacent to the campus's main entrance, still serves as a reminder of the barrio that eventually disappeared due to campus and city expansion. Below, the first adobe church, the original Our Lady of Mount Carmel, was built in 1880 on the site of the later Sun Devil Stadium. St. Mary's was built in 1903 to accommodate the growing parish and needs of Catholic normal school students and employees. (Above, courtesy of THM; below, Newman Center.)

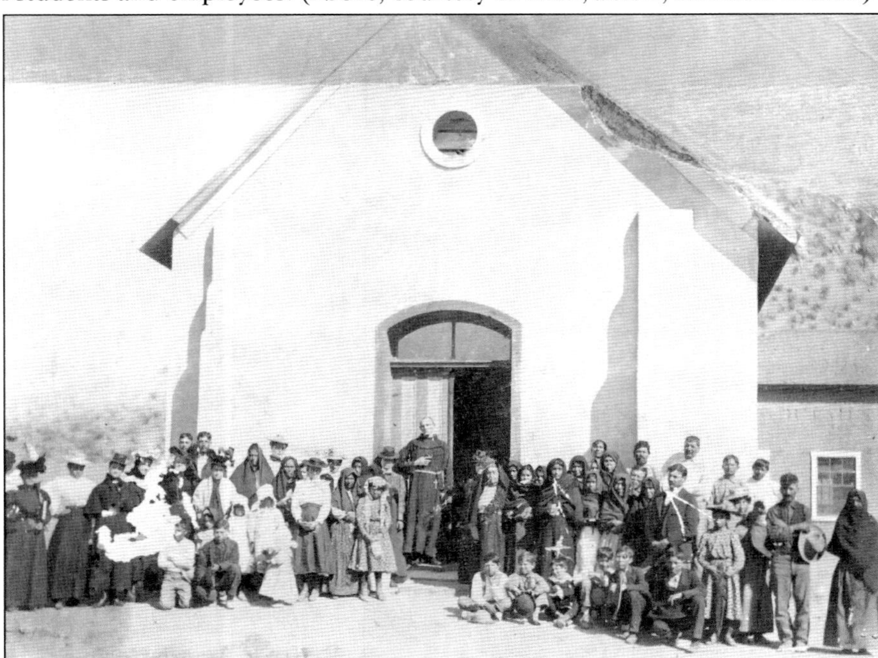

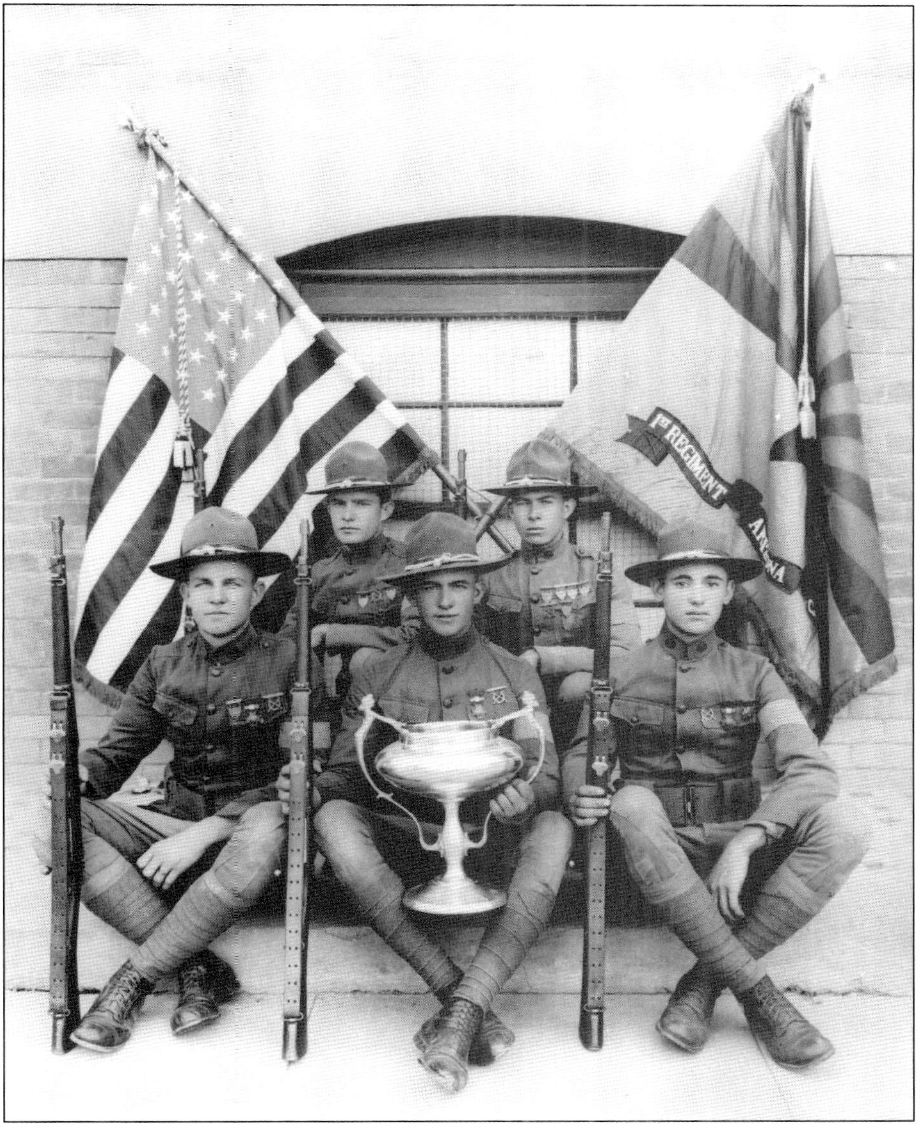

The presence of tight lines of neatly dressed young men participating in military drills was a common sight at the normal school in the 1890s. James McClintock, a member of the first graduating class and first president of the alumni association, was instrumental in establishing the Normal School Cadet Company. Prior to enlisting in Roosevelt's Rough Rider Regiment and serving in the Spanish–American War, McClintock arranged for a supply of rifles from Fort Whipple for the cadets. Frederick Irish was in charge of these drills to teach young men how to be a part of a company of soldiers. In 1901, the normal school cadets served as bodyguards to President McKinley during his Phoenix visit. Soon afterward, they became part of the National Guard and went on to march in parades and win awards in competitive field exercises, as seen in this 1920 photograph. Irish sent 106 of his cadets into the armed forces. By 1926, military drills had come to an end, only to be reinstated with the inauguration of the Reserve Officers' Training Corps (ROTC) in the 1940s. (Courtesy of John Barnard.)

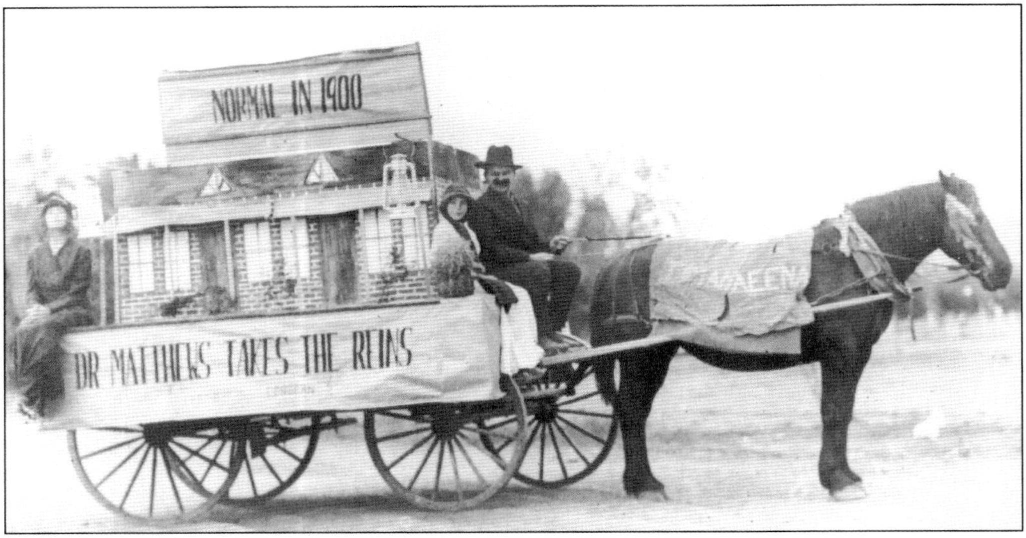

In 1900, the normal school ushered in new leadership. As the seventh principal in 14 years, Arthur John Matthews brought much needed stability and national attention to an institution that he went on to shape for the next 30 years. He was not only the administrative leader and the first to be called president, but he also served as registrar, business manager, and instructor of law, economics, and mathematics. (Courtesy of UAASUL.)

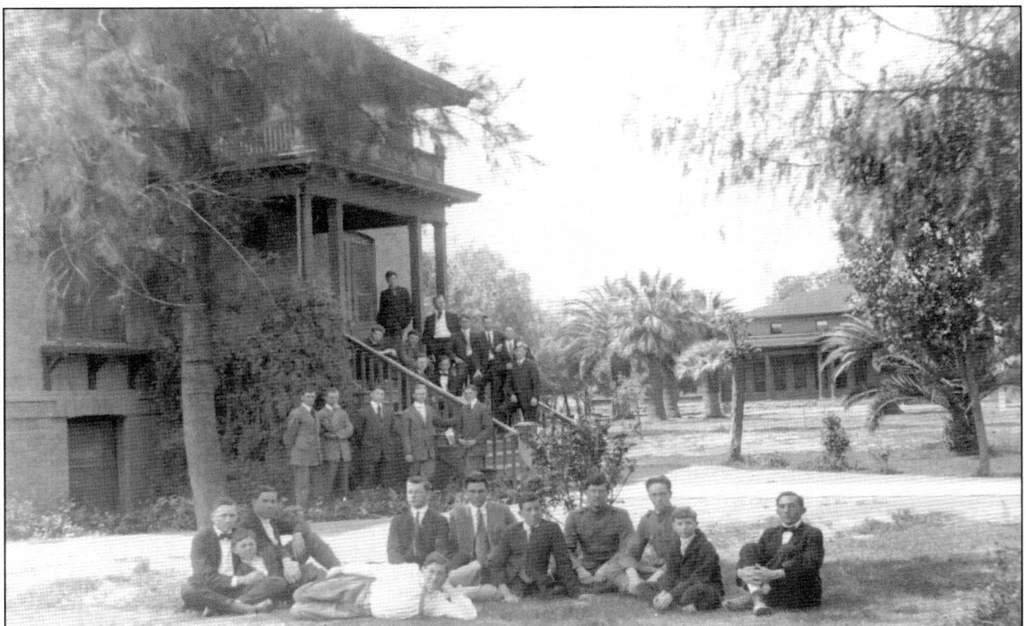

One of the first developments of the Matthews administration was Alpha Hall in 1902. Formerly a boarding club founded in 1898, it was the first campus dormitory that housed 25 women until East Hall was built the following year. This 1914 photograph shows residents of Alpha Hall after it became a male dormitory. On-campus dormitories were met with contention by many Tempe residents who took in paying student borders. (Courtesy of UAASUL.)

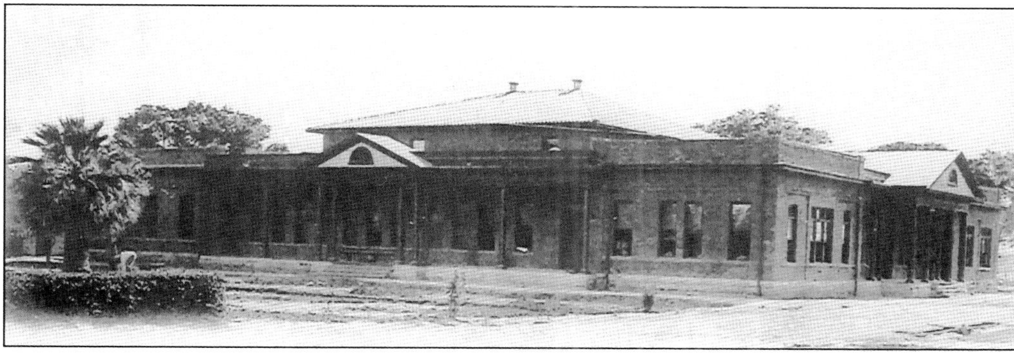

As an institution dedicated to training teachers, the normal school began operating a training program in 1895 that had an arrangement with the Tempe Grammar School, allowing student-teachers to "practice teach" under close observation of "critic teachers." In 1906, Matthews expanded the program by constructing the R.H.H. Blome Training School, pictured above in the location of the original normal school building, which was demolished. The new building contained 10 classrooms, an assembly room, and two manual training rooms. Dr. R.H.H. Blome, seen below instructing a mathematics class, was a German-born professor with a background in psychology and pedagogy who served as the training school's director from 1900 to 1909. Significantly, the school's course offerings had grown to 90 by 1913, with 18 academic departments teaching in a diverse array of disciplines. (Above, courtesy of Tempe Historic Preservation Office; below, UAASUL.)

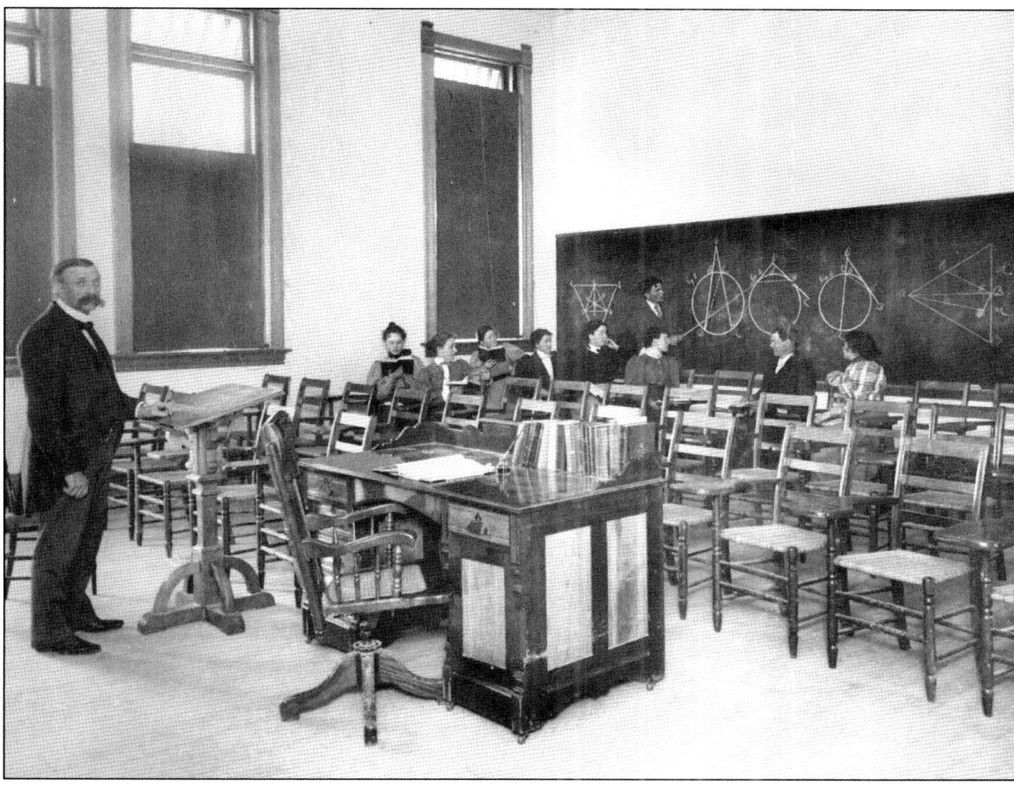

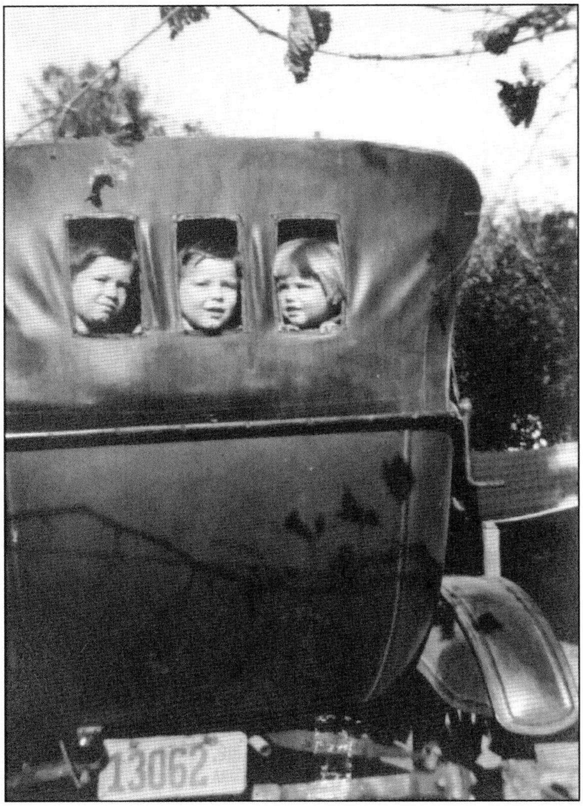

In 1911, Ira D. Payne became the new director of the training school, where he remained for another 40 years, training teachers and helping secure them positions. In 1929, the Blome Training School was razed and the Payne Training School was constructed. The presence of children on campus was commonplace; the image at left captures young students at the end of their school day. Other training schools operated off campus, such as the Rural and the Eighth Street Training Schools. The Eighth Street Training School, pictured below, gained national attention when a parent's 1925 lawsuit challenged its operation as a segregated Mexican school. Although the parent won the right to enroll his children elsewhere, the district continued running the school under the "separate but equal" doctrine until its closure in 1945. (Left, courtesy of Ida Woolf O'Connor, UAASUL; below, UAASUL.)

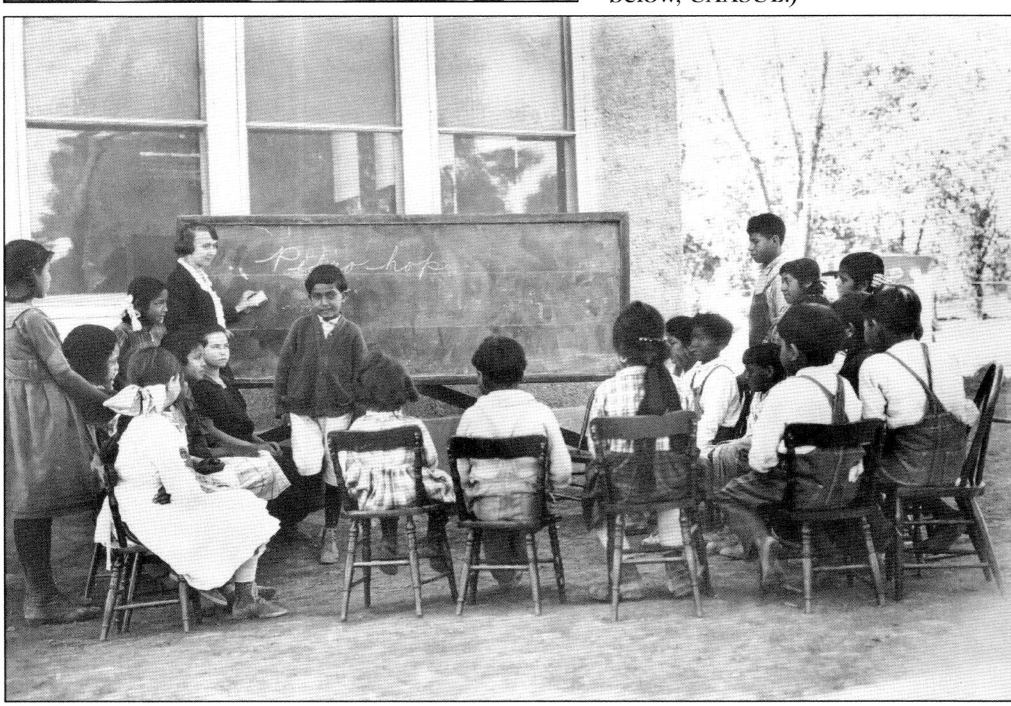

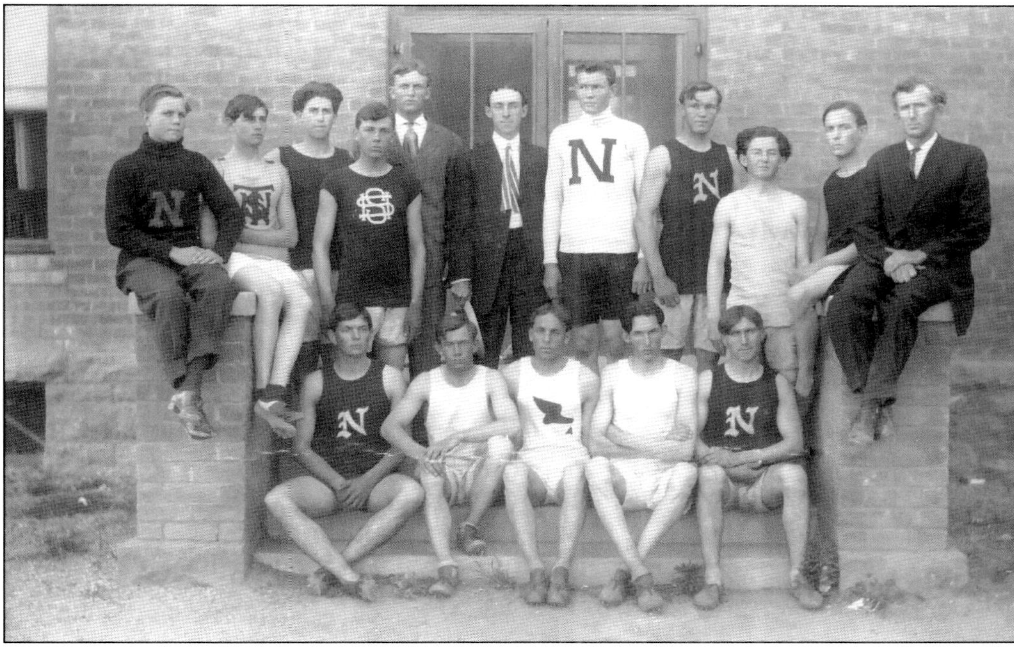

Under the Matthews administration, the institution underwent a change of identity. Initially referred to as the Arizona Territorial Normal School, at different times it was also identified as the Tempe Normal School or the Normal School of Arizona. The shirt designs of this 1910 track team speak to the inconsistency in names. Matthews sought to address this, stressing cohesion through rich symbols, such as the building of a large 36-by-36-foot "N" on the side of Tempe Butte in 1918. Matthews also tightened enrollment requirements, which previously admitted students as young as 16 years old. These students, called "subnormals," had their own high school–level courses offered on campus, such as this 1913 typing class. Matthews discouraged the enrollment of subnormals and lobbied for the founding of high schools to serve them instead. (Above, courtesy of UAASUL; below, THM.)

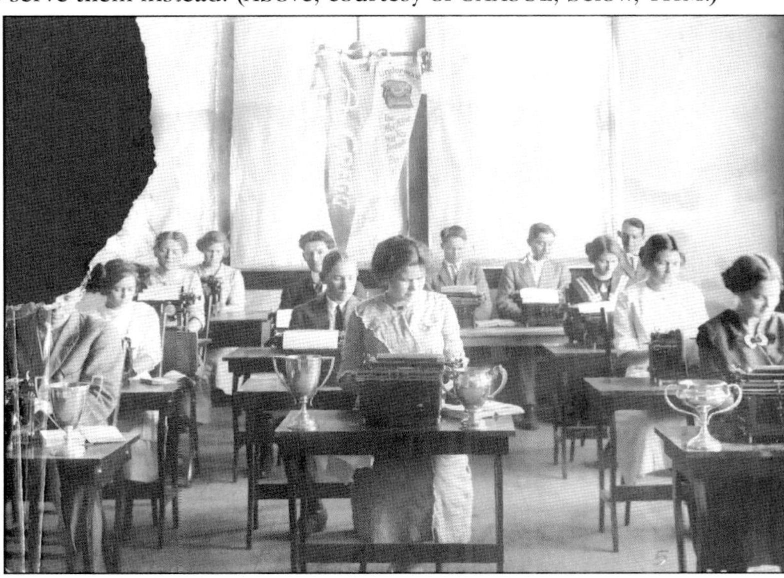

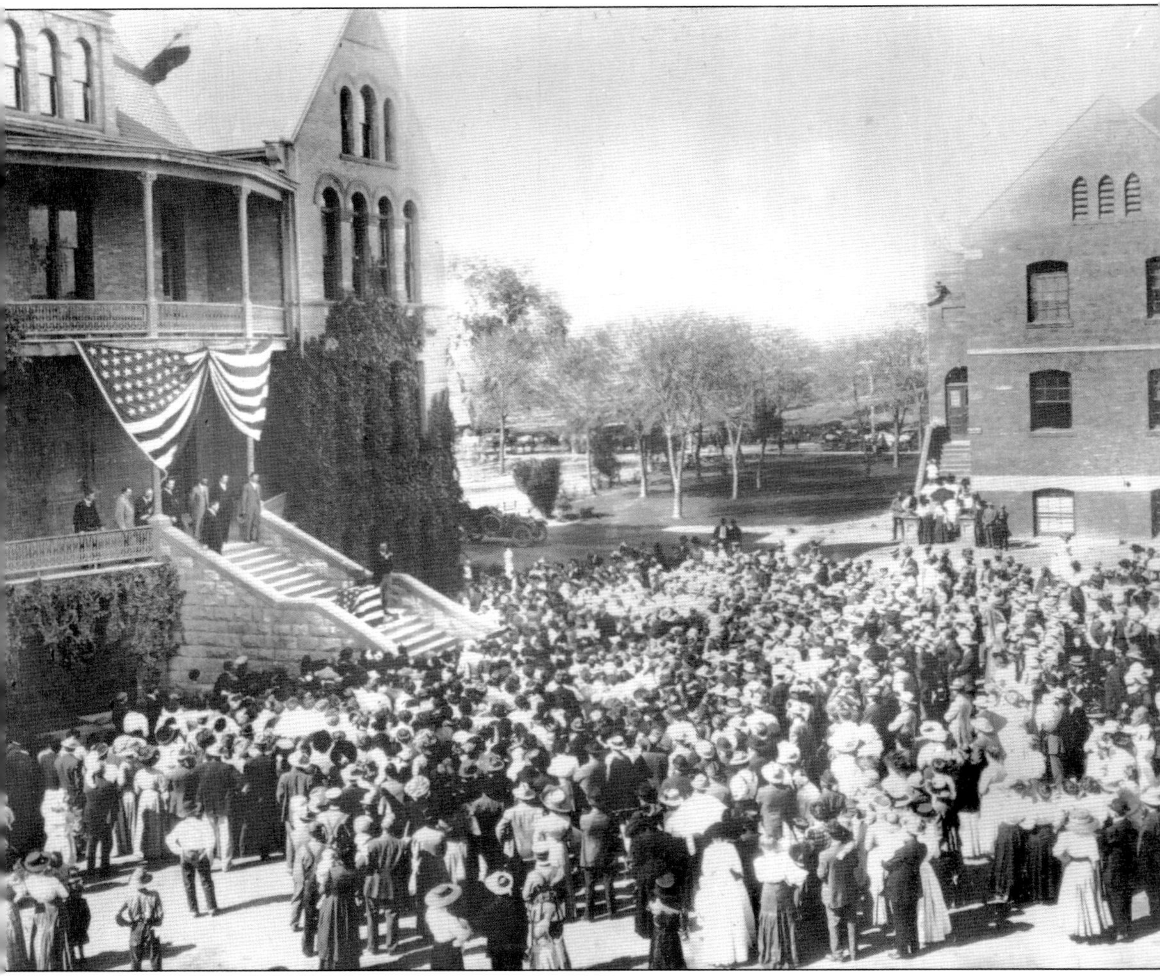

In 1911, the course of Arizona's history was determined with the completion of the Roosevelt Dam. The largest masonry dam in the world created the biggest artificial lake in its time. The newly abundant water source precipitated a massive population influx into the Phoenix valley, accelerating the growth of the normal school. Former president Theodore Roosevelt arrived for the dedication of the dam and delivered a speech on the steps of Old Main, with the auditorium built in 1909 to the right. "I have a special feeling for this institution," Roosevelt declared, reflecting on some of the alumni who fought in the Spanish–American War. He also commented on the accomplishments of the territorial residents in establishing a system of education, claiming, "If I had had my way, you would have been a state a long time ago." With the help of normal school president Matthews, who wrote the education section of the new constitution, Arizona became the 48th state the following year. (Courtesy of UAASUL.)

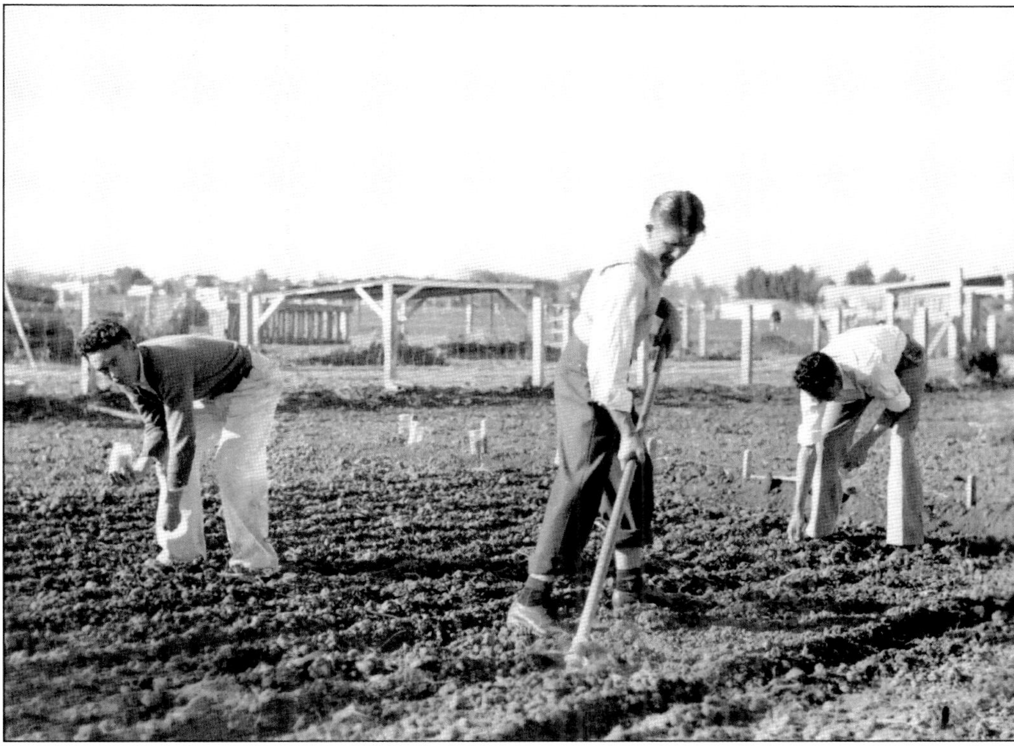

Agriculture had already been a large part of life in Tempe; however, with better access to water, farms prospered, and residents pressured the normal school for coursework on farming. By 1912, courses in agriculture and, later, husbandry were offered to normal school students, who also taught training school children, as demonstrated below in 1926. More than 50 acres were acquired for school gardens and the raising of livestock. The introduction of a curriculum in agriculture can arguably be identified as the root of early tension and competition between the Tempe school and the University of Arizona in Tucson. The university was a land grant institution already offering courses in agriculture, and many saw this shift in the normal school curriculum as an indication of interest in programs of study outside of teacher training. (Above, courtesy of JT, UAASUL; below, THM.)

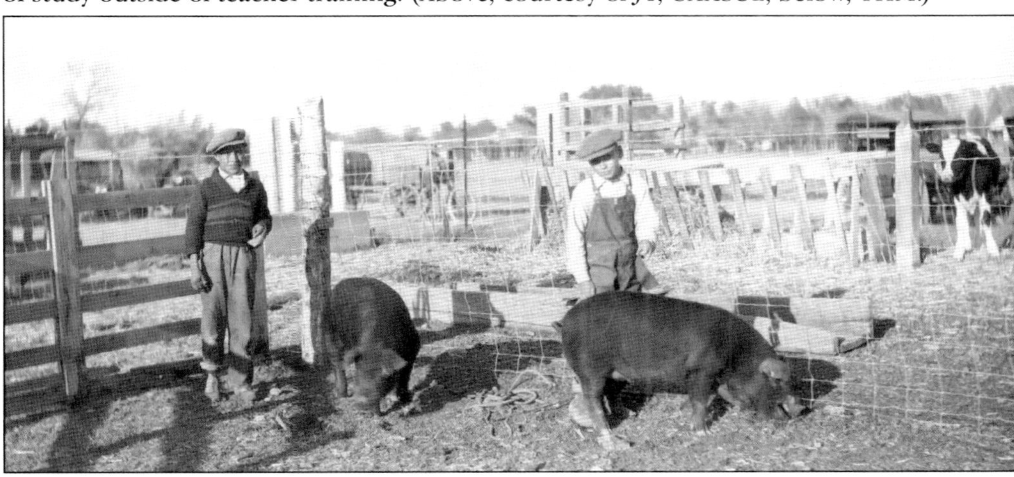

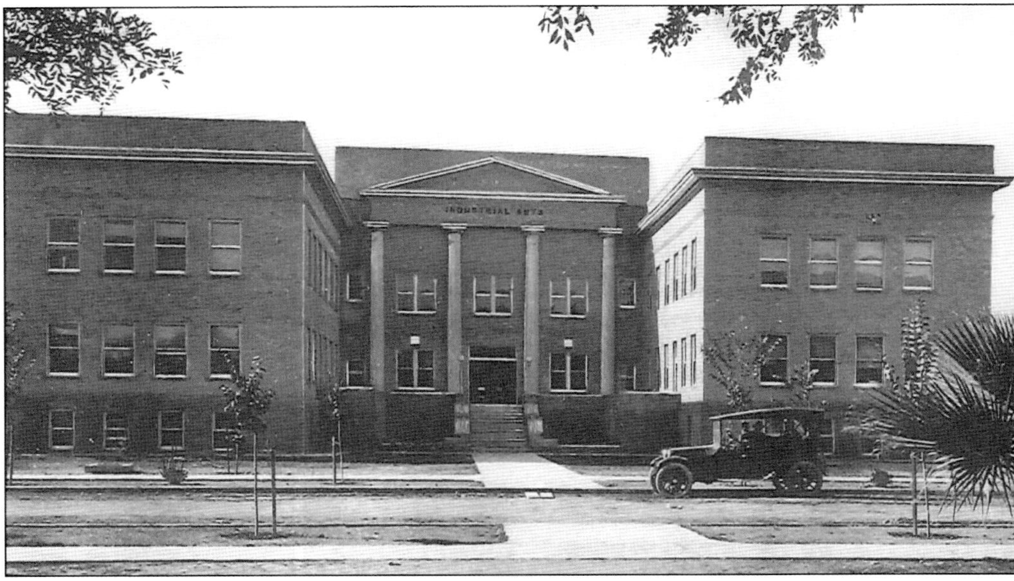

Indeed, the normal school already offered vocational training to students who had no plans to become teachers but wanted specialized training in another field. As early as 1906, mechanical art classes were taught, and they increased in popularity over the years until it became a department of its own. In order to accommodate the growing demand and need for space, the Industrial Arts Building, which would later become the Art Building and then housed Anthropology, was built in 1914. The Neoclassical building, designed by Norman Marsh, came with large workspaces and $7,000 worth of shop equipment. The increase in the normal school's enrollment to 450 students by 1917, along with the physical and curricular expansion, was just one of many indicators of an impending shift to collegiate status. (Above, courtesy of Tempe Historic Preservation Office; below, UAASUL.)

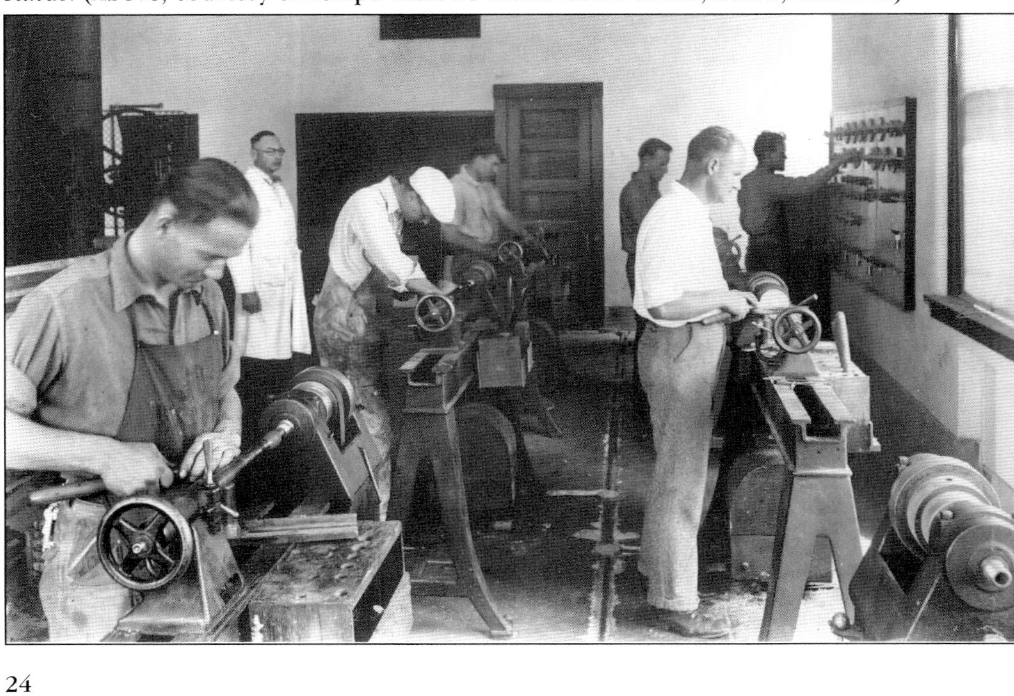

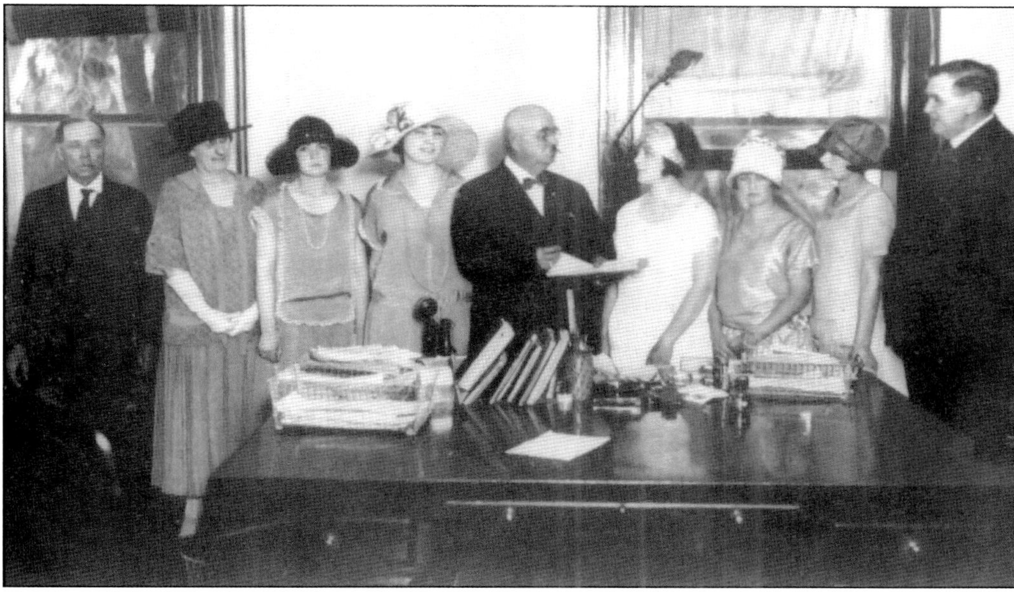

By the 1920s, Ira Payne brought a national trend to the attention of Matthews: many normal schools were transitioning to four-year state teachers colleges. Not wanting students to be disadvantaged in competing for jobs, Matthews approached the Arizona legislature with a request for collegiate status. After a bitter fight with opponents disapproving of having another bachelor's degree-granting institution in Arizona, Gov. George W.P. Hunt (above center) signed the bill creating the Tempe State Teachers College in 1925, allowing it to award bachelor of education degrees. Students paraded in the streets in celebration of the news, pictured below; however, the victory was bittersweet. The new name failed to associate the school with the state of Arizona, and the degree it was allowed to grant was not the preferred bachelor of arts in education offered by the University of Arizona. (Both courtesy of UAASUL.)

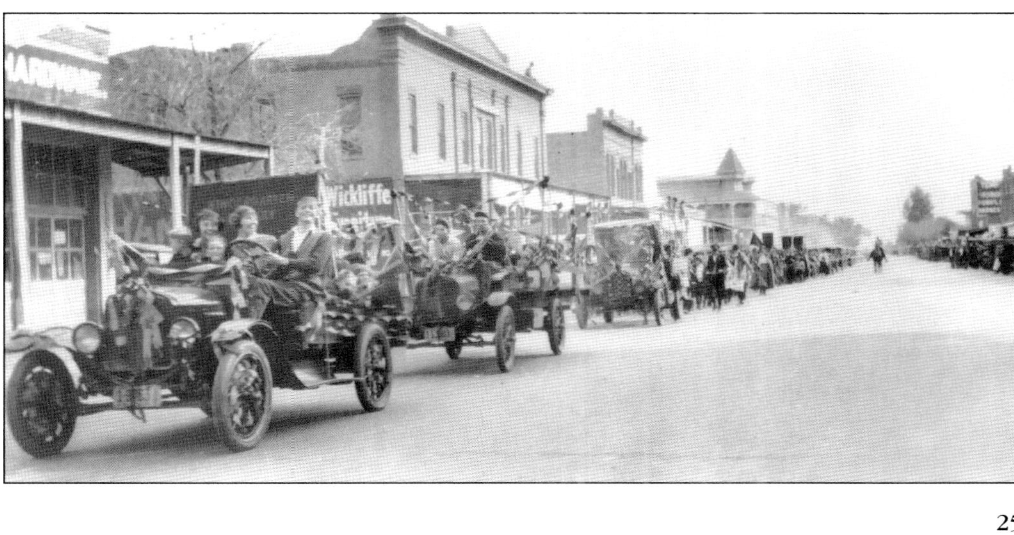

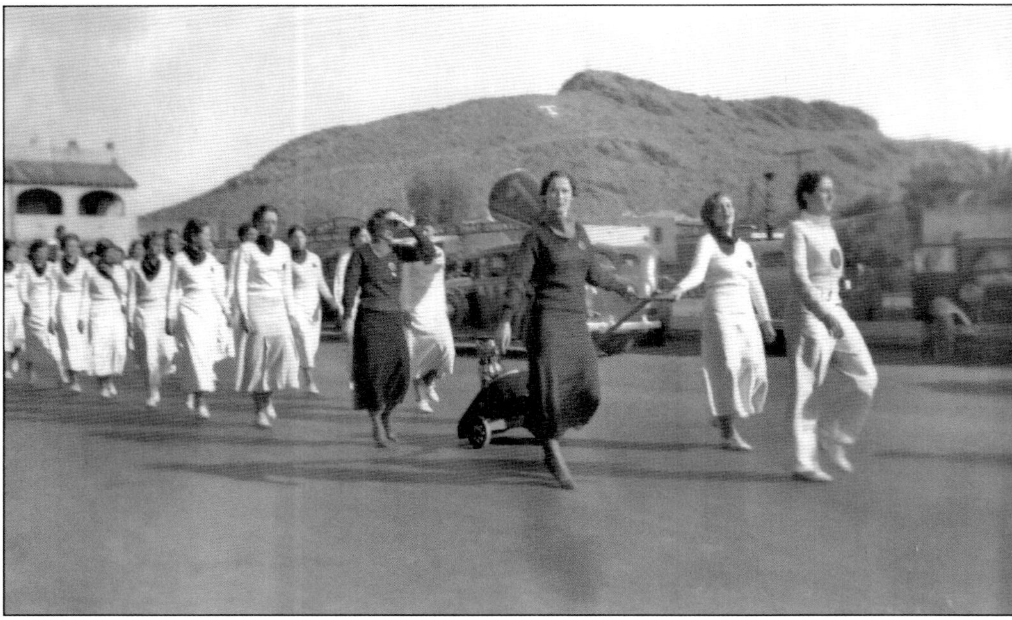

In 1926, students replaced the "N" that was previously built on the butte with a "T" to signify the change to Tempe State Teachers College. By 1929, however, the school's name changed once again to Arizona State Teachers College, at which time it began granting bachelor of arts degrees in education. This homecoming parade photograph was taken in 1935, a few years before the "A" was built. (Courtesy of JT, UAASUL.)

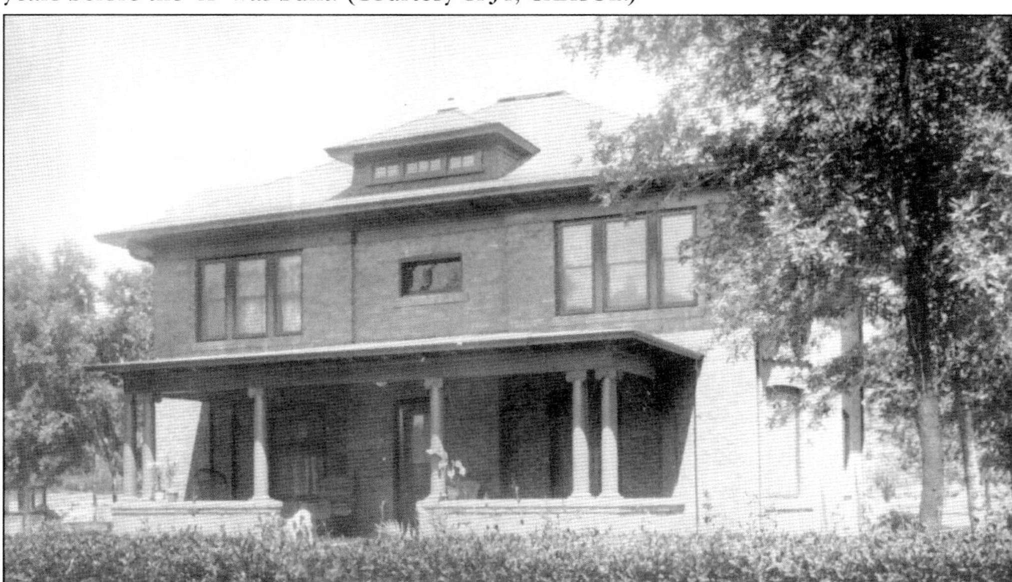

As a testament to his commitment to the institution, President Matthews lived on campus in a house that was built in 1907 and became known as the President's Cottage. Located on the corner of Palm Walk and Tyler Mall, it was home to each of the school's presidents until 1959. It went on to serve as an archive repository and is now the Virginia G. Piper Center for Creative Writing. (Courtesy of UAASUL.)

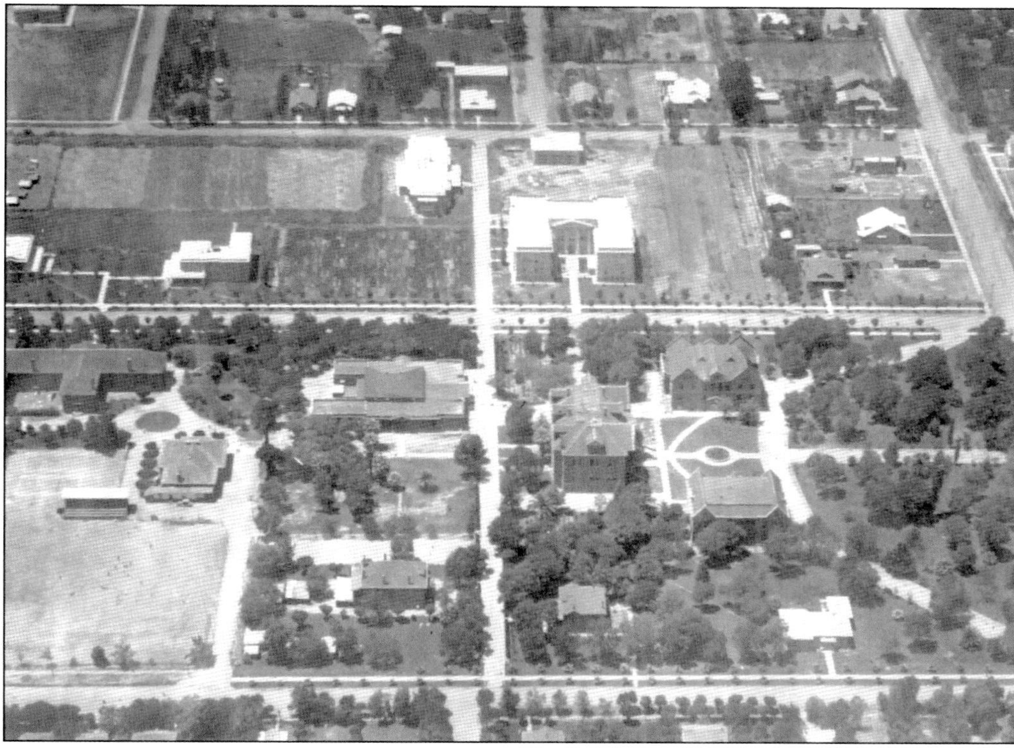

During the Matthews presidency, 18 buildings were constructed, and he oversaw the planting of thousands of trees (including Palm Walk), hedges, shrubs, and flowers. This 1919 aerial photograph offers a glimpse of the quadrangle, or "old quad," in the right center, which made up the heart of the campus comprised of Old Main; the Science Hall, built in 1908 and now the University Club; and the auditorium/gymnasium, opened in 1909 and razed in 1956. (Courtesy of JT, UAASUL.)

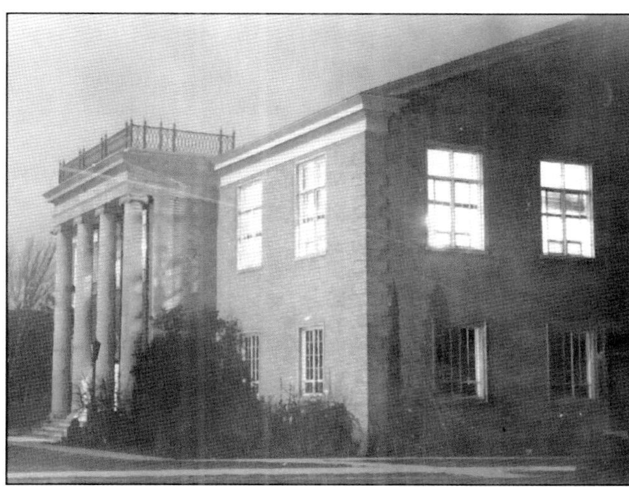

The Matthews Library was completed in 1930, the same year he retired. The school's book collection of 14,306 volumes had outgrown the space designated for it in Old Main. Faculty, staff, and students agreed that the library dedication was an appropriate way to honor the man who elevated ASTC to a Class-A rating with the American Association of Teachers Colleges. The library was the pride and joy of the campus. (Courtesy of JT, UAASUL.)

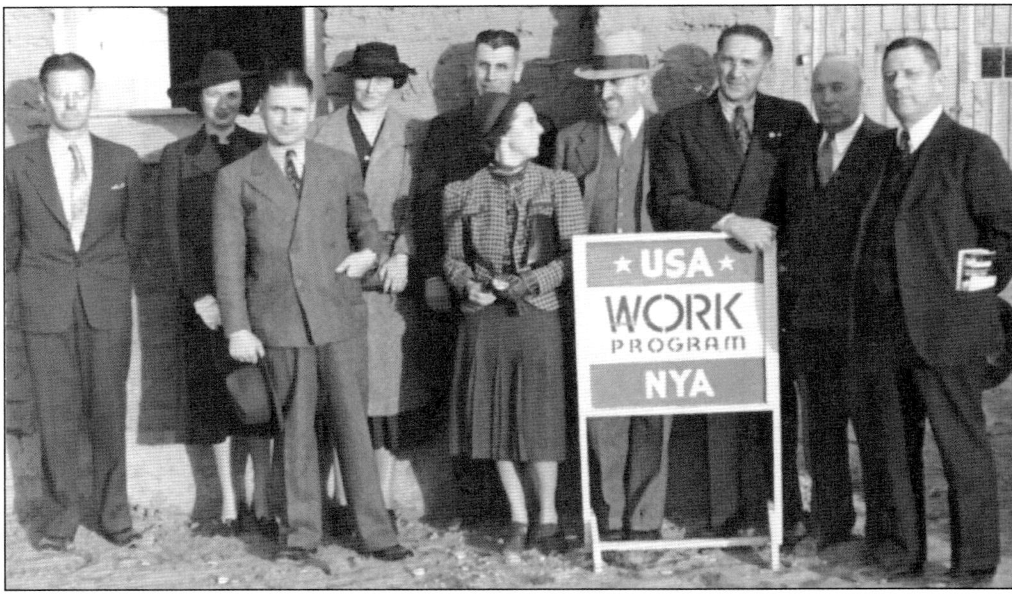

Matthews retired in 1930. The following three years were arguably the most difficult in the school's history. The nation was in an economic depression, and Ralph Swetman became the new president who had to make tough decisions, including dismissing 31 of the 56 faculty. By the time Grady Gammage arrived to take Swetman's place in 1933, morale was low and the physical campus had fallen into disarray. Gammage started by applying to federal New Deal programs for new campus buildings and art forms. Gammage, in the hat, poses above with Tempe physician and state governor Benjamin Moeur (second from right) and some Work Program staff. Some of the funding directed to the Arizona State Teachers College commissioned artists to paint murals. Emry Kopata, an Austrian sculptor, was even hired to design the Hopi Flute Ceremony–inspired fountain installed in the old quad fish pond. (Both courtesy of THM.)

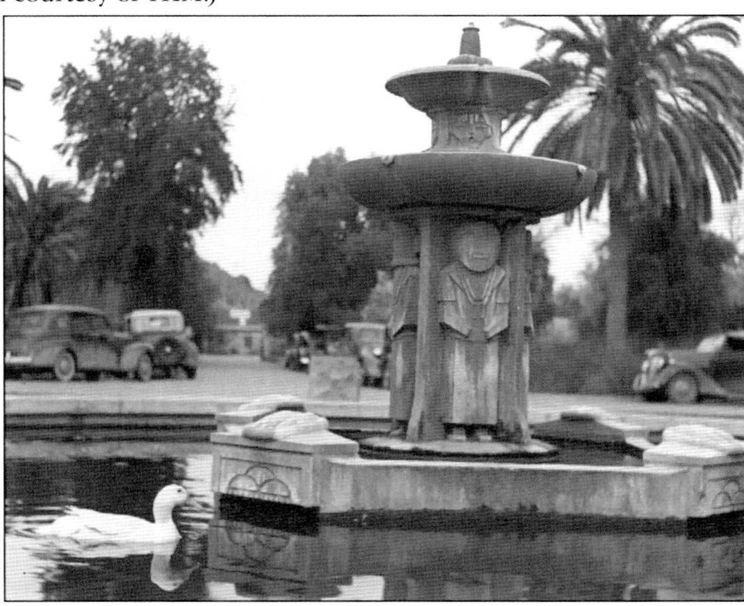

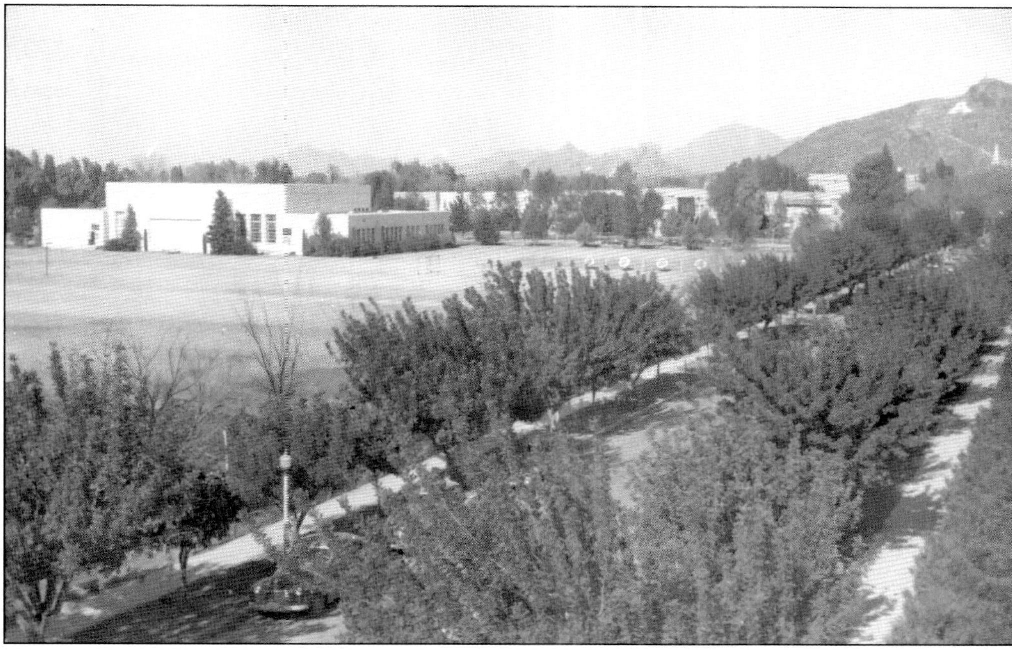

Over the course of a six-year building boom on campus, the institution received $1,745,000 in federal funds. In 1935, the Matthews Library was expanded, and in the years following, West Hall, the dining hall expansion, a new heating plant, Irish Hall, and Dixie Gammage Hall were also built. The largest Works Progress Administration (WPA) structure in the state was the Moeur Activity Building, above, which was completed in 1938 and served as a women's gymnasium. It is the only adobe building on campus and was completed through the generosity of local businesses that donated the windows (including treatments), floors, wiring, and fixtures. Murals depicting women engaged in sports, art, music, and dance, right and on page 39, were painted in a few locations within the building. This historic and unique building later became the Mars Space Flight Facility. (Above, courtesy of Shirley G. Schmitz; right, THM.)

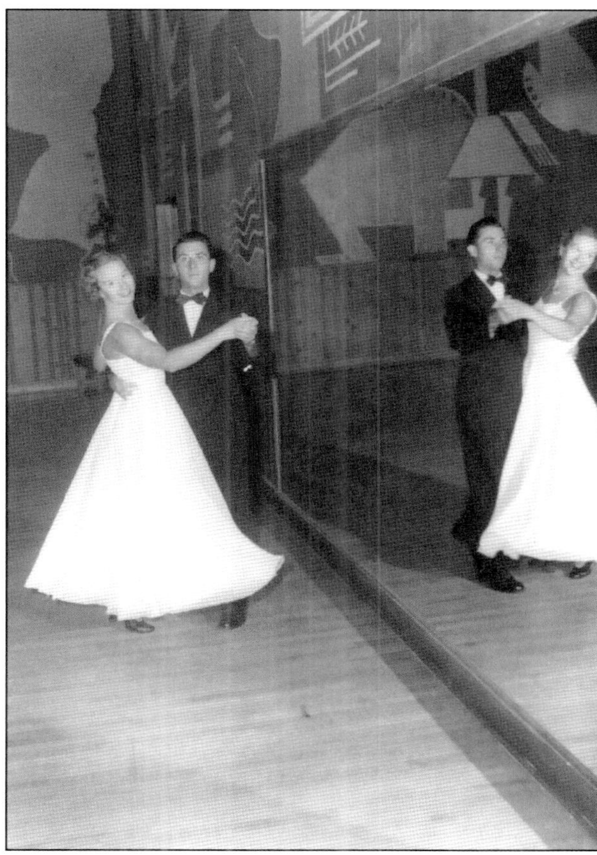

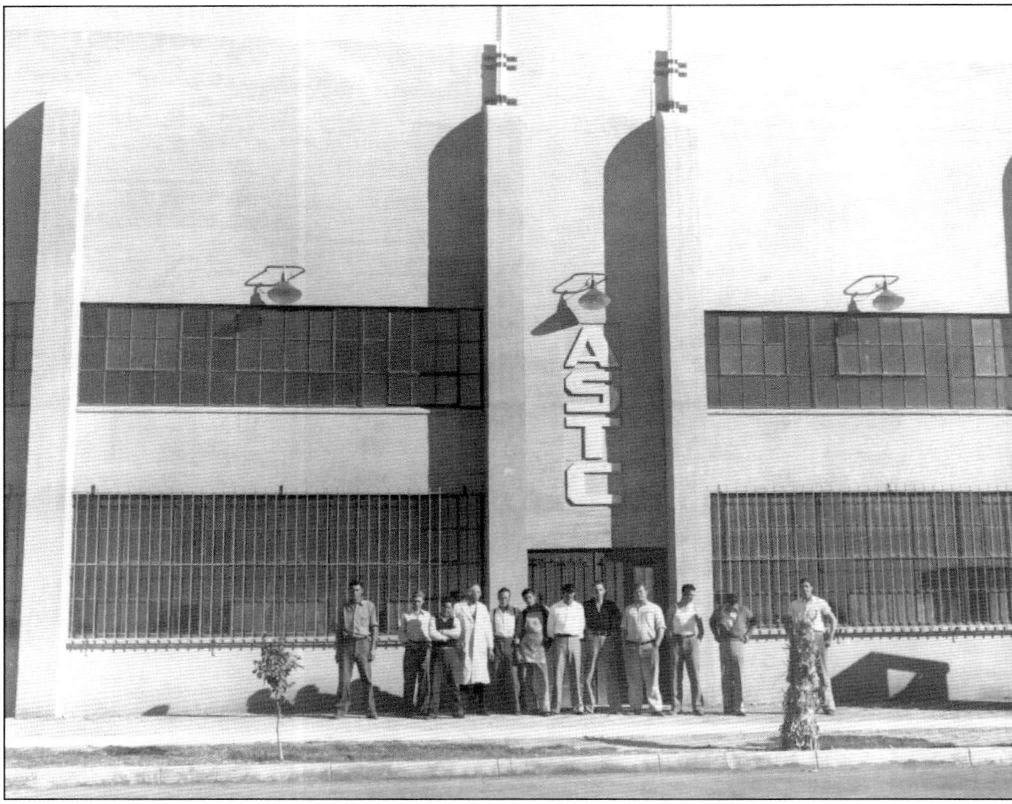

Another noteworthy product of the 1930s building boom was Goodwin Stadium, seen above with students and faculty. Completed in 1936, the stadium was named after Garfield Goodwin, an early alumnus and ardent football supporter, and served the Arizona State Teachers College football team until it was replaced by the Sun Devil Stadium in 1958. A men's dormitory was located on the east side of the facility. (Courtesy of THM.)

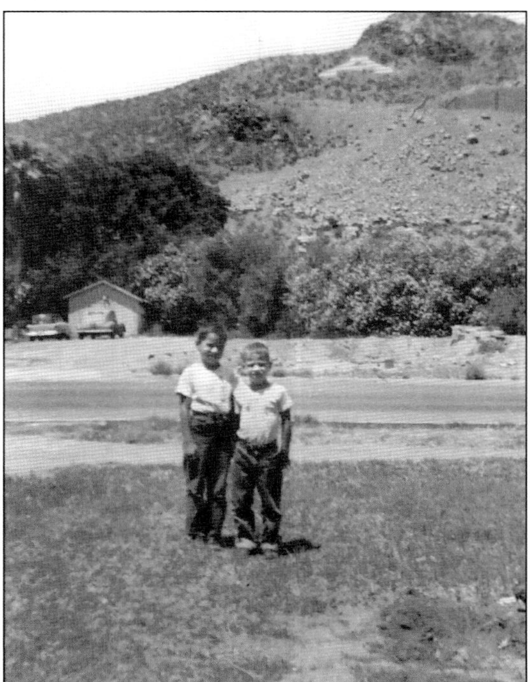

As the physical campus grew, the enrollment swelled to 1,341 students by the fall of 1940. Tempe residents certainly felt the results of this expansion. This 1950s photograph shows two young boys in front of their home, located just below "A" mountain, which replaced the "T" in 1938. Students annually climbed the butte in droves to whitewash and maintain the school symbol. (Courtesy of Kimberly Fuqua.)

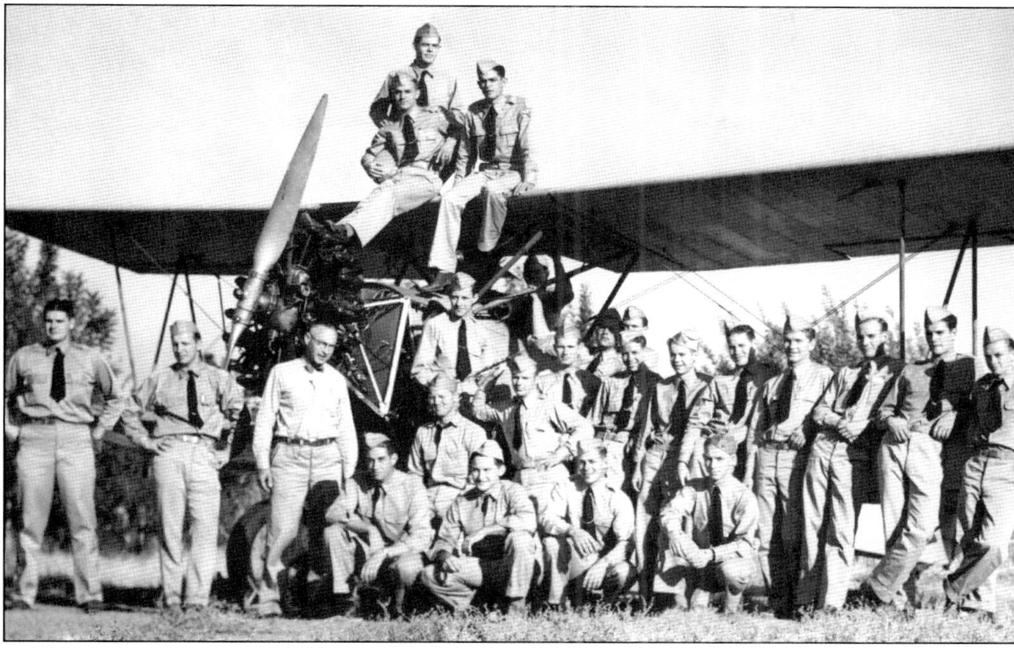

The onslaught of World War II brought many changes to the campus, including the revival of a visible military presence not seen since the 1920s. In 1943, the 315th Army Air Force College Training Detachment made its headquarters in the Matthews Library, and hundreds of cadets learned about aircraft engines and controls from Lewis Neeb. Some female students, along with courses in sewing and home economics, also took courses within the Department of Industrial Arts to train for positions within the aircraft industry. Initially founded in the 1930s, the Department of Military Science has a long history at the institution, training students for leadership positions within the US Army and offering required courses until the late 1960s. As of 2012, what later became the Sun Devil Battalion has received five Gen. Douglas MacArthur awards. (Both courtesy of THM.)

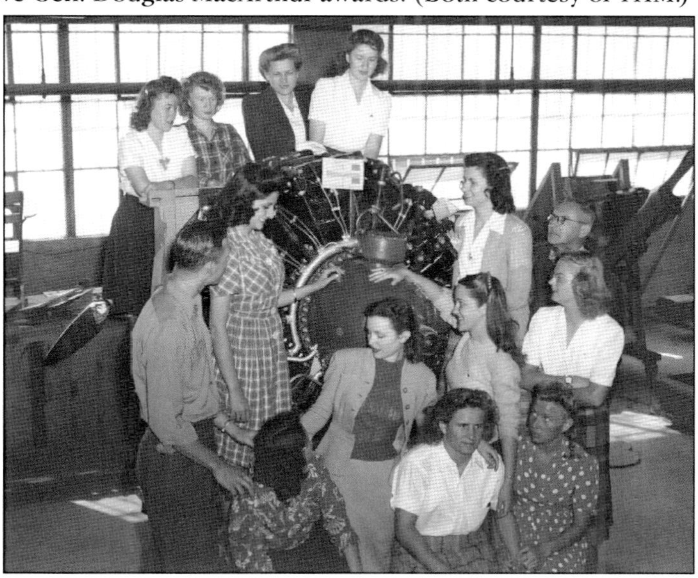

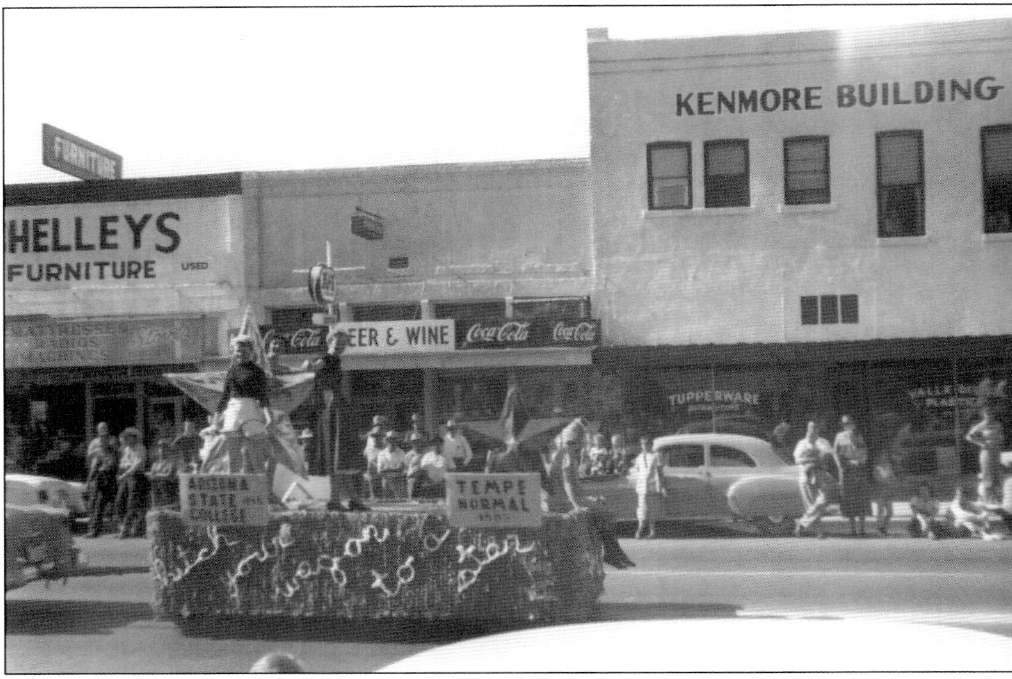

In 1945, Arizona State Teachers College went through another name change when it became Arizona State College, as celebrated on this float. This was a result of Gammage anticipating an influx of returning GIs from World War II who would be looking to receive a higher education. Arguing that the University of Arizona would be unable to fill the demand, he lobbied the legislature to become a multi-degree granting institution. (Courtesy of UAASUL.)

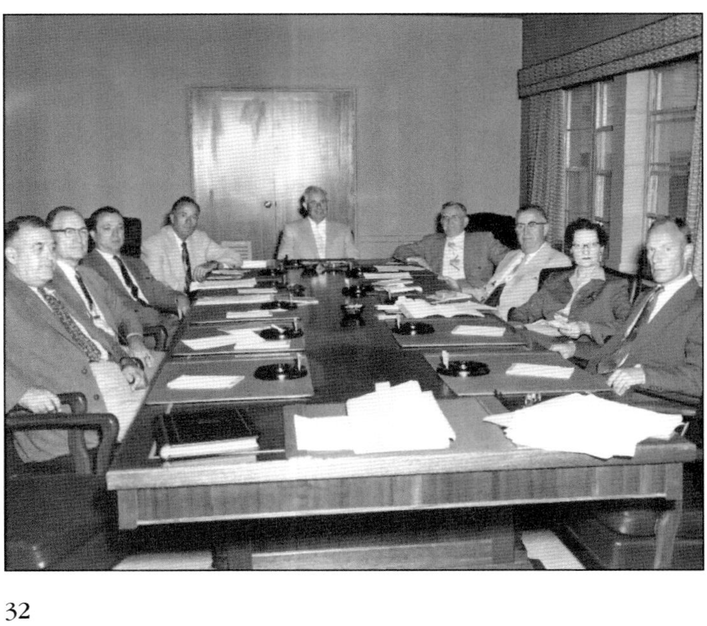

Gov. Ernest McFarland, at the head of the table, signed the bill to eliminate the school's status as a teachers college. That same year, he also united the governing boards of the university in Tucson and the state colleges in Tempe and Flagstaff as the Arizona Board of Regents (ABOR). This 1955 meeting depicts the three presidents and others making decisions about the future of higher education in the state. (Courtesy of Grady Gammage Jr.)

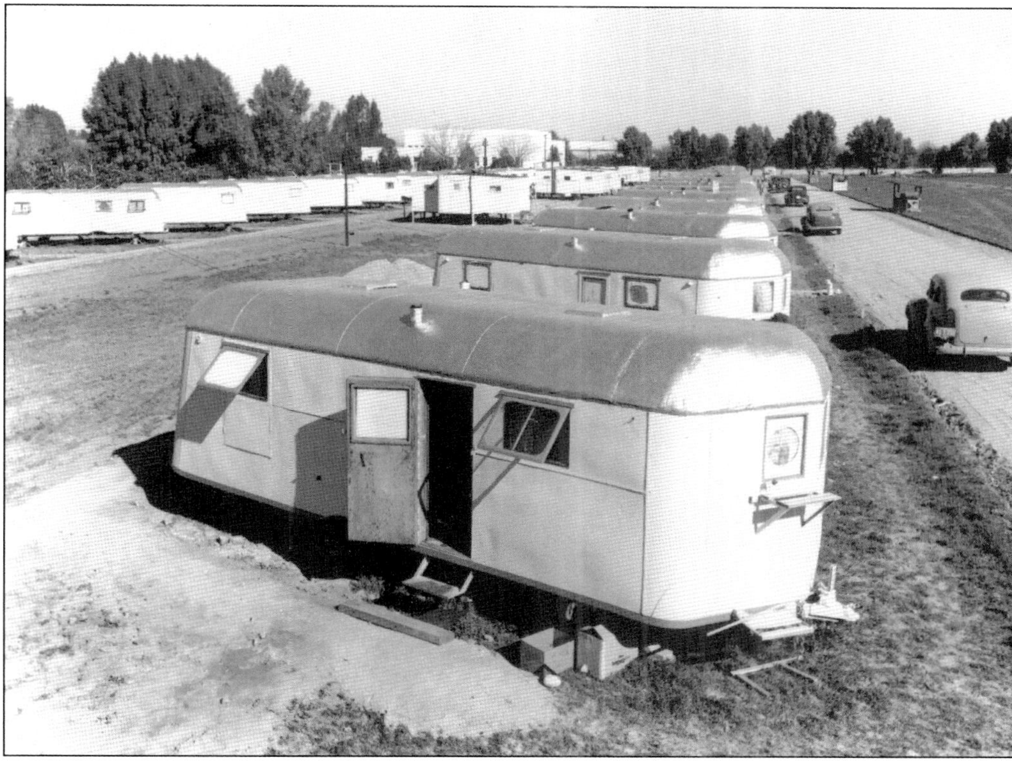

Gammage was right to anticipate an influx of new students following the war. From 1946 to 1950, the enrollment grew from a low 553 students to an extraordinary 4,094. Two thirds of these students were men, the majority of whom were veterans, and many had their own families. With the dormitories full of single students, the administration faced the challenge of where to house married students and their families. In 1946, Gilbert Cady purchased 50 used trailers and 20 knockdown apartments, set up on the southwest corner of campus near the present location of Gammage Auditorium. Victory Village, as it was called, offered tenants a heating system, stoves, sinks, bathrooms, and two pull-out couches per unit that could sleep four. Long stretches of clotheslines and children playing in the dusty field were common sights. (Both courtesy of UAASUL.)

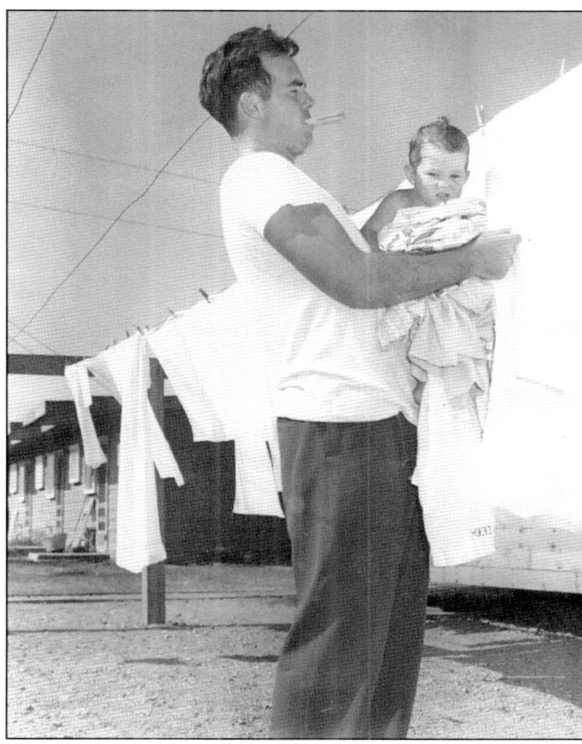

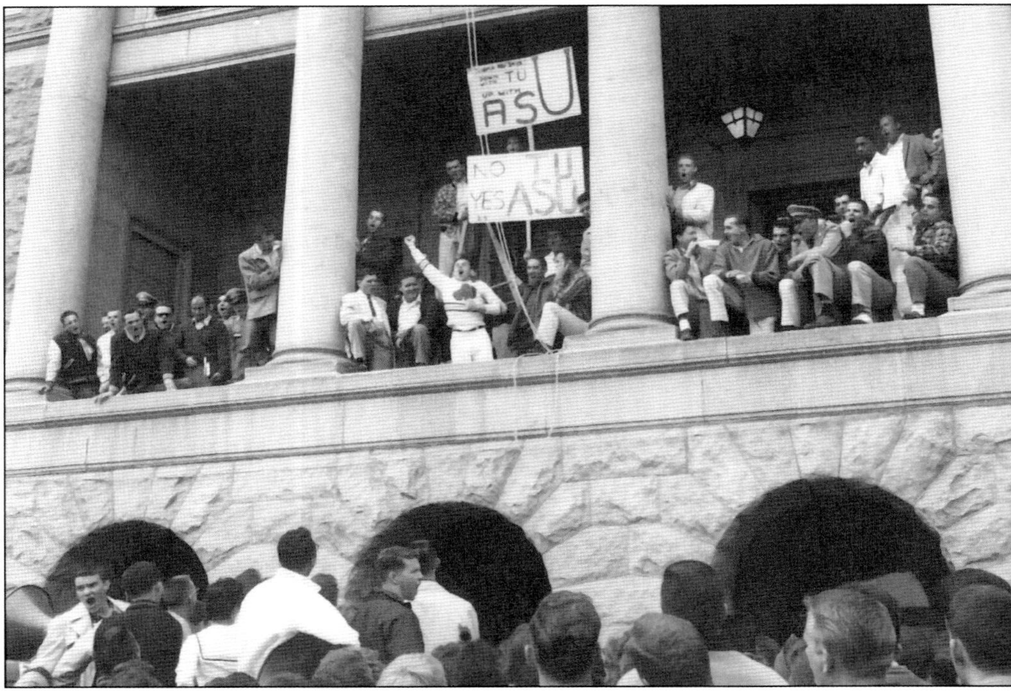

Arizona State College entered the 1950s as a more mature institution. A 1954 US Department of Education report even acknowledged that it was "rapidly becoming a university." The Gammage administration once again positioned for a shift in status; however, the predictable pattern of opposition prevailed. University of Arizona officials, alumni, and advocates rejected proposals that placed ASC on equal footing with the existing university. Attempts to gain university status met one challenge after another until one sympathetic legislator introduced a compromise bill proposing to rename the school Tempe University. Students rejected this name, which downplayed the statewide importance of the school, protesting at the state capitol, as seen in the photograph above. Soon after, a petition campaign to put the name change measure on the ballot was successfully launched, and Proposition 200 was born. (Above, courtesy of UAASUL; below, Reg Manning Collection, Arizona Collection, ASU.)

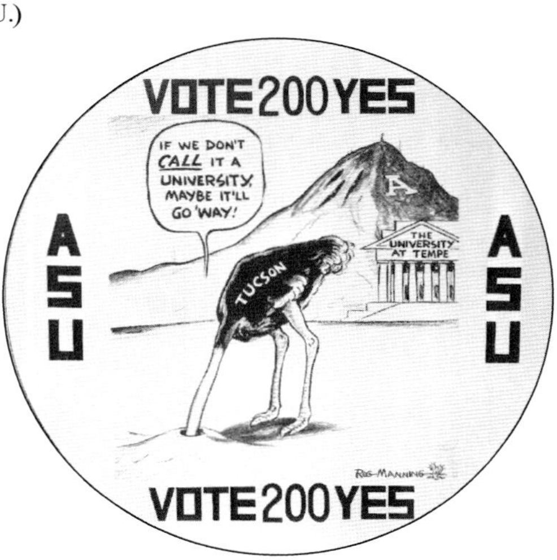

The name change campaign swept the state with a force. Students and alumni organized phone banks, funded billboards and television commercials, and distributed bumper stickers, buttons, and brochures. Gammage gave speeches across the state, and an airplane was even flown above several towns urging citizens to vote "yes" for Proposition 200. The campaign served to unify students and generated a camaraderie that was talked about years later. (Courtesy of UAASUL.)

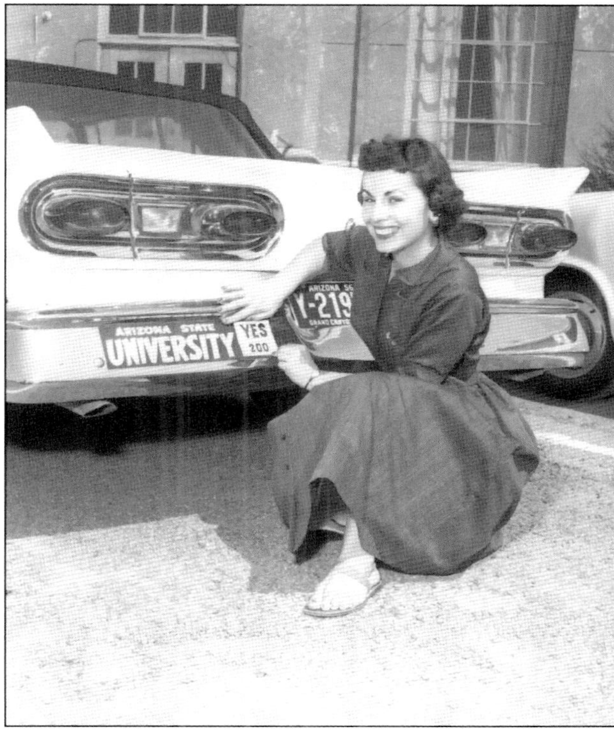

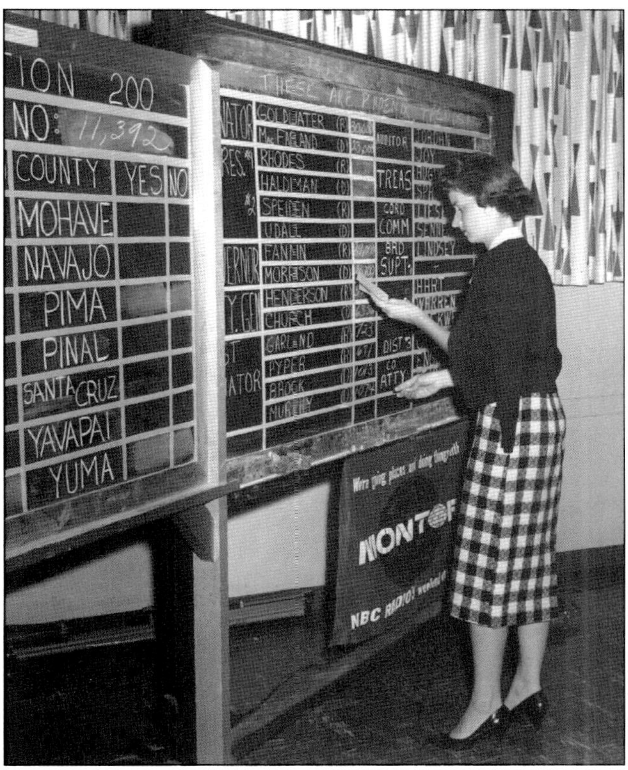

The moment of truth arrived on November 4, 1958. The name change campaign had aroused such interest in Arizona citizens, partially because the University of Arizona had launched its own aggressive anti–Proposition 200 campaign, that the voter turnout was a high 72 percent. The Memorial Union was the ASC headquarters, where students tallied votes as they were reported late into the night. (Courtesy of UAASUL.)

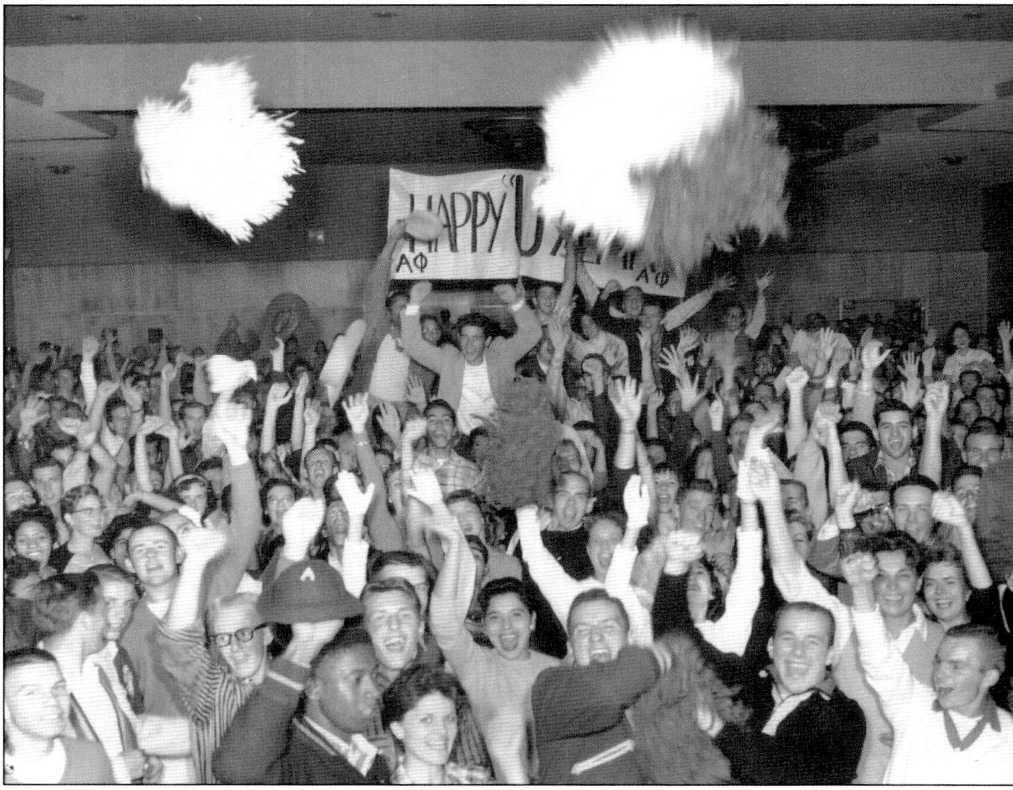

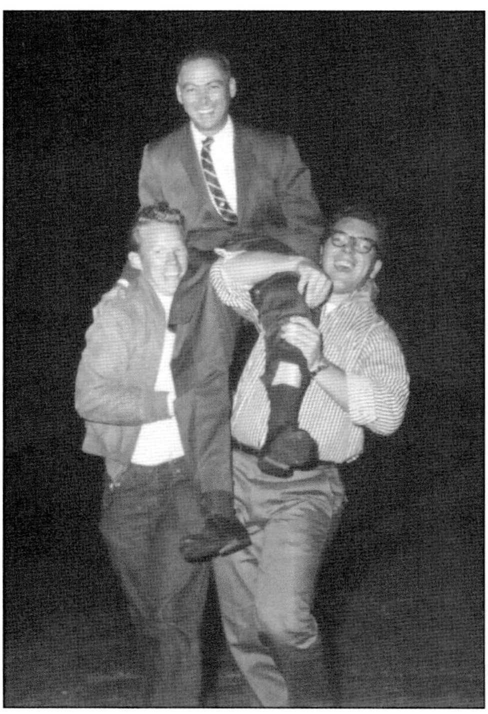

The final vote for Proposition 200 was 101,881 in favor of the name change and 51,471 against it. Arizona State University officially stepped into the world, the first time in national history that a university had been named under such circumstances. Cheers erupted across campus, and Gammage spoke to the celebrating students, alumni, staff, and faculty as they reveled in "ASU's finest hour." (Courtesy of UAASUL.)

The name change campaign succeeded due to the tireless work of leaders like alumni association director James Creasman, pictured at left as he is carried by celebrating students. Creasman was relentless, delivering speeches around the state along with others like new head football coach Frank Kush and organizing volunteer activities. Governor McFarland even praised his work with the alumni association as being "second to none." (Courtesy of UAASUL.)

Two

Academic Glimpses

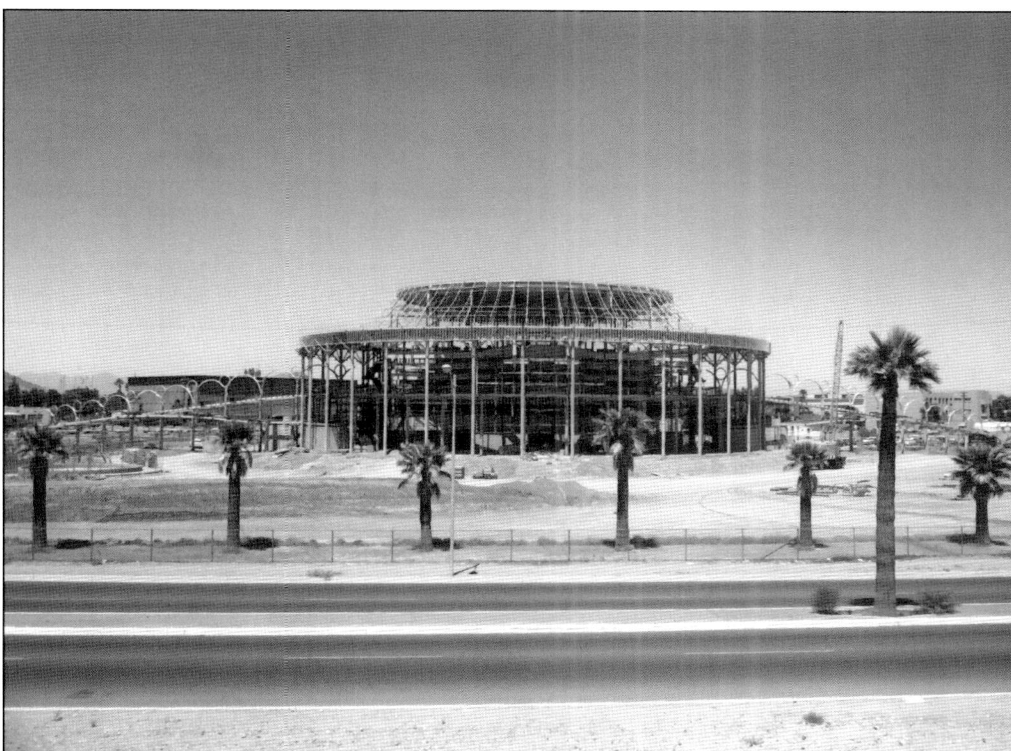

The name change reflected both shifting demographics and the hard work of the faculty, staff, students, and alumni. Their effort laid the excellent foundation on which the next waves of Sun Devils built, symbolized above by the construction of the Grady Gammage Memorial Auditorium in 1964. In the next decades, ASU continued to respond to and help shape the community agendas and quality of life in the valley. (Courtesy of UAASUL.)

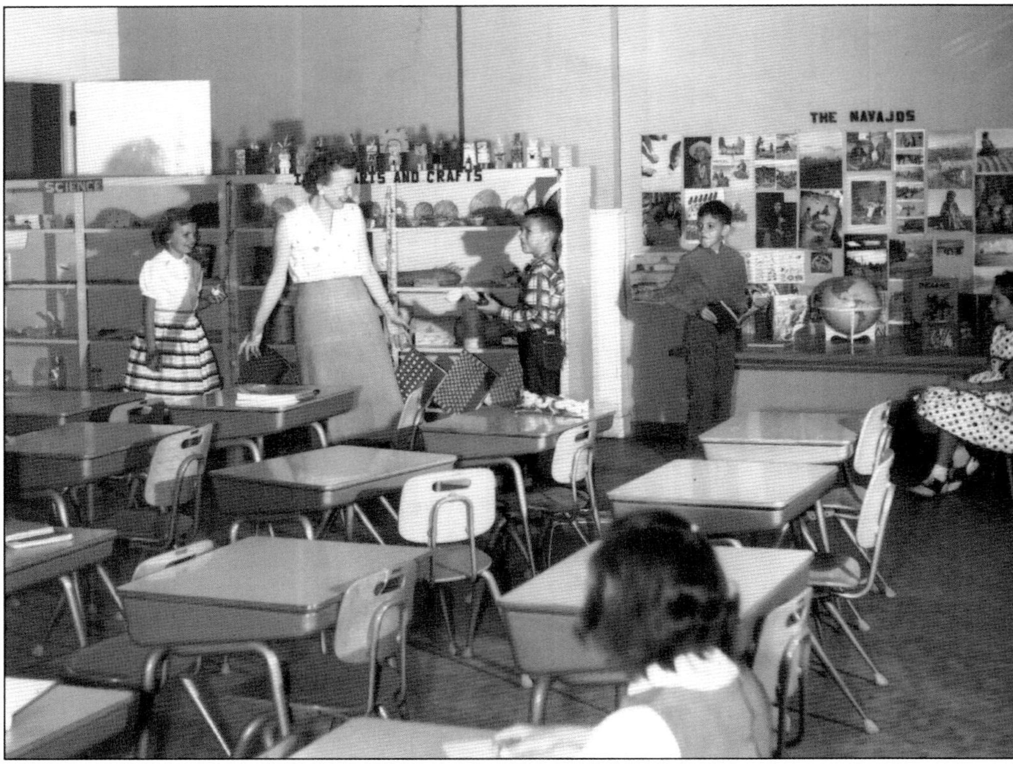

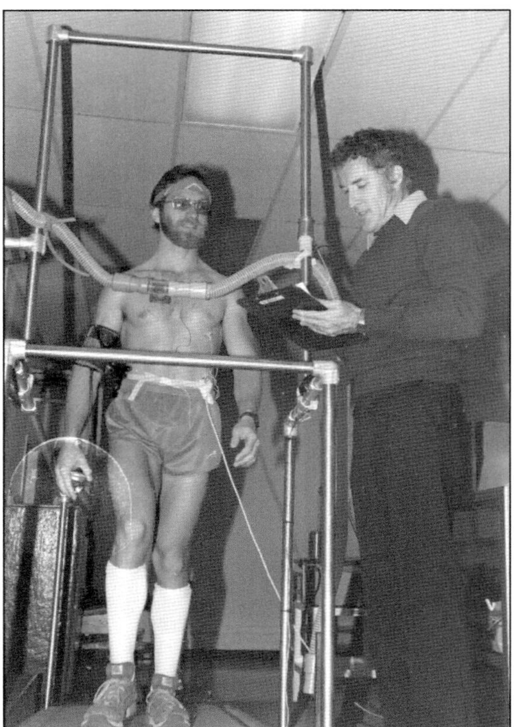

ASU continued to train teachers, as in this 1960s Payne Training School classroom. The faculty of the current Mary Lou Fulton Teachers College conducts research to understand and solve issues that affect education from preschool onward. Beyond undergraduate degrees since 1925, it has offered a master's degree since 1937; the first doctorate in education was granted in 1954. The first undergraduate degrees in non-education fields were awarded in 1946. (Courtesy of UAASUL.)

From early physical activities, required for graduation until 1967, the Department of Physical Education formed in 1928. Now known as the Kinesiology Program, scholars study how movement relates to health, disease, and prevention. The department was among the best when, for instance, nine of the National Academy of Kinesiology's members, limited to 100 top scholars, were from ASU. At left, William Stone conducts an exercise study. (Courtesy of Gary Krahenbuhl.)

Early dancing activities led to a dance program in 1954. Later, dance would split off from Physical Education. Margaret Gisolo (right), a multisport athlete and former naval officer, directed the program from 1954 to 1977, building undergraduate degrees by 1969 and forming a student dance company. Her excellence in teaching and administering resulted in many awards, including honorary doctorates and hall of fame inductions. Interpretive dance tested the boundaries of the older generation at ASTC's first public modern dance performance in 1939. Outreach to local schools educated and recruited students to a program that now receives national recognition for its choreography, education, and production. Dance, along with the other arts, are now administratively housed in the Herberger Institute for Design and the Arts. Below, a dance class practices in the Moeur Building. (Right, courtesy of Beth Lessard; below, THM.)

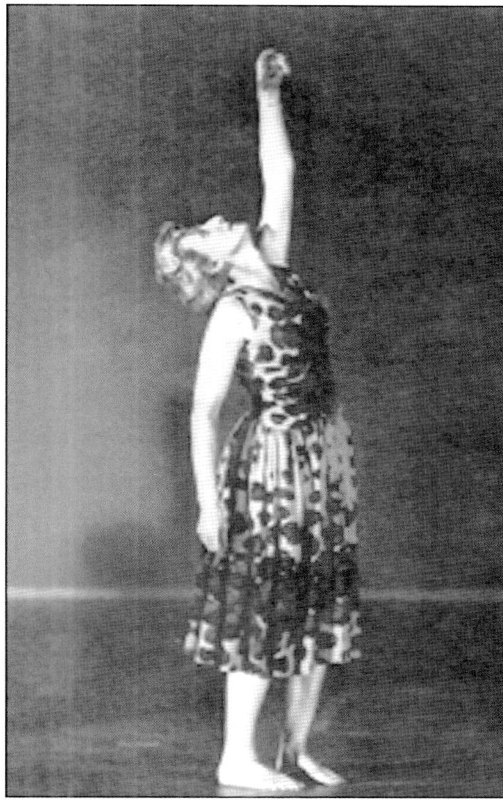

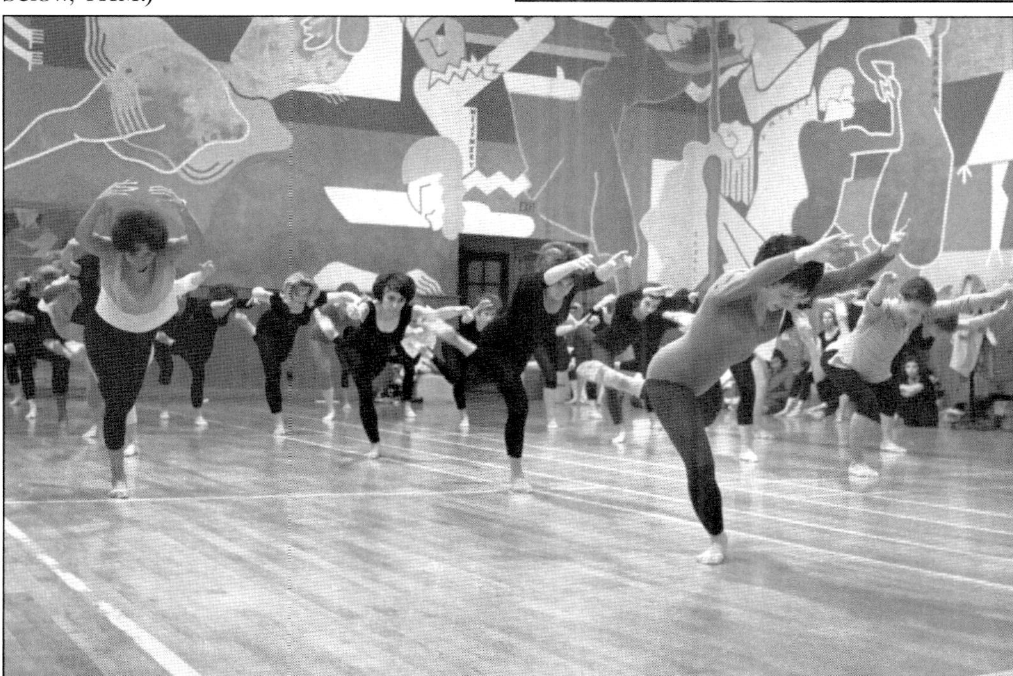

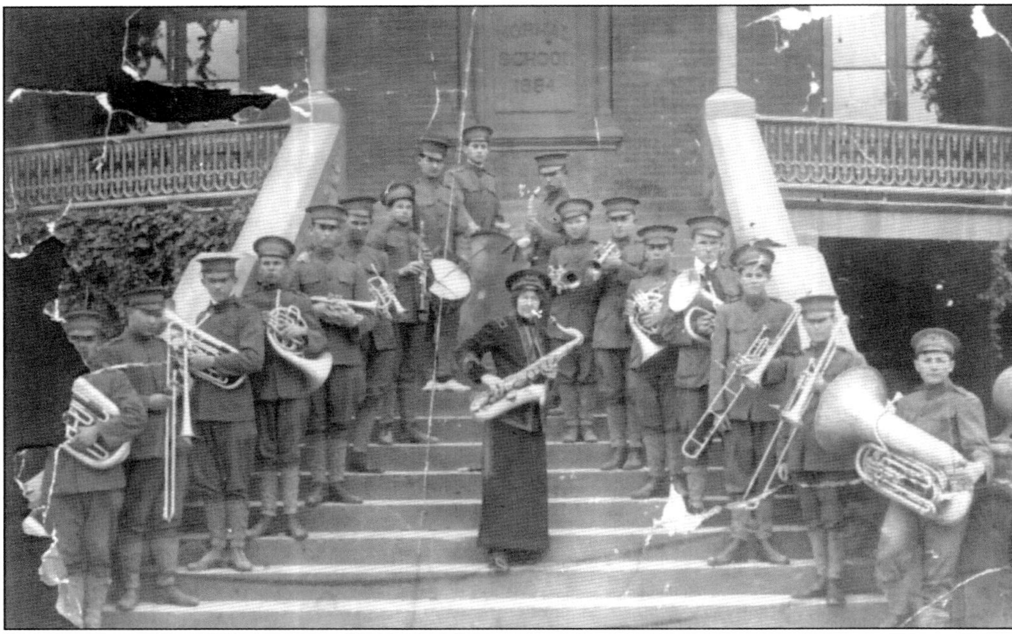

Music and voice have long been a part of ASU. As early as 1895, voice lessons were offered for $1 per lesson, and in 1900, a better piano was purchased for $1,000—a staggering sum in those days. Lillian Williams, above, was hired to offer instruction in orchestral and band instruments, leading to the formation of the first marching band in 1915. The Milkmaids Chorus, below, poses with the championship dairy cow in 1926 on the north steps of the current University Club, previously known as the Science-Administration Building, then, later, as the Fine Arts Annex. In the 1960s, the 12–14 members of the University Singers often performed for the public. Whether interested in band, orchestra, opera, or musical theater, ASU students now can learn all angles of music, including composition, conducting, performance, and music therapy in state-of-the-art facilities. (Both courtesy of UAASUL.)

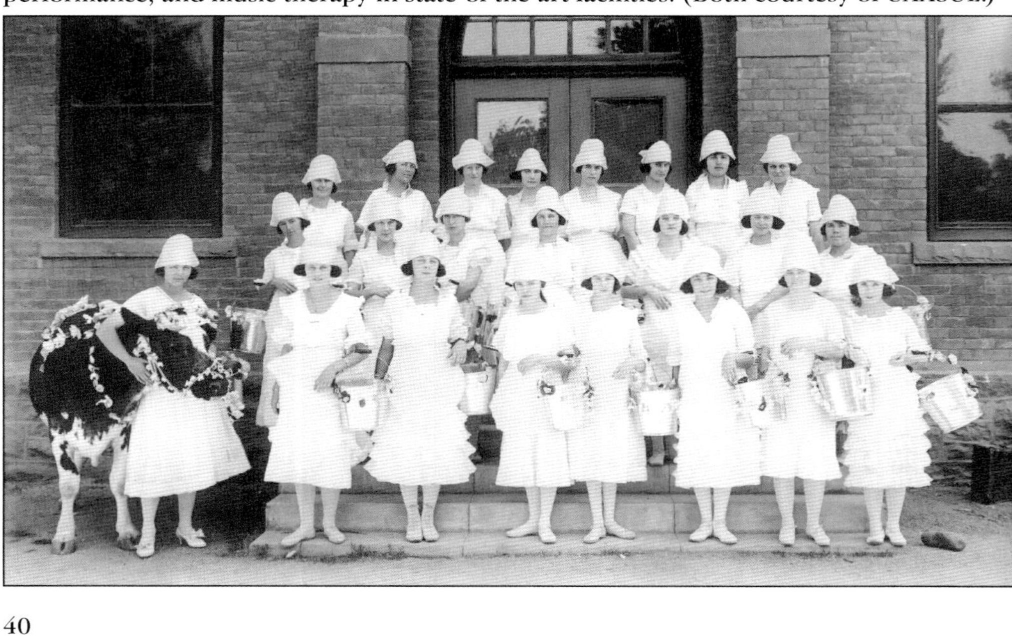

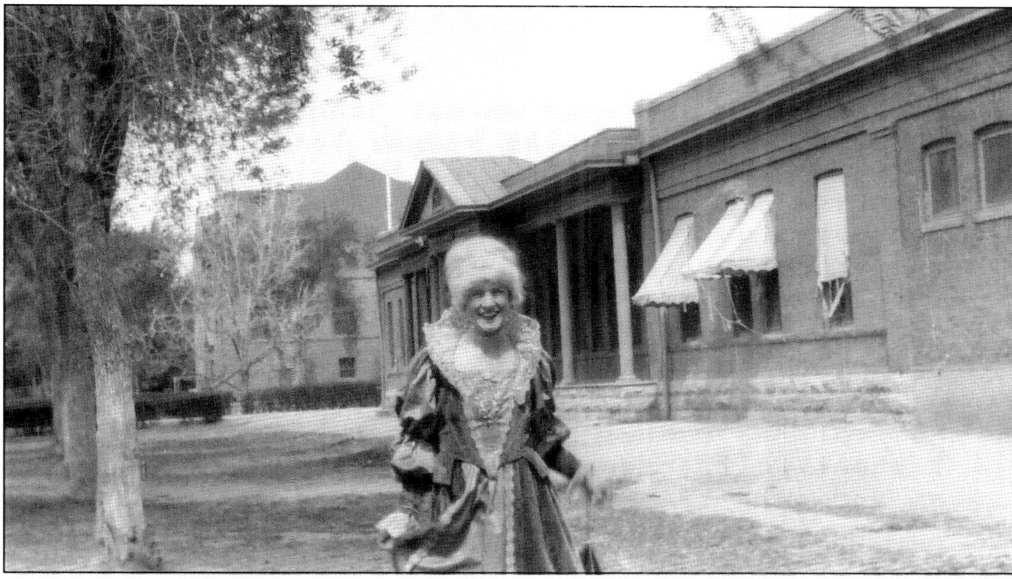

Above, a student runs by the Blome Training School on her way to a performance. Early plays and pageants with normal school students and their young pupils laid the foundation for the Theatre Department, which now educates in technical aspects of theater, design, acting, makeup, playwriting, and more. Beryl Simpson, hired in 1930 to the Division of Drama in English, was key in developing drama and involving the community through, for instance, playwriting contests. Theatre split off from English and evolved with the guidance of faculty like James Yeater and alumnus Don Doyle. Doyle returned to ASU as faculty, establishing the internationally known Theatre for Youth program. ASU also draws researchers to its large, one-of-a-kind Child Drama Collection, tracing back to the 17th century. The 1963 photograph below shows *Rumpelstiltskin* in the Playhouse in the Lyceum Building. (Above, courtesy of THM; below, Child Drama/UAASUL.)

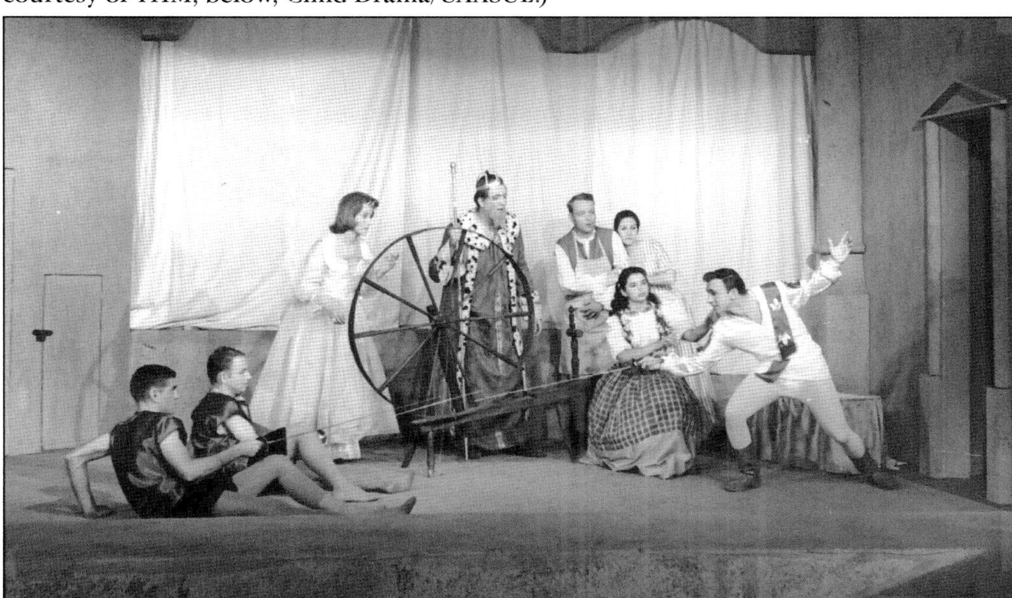

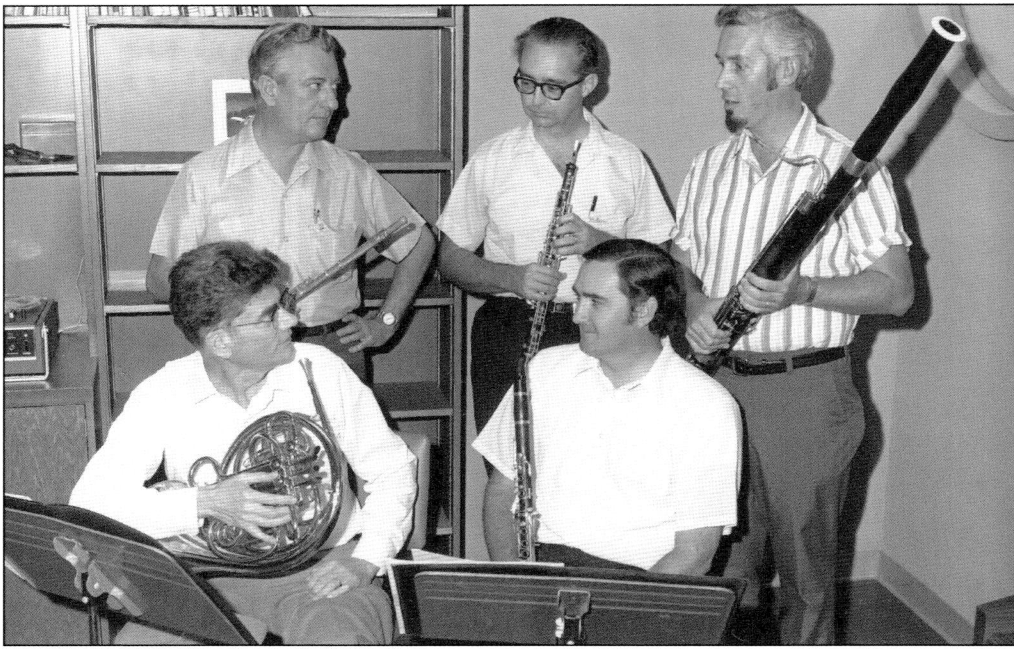

In the early 1960s, faculty formed cohesive groups that practiced and performed together regularly for schools and in the broader community. There was usually no cost for admission though a nominal fee was sometimes charged that was used for scholarships. The Gammage Woodwind Quintet, above in their practice attire, included, from left to right, (first row) John Barrows (French horn) and Jack Ratterree (clarinet); (second row) Edwin Putnik (flute), Frank Stalzer (oboe), and Jack Rausch (bassoon). The New Art String Quartet, below in their performance attire, was comprised of, from left to right, Frank Spinoza (violin), Eugene Lombardi (violin), Gabriel Gruber (viola), and Takayori Atsumi (cello). The music program was visited by world-famous musicians like cellists Pablo Casals and Gregor Piatigorsky. The faculty also included composers like Robert Lamm, Wendell Rider, and Grant Fletcher. Many music faculty members also performed with the Phoenix Symphony. (Above, courtesy of Frank Stalzer; below, Sally Atsumi.)

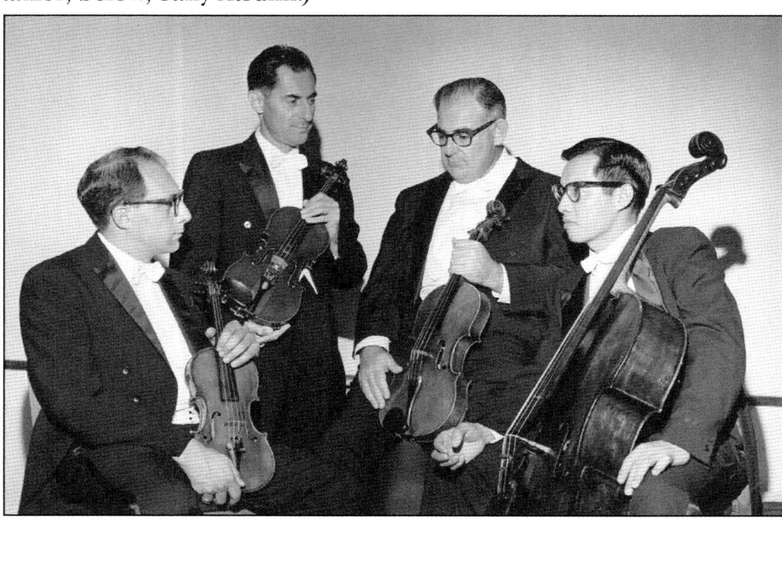

West Side Story, with students JoAnn Yeoman (left in the photograph at right), who later returned as faculty, playing Anita and Norma Yeary as Maria, was the first regular season musical in the Gammage Memorial Auditorium, built in 1964. Don Doyle was the director, and Kenneth Seipp was the musical director; 1964 also marked the year Seipp started the Lyric Opera Theatre. Back then, the Music, Theatre, and Dance Departments regularly cooperated on productions. Gammage Auditorium, the last public design of famed architect Frank Lloyd Wright, initially provided a great opportunity for students to cross train and perform on a world-class stage. That changed as more traveling shows visited, the first of which was the Philadelphia Orchestra in 1964. Theater directors like the early David Scoular and the longtime Clyde Parker are indispensable, whether Gammage hosts an ASU ceremony, a major show, or a presidential debate. (Right, courtesy of JoAnn Yeoman Tongret; below, UAASUL.)

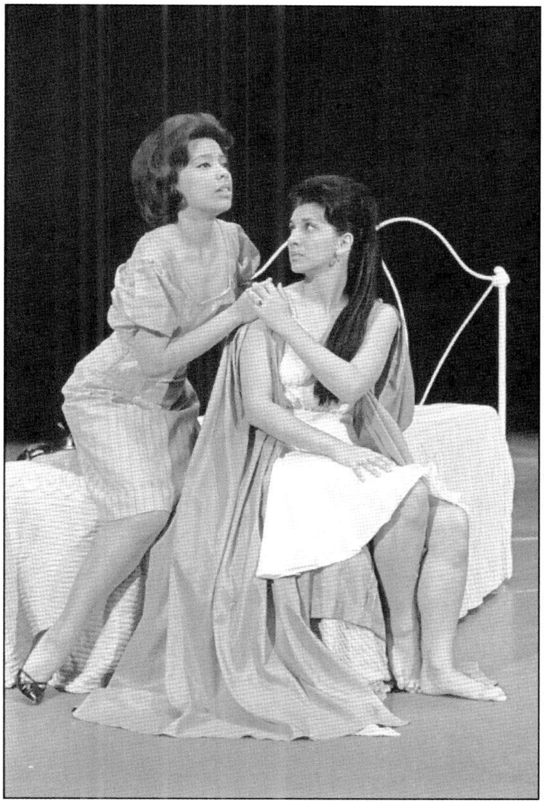

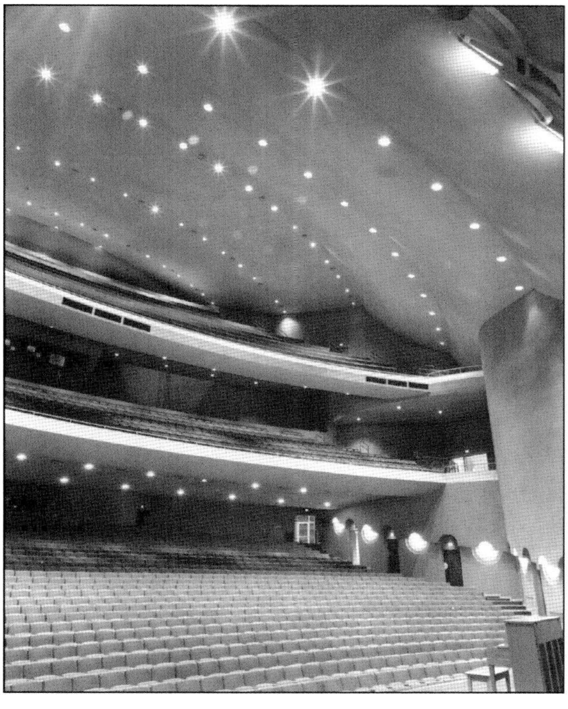

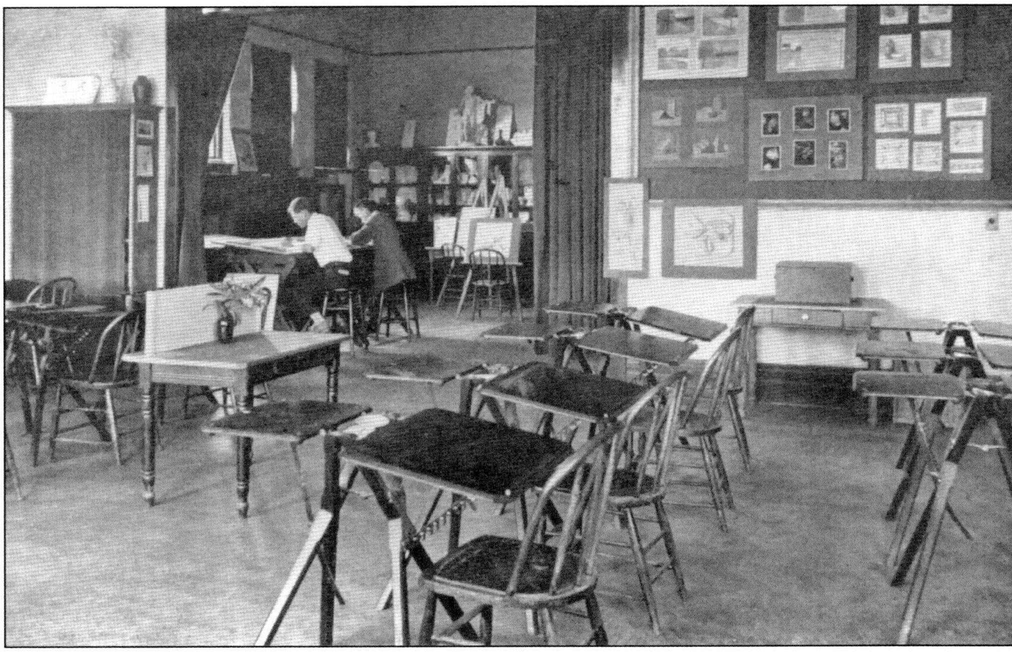

The 1911 normal school Art Department, pictured above, was well equipped. Learning how to teach art later expanded to include scholarly research and creative activities relating to art history and forms of art beyond drawing, painting, and sculpture to include printmaking, ceramics, fibers, metals, wood, and photography. The Harry Wood Gallery was named after a late-1950s faculty member who helped shepherd the program through various changes. Each program in what is now the Herberger Institute School of Design and the Arts has established a strong reputation. For example, the photography program regularly ranks in the top 10 in the country. Students learn traditional and new photographic processes and engage in cultural analysis. Along with the wider community, they can explore the Northlight Gallery's extensive collection of prints spanning the history of photography media back to 1840. (Above, courtesy of THM; below, Neil Miller.)

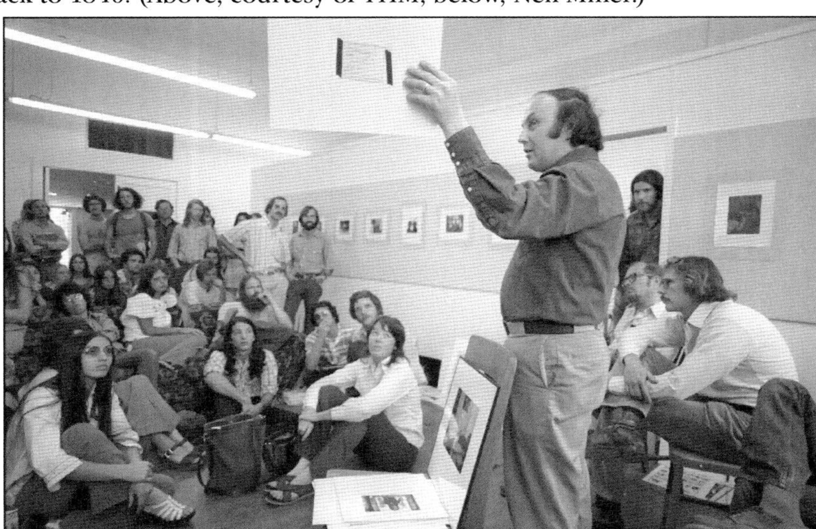

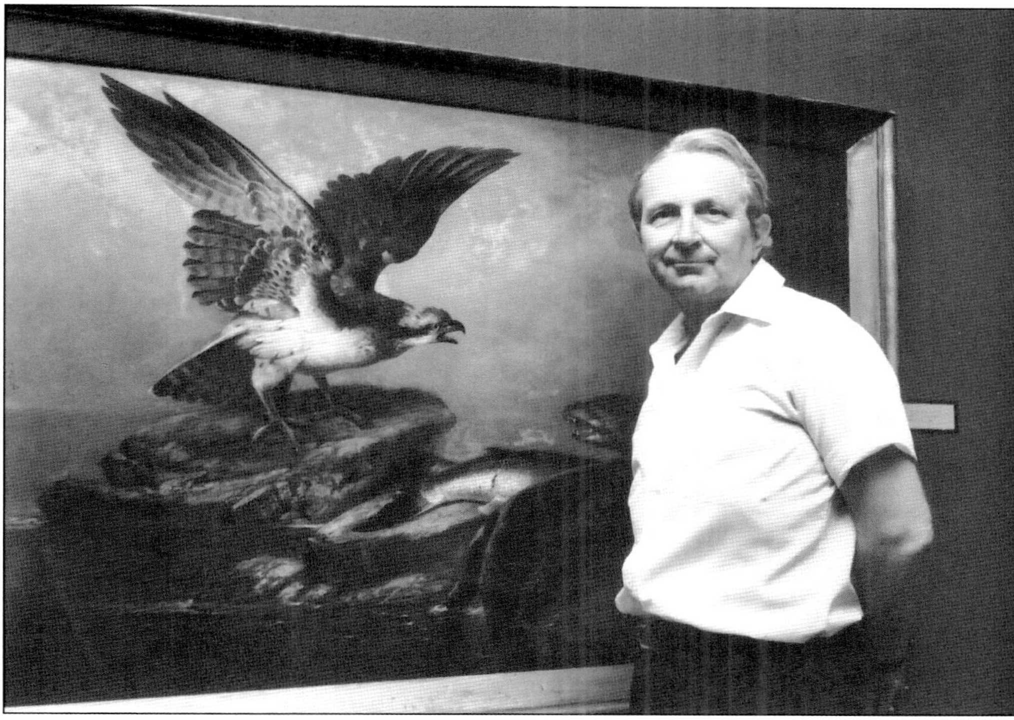

Galleries grew since 1950. Rudy Turk, above with an Audubon painting, directed the art collections from 1967 to 1992 and helped start the ASU Art Museum. During his 25 years, Turk was instrumental in building the Ceramic Research Center, an international resource, and one of the most prominent print collections in the southwest, which includes Latin American Art, one of the first museums in the United States to do so. (Courtesy of Ceramics Research Center.)

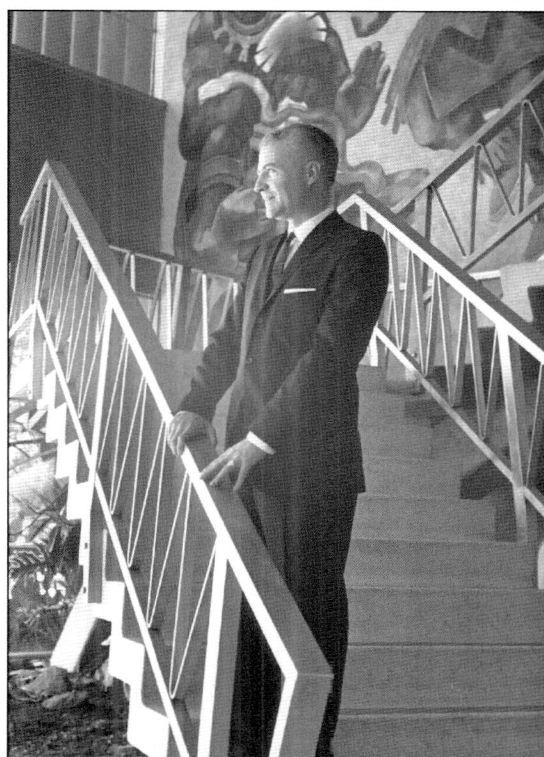

Pres. G. Homer Durham (1960–1969) is remembered as a friend to the arts. He built programs like Gammage built buildings as the new university continued to grow. Durham wrote that ASU "must be a center of academic integrity and freedom in the pursuit of knowledge and truth . . . beauty, goodness. This role is limited chiefly by character and quality, and the condition of support and freedom under which a university attempts to flourish." (Courtesy of UAASUL.)

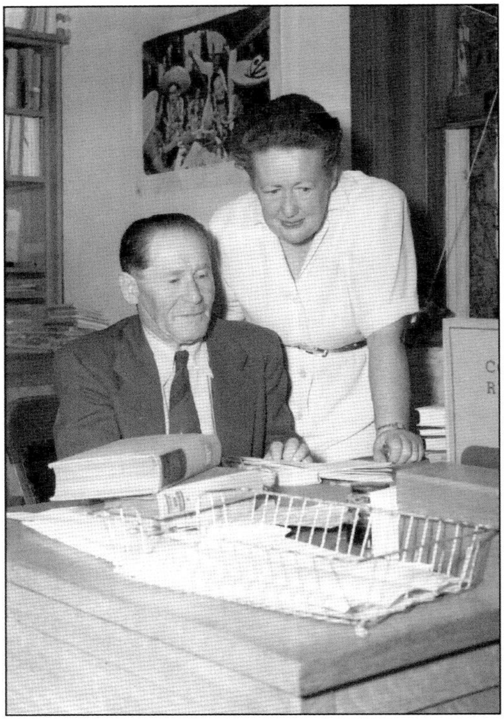

George and Collice Portnoff, at left, were brought to ASC from Flagstaff by Grady Gammage in 1945. George, a linguist, chaired the Foreign Language Department. Sadly, he passed in 1948. Collice, a friend of arts patron Louise Lincoln Kerr, was a founding member of the Arizona Cello Society and the Valley Shakespeare Theatre. She joined the English Department, which she chaired from 1958 to 1964. She remained in the English Department until retiring from ASU in 1969. Many years later, Foreign Languages would form the School of International Letters and Cultures, which, in an ever more global environment, now offers the study of many languages and cultures. In 1958, the McCune Foundation donated $80,000 in television equipment that opened up more educational and broadcasting possibilities, to the benefit of the students and community. Quino E. Martinez, below, presents a Spanish language program on Channel 8. (Left, courtesy of Lisa Portnoff Crehan; below, UAASUL.)

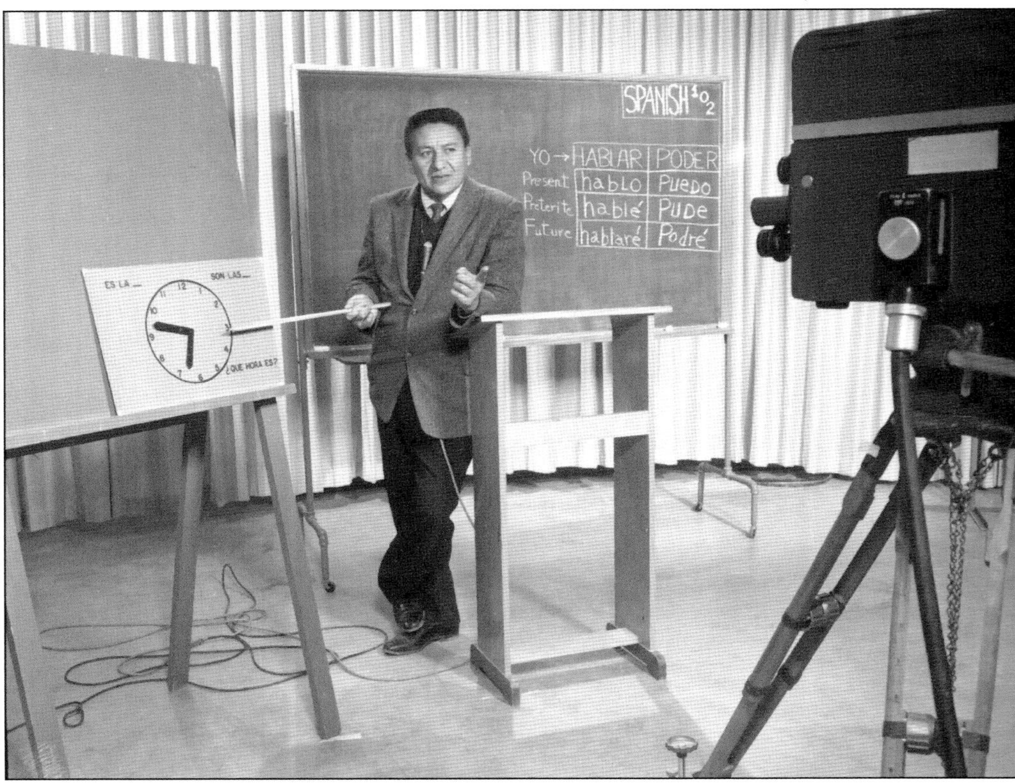

English also grew into a richly varied, award-winning unit building on the seeds of the first normal school curriculum, which included courses on literary classics. Nicholas Salerno, English faculty from 1961 to 1991 (chair from 1982 to 1988), had a cinema classics show on Channel 8, KAET, that aired locally for 10 years and for three years nationally on PBS. KAET, a PBS station, began broadcasting in 1961 with Robert Ellis in charge. A beloved part of ASU and the community, it provides educational, cultural, and news programming of the highest caliber, with Emmy Awards to prove it. It competed with few other television stations then, and local residences told their families back home about it, influencing some early faculty members to move west. Below, Ellis, far right in the first row, helps celebrate a Diamond Jubilee event honoring the return of alumni from 50 years prior. (Right, courtesy of Gary Krahenbuhl; below, UAASUL.)

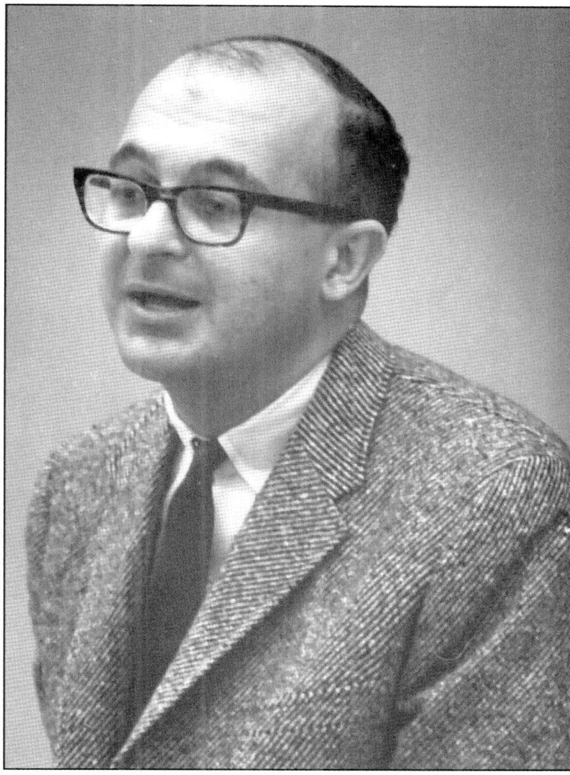

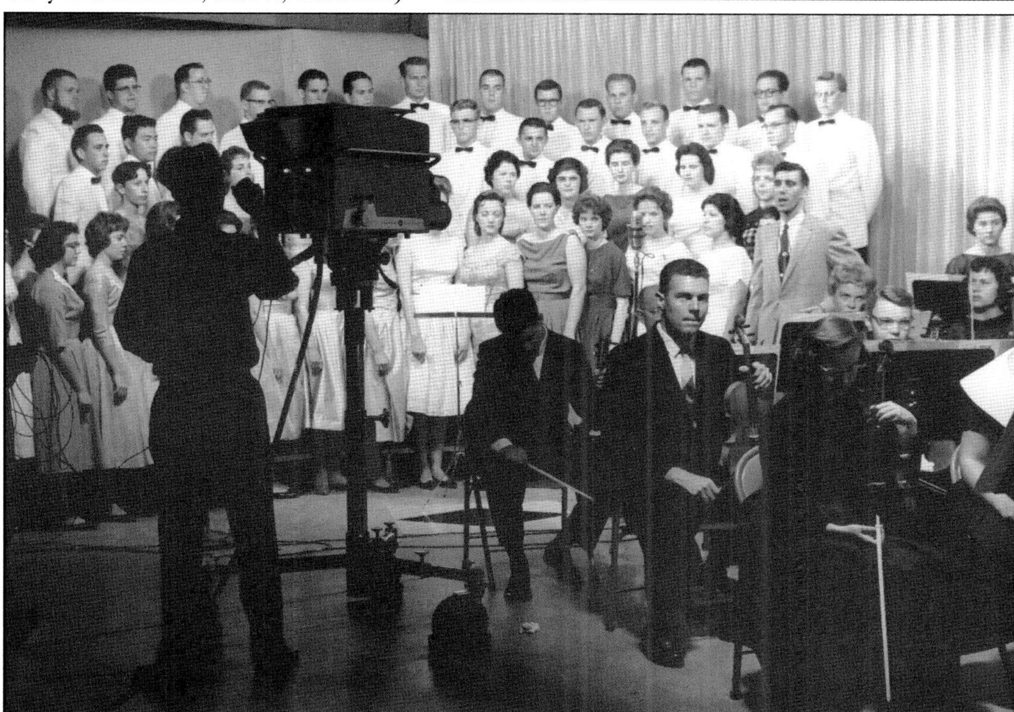

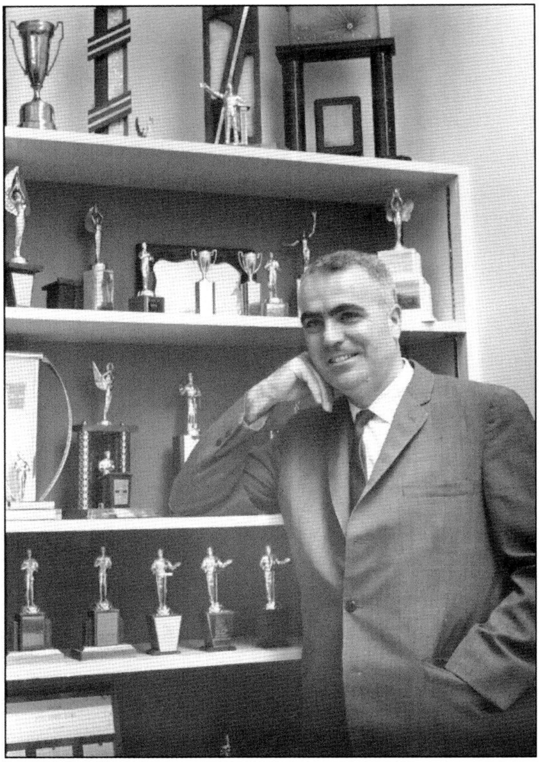

Gale Richards, chair of Speech and Drama (1965–1973), continued the tradition of debate that developed in the normal school early on. As fields grew, theater, communication, and speech pathology each developed separate departments. Rhetoric grew to include intercultural, interpersonal, and organizational communication scholars. In 1999, after years in the College of Public Programs, they became the Hugh Downs School of Human Communication, named after the well-loved broadcaster. (Courtesy of UAASUL.)

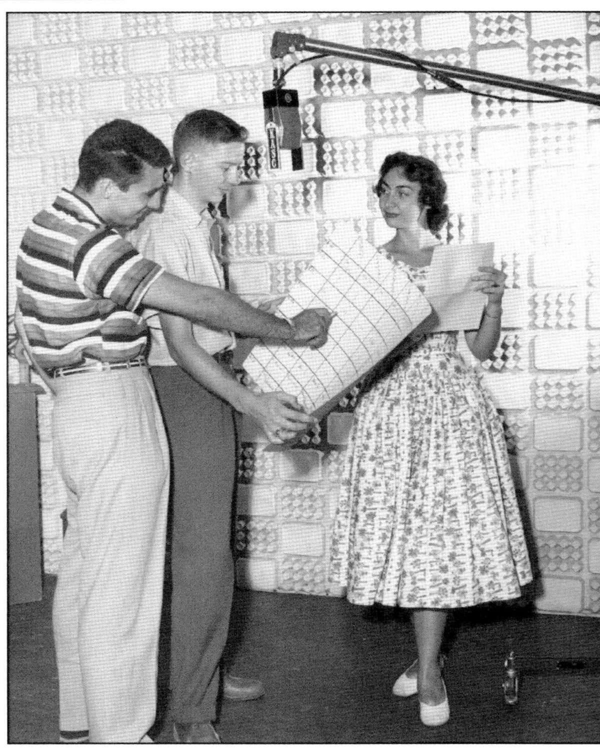

Campus radio station KASC contributed to the development of a radio/television major, first available in 1954. While journalism courses were offered since 1936, Ernest J. Hopkins was, in 1949, the first faculty member with the word "journalism" in his title. Journalism broke from English in 1957 and eventually became the Walter Cronkite School of Journalism and Mass Communication in 1984, named after the famed anchorman It is now on ASU's Downtown Phoenix campus, which opened in 2006. (Courtesy of UAASUL.)

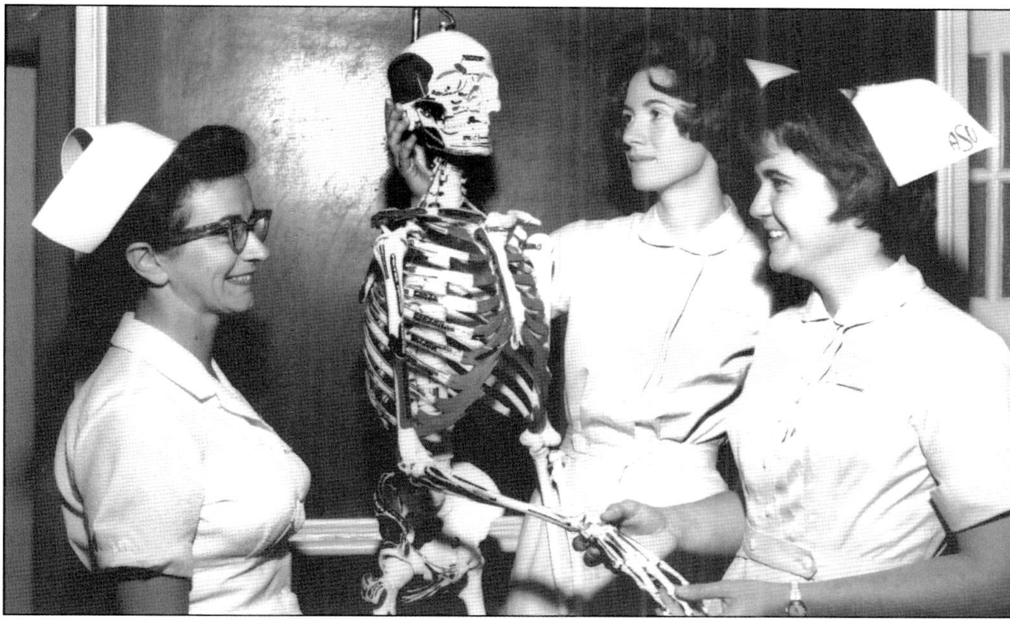

The College of Public Programs, whose founding dean was Frank Sackton, also moved downtown, as did Nursing. Health-related classes were an early part of the institution's history. By 1943, the students and community actively sought more than general education classes. George Bateman requested that the School of Nursing be formed within Liberal Arts in 1957, and in 1960, the first six students graduated. Nursing's first building, below, was a welcome addition in 1959 after two years in the basement of Matthews Library. It became a college of its own in 1964 and is now the impressive College of Nursing and Heath Innovation. The scholars and educators there contribute greatly to the body of knowledge within the field of healthcare and to the community by graduating thousands of healthcare providers and researchers. (Both courtesy of UAASUL.)

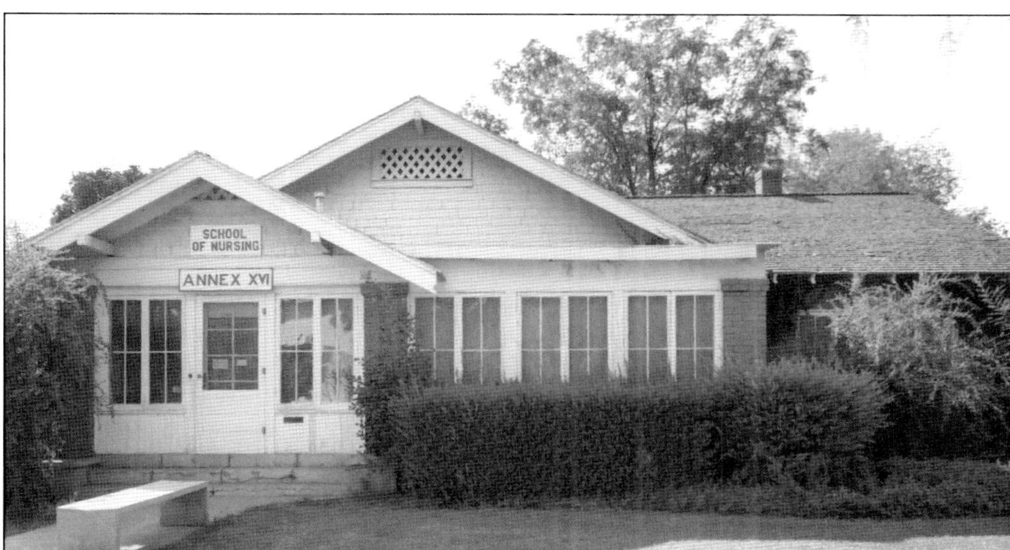

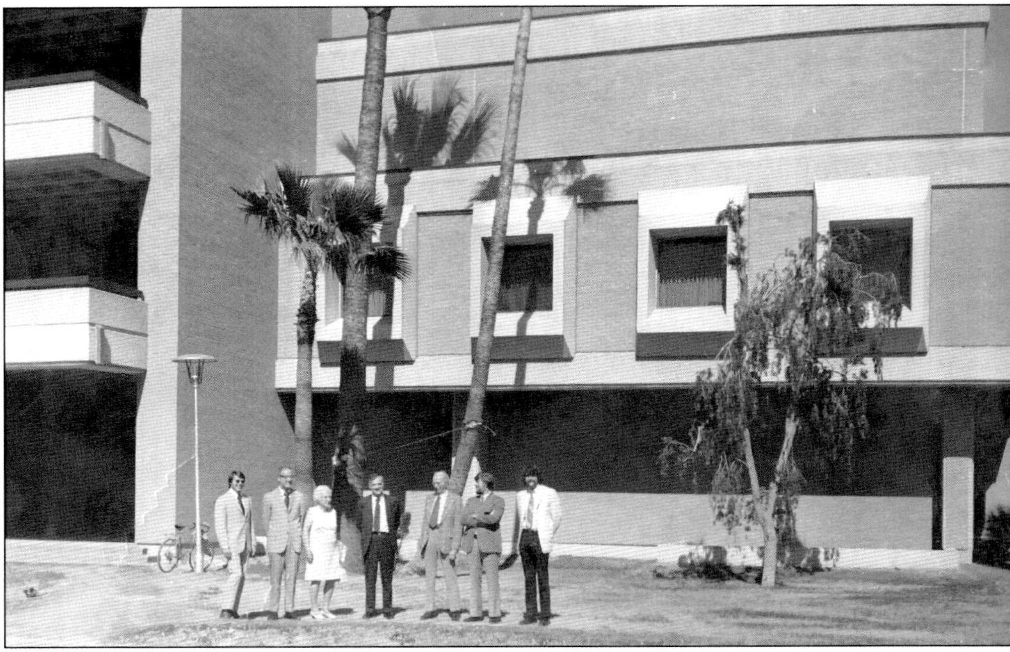

Psychology has early roots within the institution. Early figures like James McNaughton, John Grimes, Herbert Gurnee, and Rachel Ball taught psychology, with offerings increasing until a department formed in 1931, graduate courses were first offered in 1937, and behavioral research started as early as the 1950s. An outpatient clinic was established as a training facility in 1959. Psychology grew so rapidly in research and teaching that it was granted its own building in 1971, pictured above with noted learning theorist Ernest Hilgard (center) as dedication speaker in 1973. The field has both social science and physical science components; thus, the program offers graduate degrees in developmental, social, clinical, cognitive, behavioral neuroscience, and quantitative methods, with tools and insights applied in many other fields. Hudson Jost, Psychology Department chair from 1959 to 1962, conducts a stress test in the photograph below. (Above, courtesy of Stanley Parkinson; below, UAASUL.)

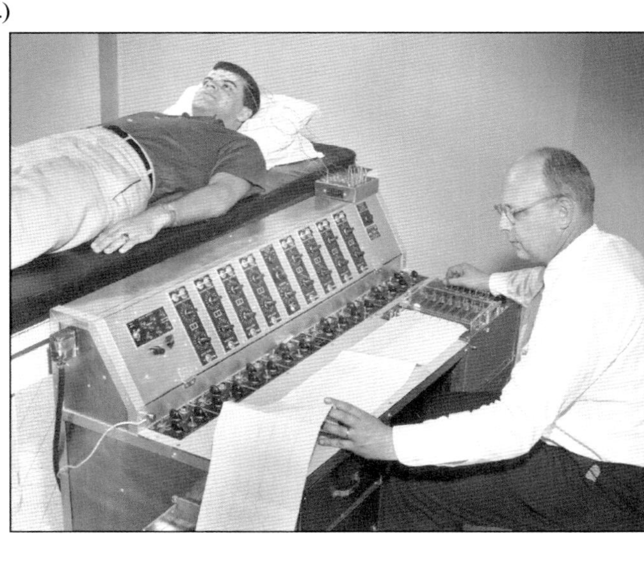

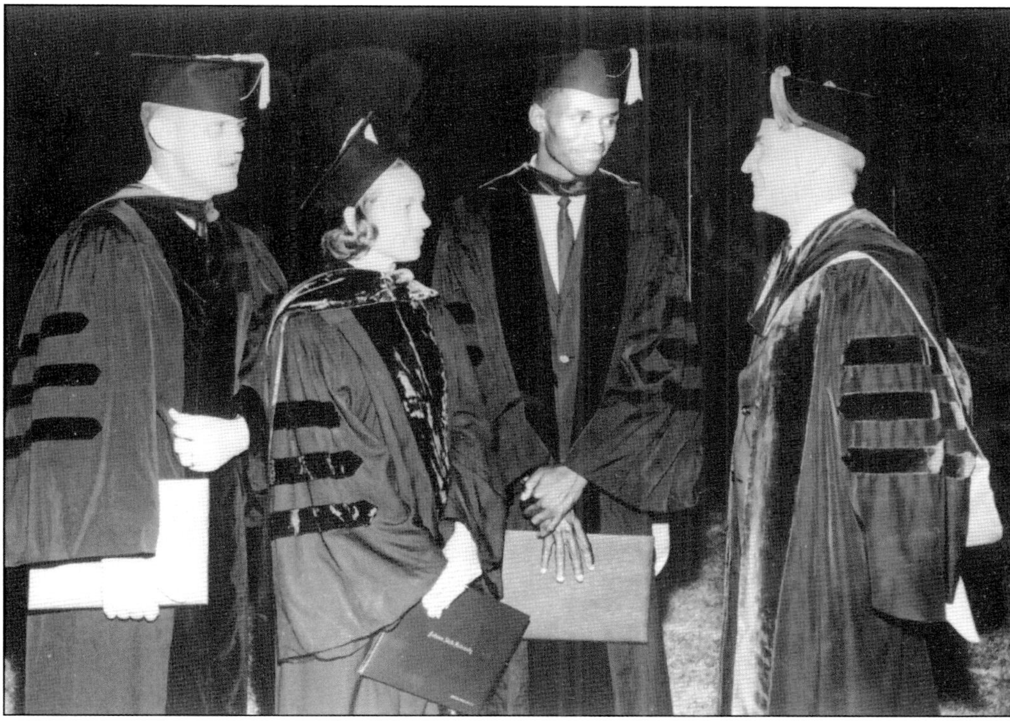

Three of the first four students to graduate with PhDs from ASU in 1963 were from the Psychology Department; they pose above with President Durham. Graduate education is often interdisciplinary. For instance, psychologist Stanley Parkinson served on the master's committee for Temple Grandin, an animal science major who later became an international spokesperson for autism and a leading animal rights advocate, especially as relates to livestock facilities design and humane slaughter. (Courtesy of CC, UAASUL.)

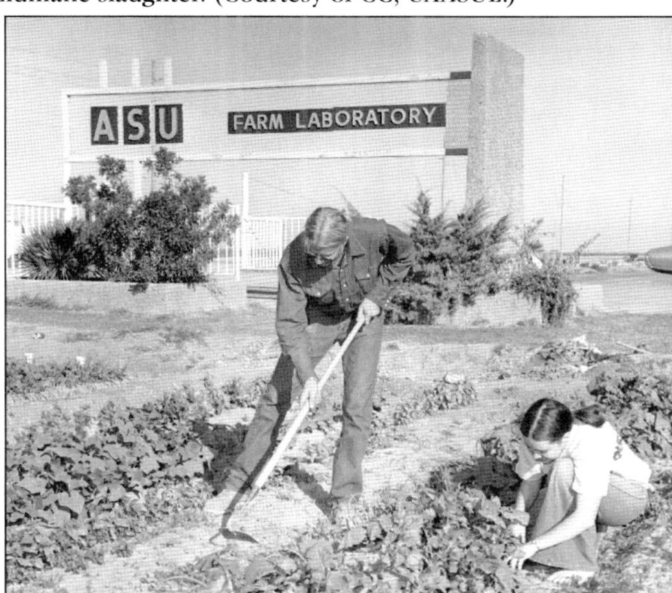

The institution's early teachings about agriculture and livestock led to the 1956 development of the Farm Laboratory on a 320-acre site at Elliot and Price Roads. Sheep, beef cattle, dairy cows, poultry, and pigs were raised and researched there, as were horticulture and crop rotation. The laboratory was discontinued by 1983, and the land was later developed into the ASU Research Park with the help of a board of community members like Rudy Campbell. (Courtesy of UAASUL.)

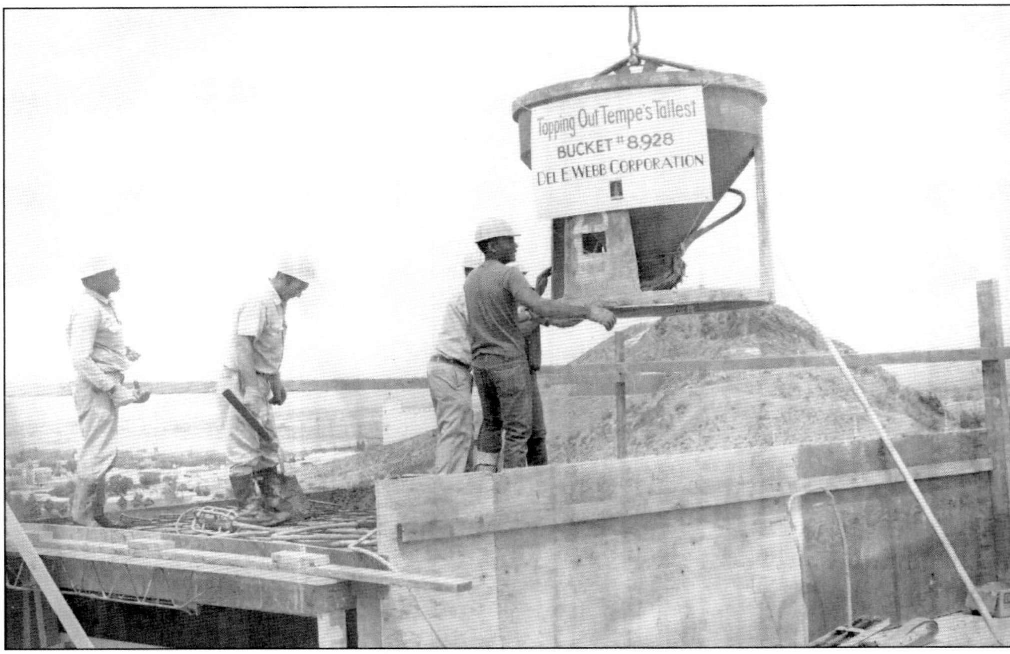

Early agriculture and industrial arts were, in 1954, grouped with architecture and engineering. Extreme growth led to a remarkable array of engineering studies and achievements and to what are now known as the Ira A. Fulton Schools of Engineering, one of which is the Del E. Webb School of Construction, named after the builder. By 1960, all of the engineering programs were accredited. Architecture began as early as 1952 and became its own college in 1966 with founding dean James Elmore. ASU students, below, learn a casting technique during internationally known architect Paolo Soleri's workshop. The exciting learning opportunities for those in what is now the Design School in ASU's Herberger Institute, whether they be architecture, landscape architecture, or graphic, industrial, interior or urban design, contribute to the public good through safe and beautiful environments. (Above, courtesy of Shirley Blanton; below, UAASUL.)

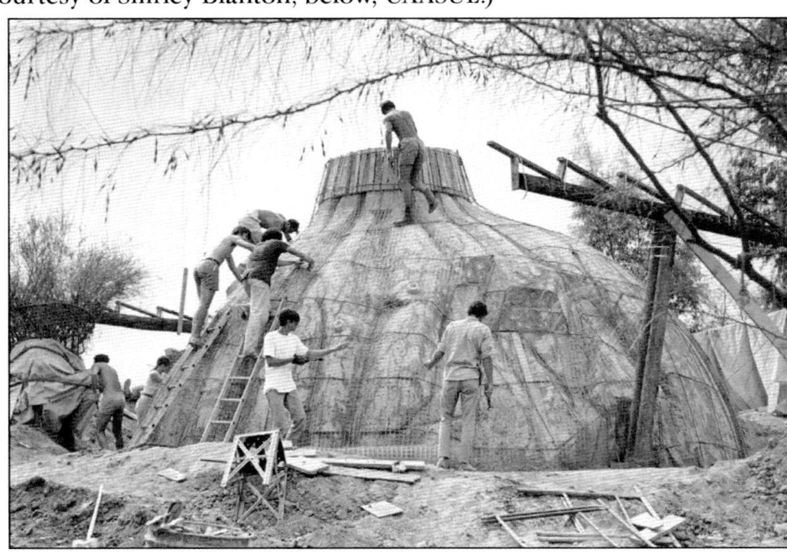

The first externally funded research at ASU was granted to the Department of Physical Sciences in 1956 but would not have been possible without engineers. The solar furnace, partly pictured above with physicist Clement Kevane, could reach 6,000 degrees Fahrenheit, permitting high-temperature research with metals. ASU has long been involved in solar-related research, and engineering faculty in 1972 created a system to allow homes to harness electricity from the sun. (Courtesy of UAASUL.)

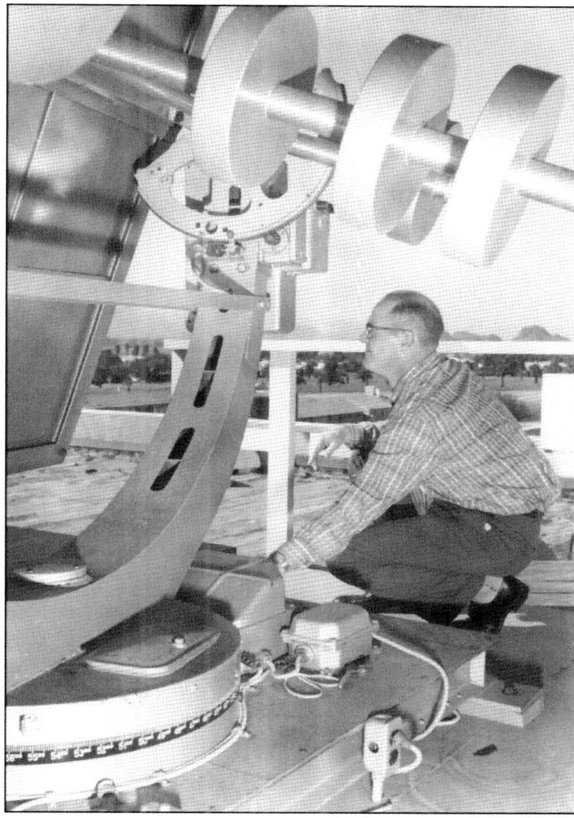

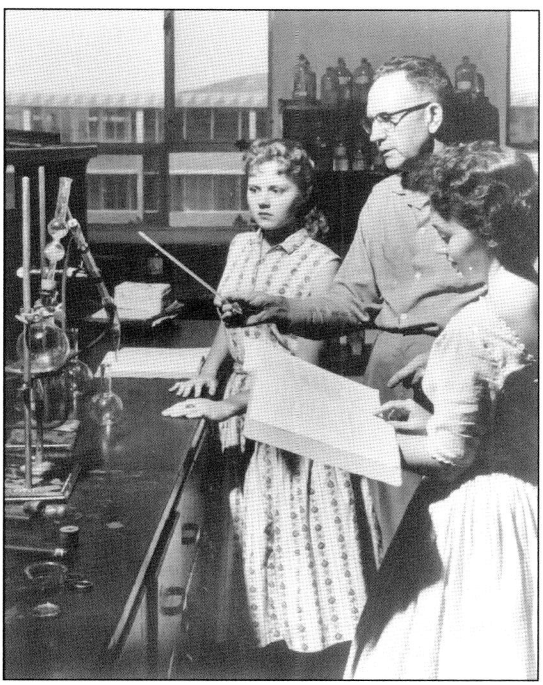

George Bateman arrived in 1927 and was the first faculty member with a PhD who was not a principal or president. During his 40-year career, he led the physical sciences for years and helped develop the Botany, Zoology, Physics, and Chemistry Departments. A chemistry doctoral student was one of the first four graduate students to earn a PhD at ASU in 1963. The Bateman Physical Sciences Center was named in his honor in 1977. (Courtesy of UAASUL.)

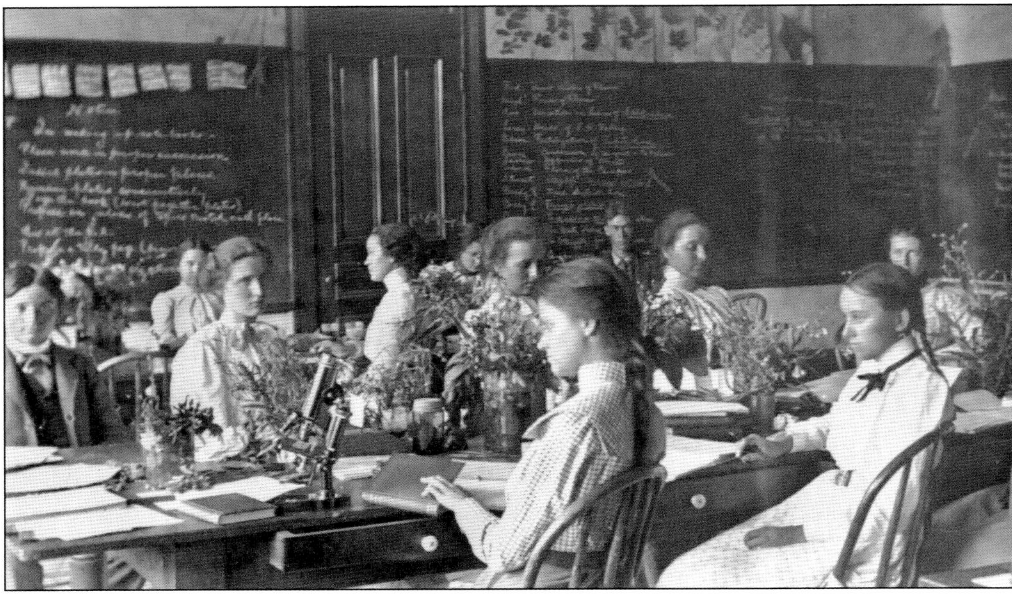

Students learn plant biology, or botany, above in a 1903 classroom in Old Main. Their teacher, Frederick Irish, pressed and documented plants that later became part of the Vascular Plant Herbarium in the Natural History Collections. ASU has numerous collections, including insects, fossil plants, reptiles, birds, lichens, and more. These help students learn and attract researchers from around the world. Milton Sommerfeld, pictured below with students at an algae pond, arrived in 1968. He later moved his lab to the East campus (now Polytechnic), which was formed in 1996 on the old Williams Air Force Base. There, in the College of Technology and Innovation, his work includes the feasibility of large-scale applications of one of his team's key discoveries: algae as a source for renewable biofuels. Forward thinking, ASU established the first school of sustainability in the United States in 2007. (Above, courtesy of UAASUL; below, Gary Krahenbuhl.)

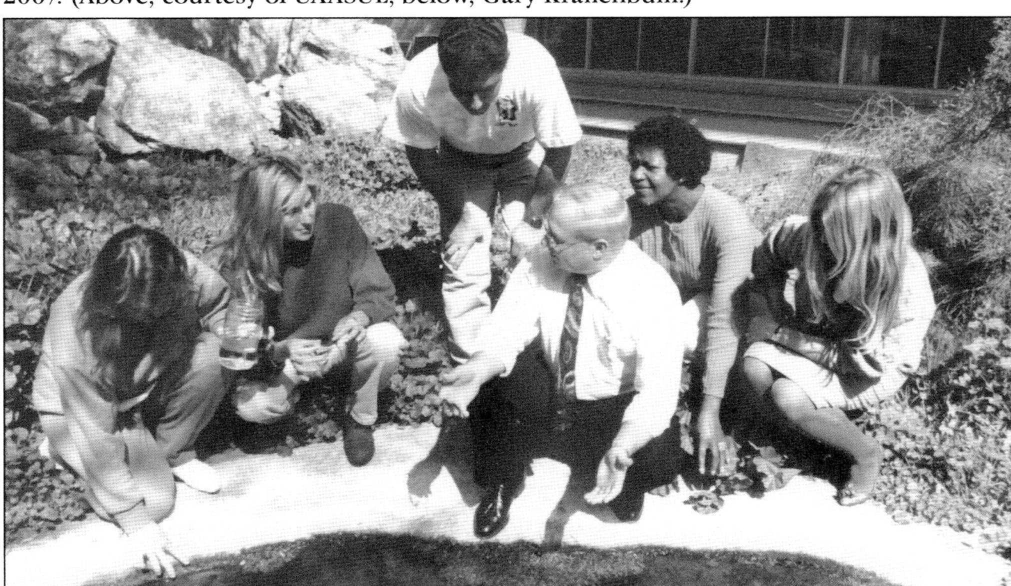

Early chemists like LeRoy Eyring, not pictured here, and Robert Pettit, on the right, helped build ASU's strong science reputation. Roland K. Robins conducted cancer research as early as 1957. In 1965, Robert Pettit arrived and began developing marine organism research that led to the creation of anti-cancer drugs and, in 1973, what became the Cancer Research Institute. Others, like zoologist Charles M. Woolf, took a genetic approach to cancer research. (Courtesy of Gary Krahenbuhl.)

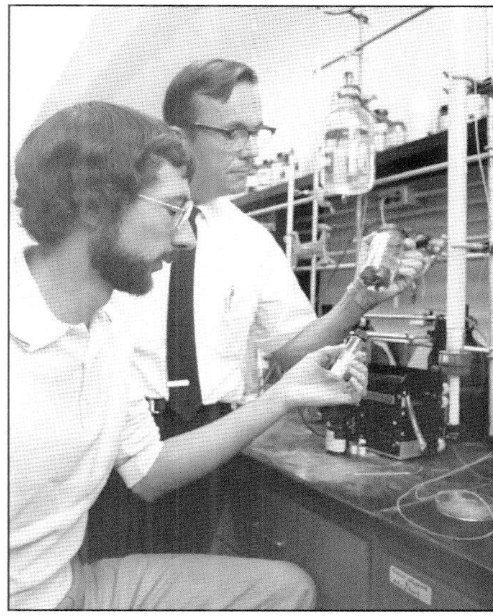

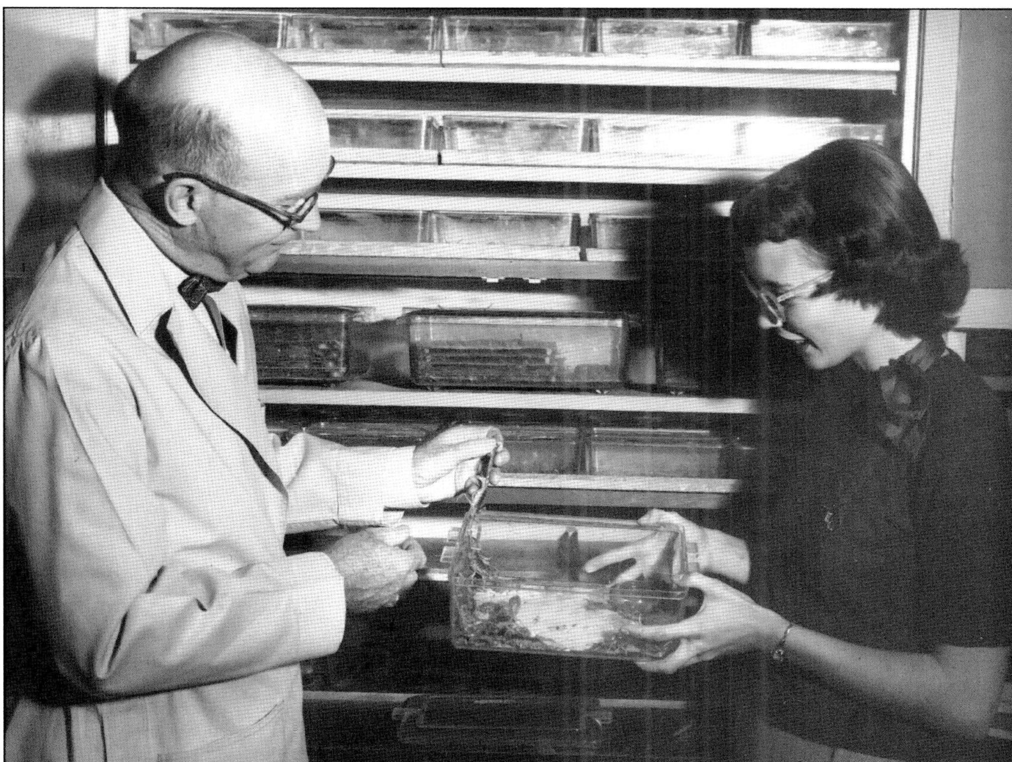

Expert venomologist Herbert Stahnke (left) arrived in 1928 for a long and fruitful career. Through direct legislative appropriations in the early 1940s, he founded the Poisonous Animal Research Laboratory to help develop antivenins to deadly scorpion stings and snakebites. The lab closed in 1972, but scorpion antivenin was produced at ASU into the 1990s. Stahnke helped start a rich tradition of solution-oriented science. (Courtesy of UAASUL.)

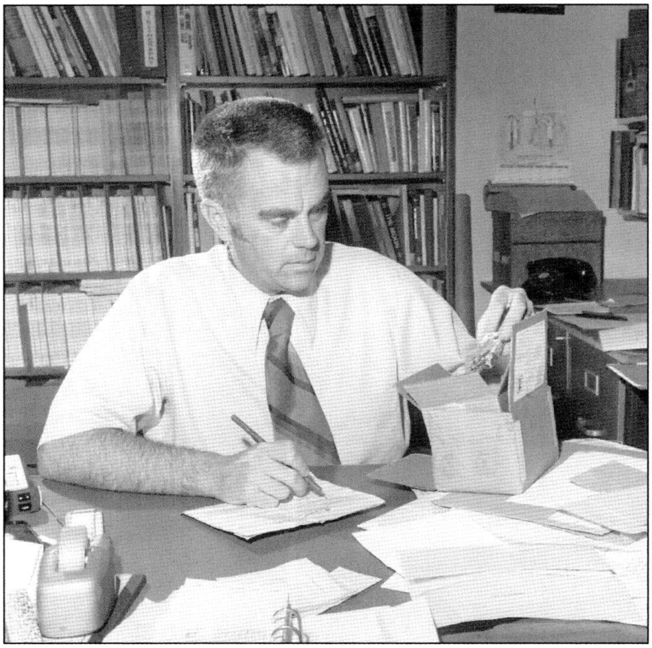

George Boyd, the first coordinator of research, helped secure a portion of Harvey H. Nininger's meteorites for ASU in 1960, making it the largest university-based meteorite collection. Geochemist Carleton Moore, pictured here, became the first director of the Center for Meteorite Study in 1961. ASU has an international reputation in astrophysics and planetary geology, having been involved in, among other things, lunar, Mars, and Crab Nebula research. (Courtesy of Gary Krahenbuhl.)

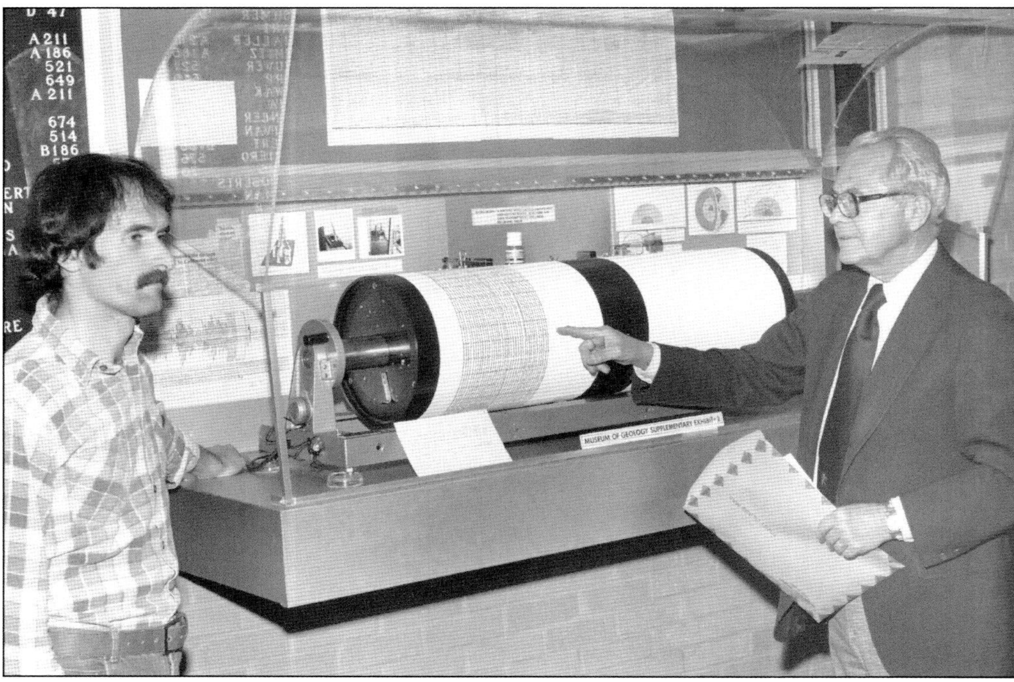

ASU researchers are also interested in the geology of the earth. For instance, early soil geologist Troy Péwé both researched arctic permafrost and mapped fissures in the southeast region of the Phoenix metropolitan area. Péwé, to the right with student Brad Archer, later curated ASU's Robert S. Dietz Museum of Geology, which has exciting items like an active seismograph, a six-story Foucault pendulum, and mammoth bones from Chandler, Arizona. (Courtesy of Gary Krahenbuhl.)

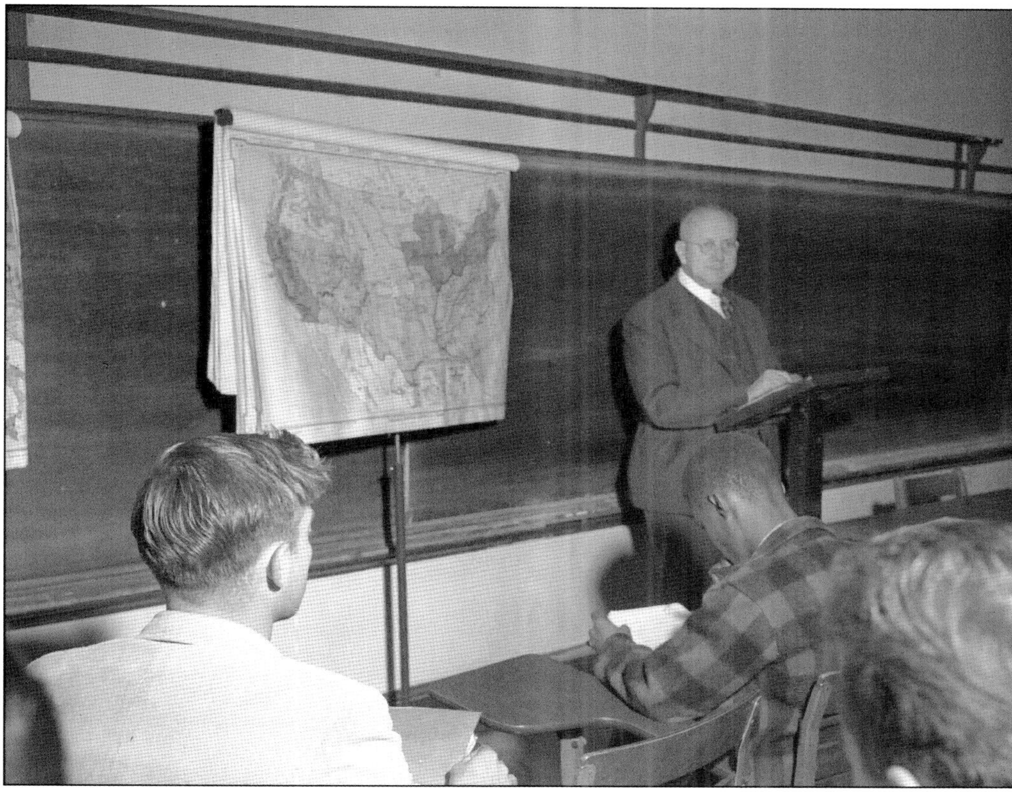

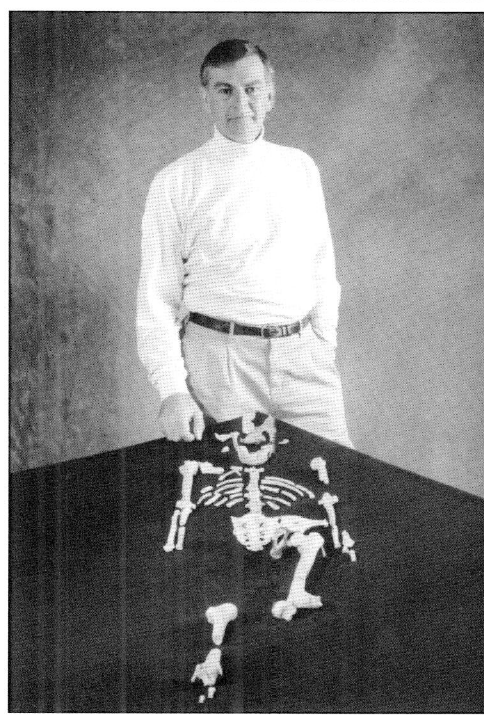

Rufus K. Wyllys (above), a historian of borderlands and Latin America, arrived in 1930 and headed the Department of Social Studies, encompassing history, economics, sociology, and political science. Later, those disciplines grew into separate powerhouses of research and education. Recently, the Sociology Department's substantial scholarly strengths were absorbed into the School of Social and Family Dynamics, where work on social institutions, ethnic and gender issues, and population dynamics continues. Once combined with Sociology, the Anthropology Department formed in 1962, building on the work of early faculty like Reynold Ruppé and Christy G. Turner II. The more than 50 members studying local and global cultures today were joined by Donald C. Johanson in 1996. Johanson, pictured at right, discovered the world-famous 3.18-million-year-old hominid bones of "Lucy" and brought the Institute of Human Origins with him to ASU. (Above, courtesy of UAASUL; right, Gary Krahenbuhl.)

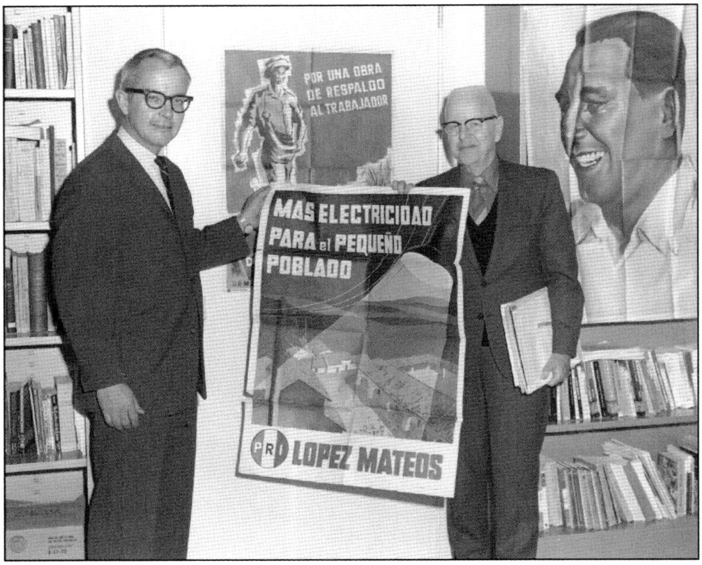

From the foundation that Wyllys laid, later faculty developed the Center for Latin American Studies in 1965. Historian and director Louis Tambs is seen to the left meeting with expert Russell Fitzgibbon. This center helped set the stage for ASU to take on ever more complex transborder issues. Numerous other centers, like the Center for the Study of Religion and Conflict, study about and contribute to local and global arenas. (Courtesy of THM.)

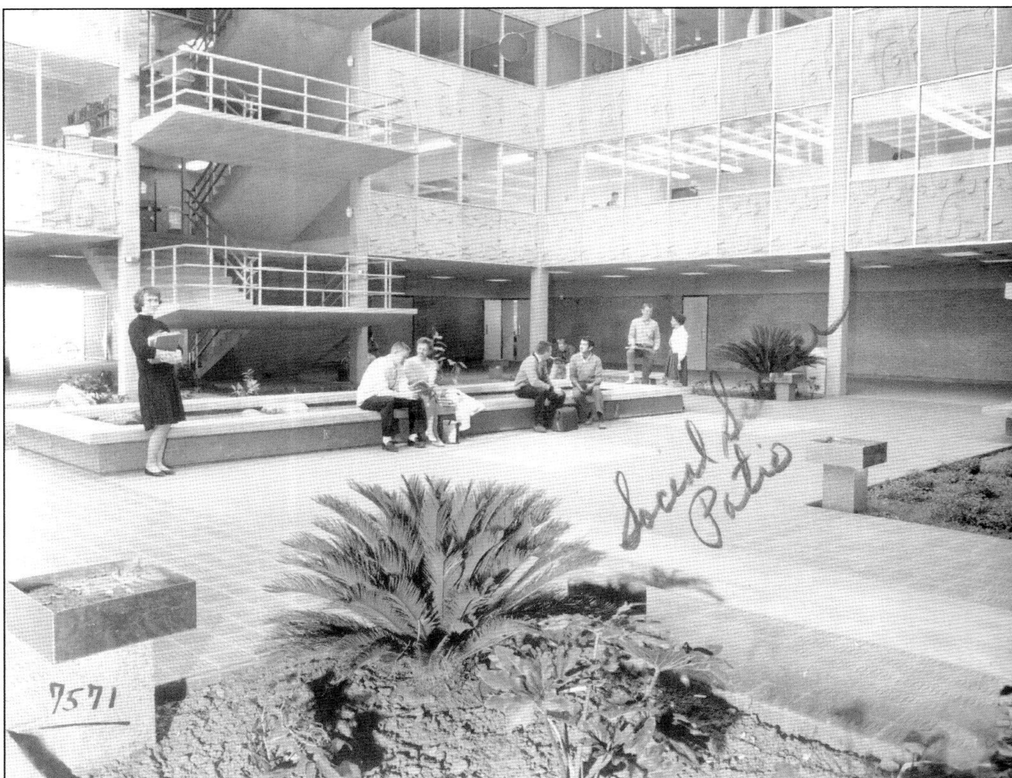

Always an issue on a growing campus, space grew so tight in the 1950s that the Lyceum Building, which was used for events and receptions (originally a campus heating facility), was refitted to hold administrators, academics, and even the Psychology Department's rat maze cages on the stage. The Social Science Building (above), dedicated in 1961, was a welcome relief and allowed the Lyceum to be remodeled as a theater. (Courtesy of UAASUL.)

Early courses in secretarial skills were part of Commerce. More modern business specialties were added as times changed. The College of Business Administration officially formed in 1954. From left to right at right, Dean Glenn Overman (1956–1981), President Durham, and Paul Oreffice, chief executive officer of Caterpillar, attend the ground-breaking ceremony of its first building in 1967. Overman guided the college to great heights, inspiring student, faculty, and community success. In 2003, noted businessman William P. Carey, grandson of ASU's founder, John Samuel Armstrong, endowed $50 million to the college. The W.P. Carey School of Business continues to honor the past and build the future with each generation of students. Below, from left to right, are business dean Larry Penley (1991–2003), W.P. Carey, John Samuel Armstrong III, and Richard Morgan, the law school dean (1989–1997). Morgan was appointed after Alan Matheson's third time as dean of law. (Right, courtesy of UAASUL; below, John S. Armstrong III.)

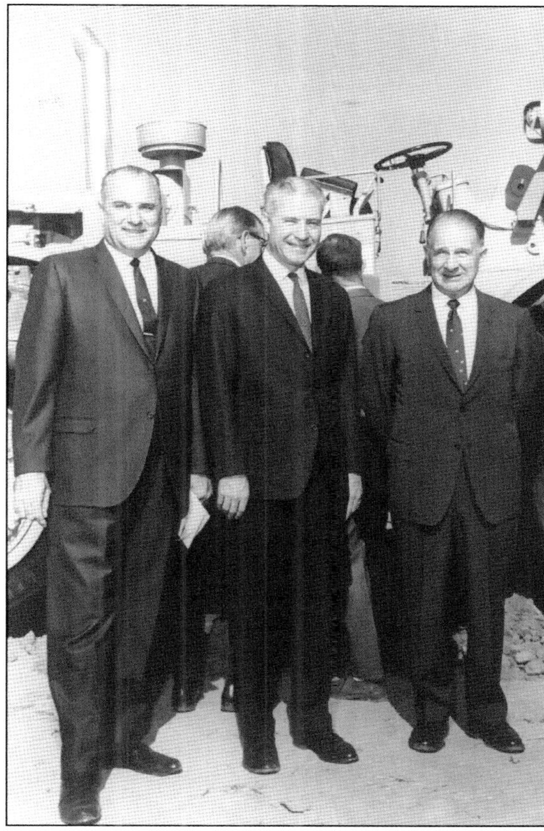

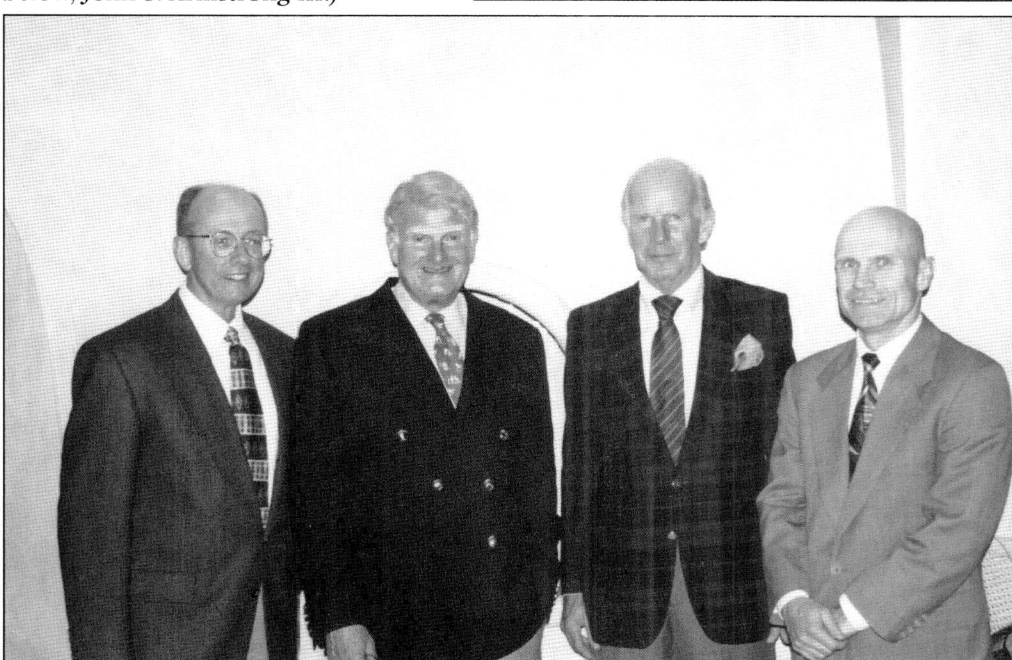

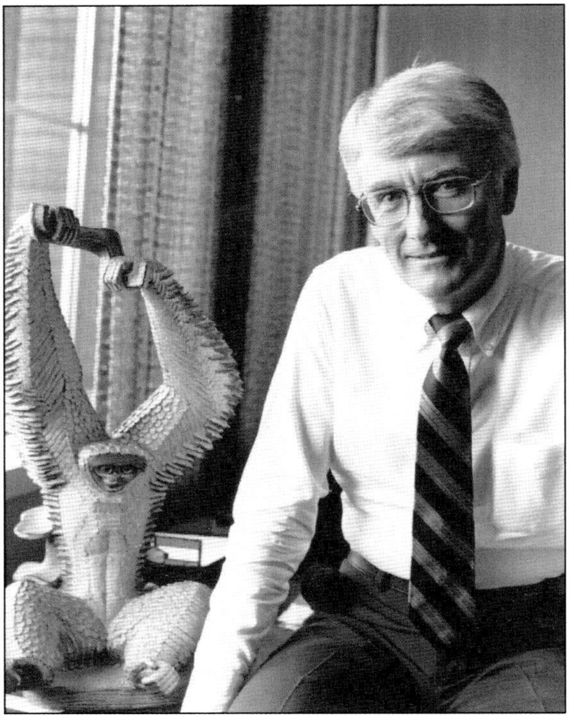

After presidents Grady Gammage (1933–1959), Harold Richardson (1959–1960), G. Homer Durham (1960–1969), Harry Newburn (1969–1971), and John Schwada (1971–1981) came J. Russell Nelson, pictured here, whose 1981–1989 presidency marked another surge in development, with student enrollment growing to 40,500 and grants doubling, further setting the stage for ASU to join the ranks of other top-notch universities. It officially did so under president Lattie Coor Jr.'s leadership (1990–2002), earning the designation Research I University in 1994. (Courtesy of the *State Press*.)

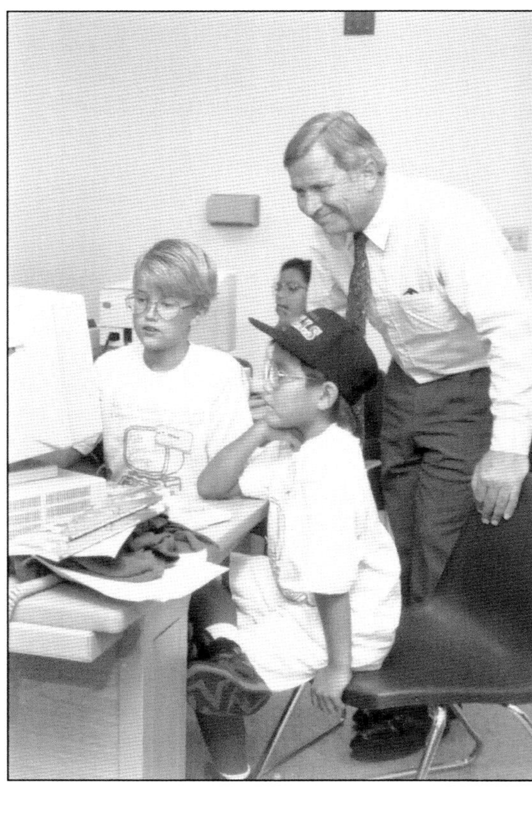

Sun Devils are part of the community, as demonstrated by Pres. Lattie Coor, pictured here at a children's computer camp at ASU's Downtown Center, a forerunner of the Downtown Phoenix campus. Programs like the School of Social Service Administration, formed in 1961 and now the School of Social Work, are exemplars of helping individuals, families, and communities. Similarly, the Department of Speech and Hearing Science's scholarly and community work has garnered it international recognition. (Courtesy of UAASUL.)

ASU was destined to expand into the west valley. An initial attempt in 1968, under Durham, to establish a campus in Litchfield Park failed to pass through the state legislature. In 1972, Barbara Ridge, a mother of four attending Glendale Community College, resurrected the idea. She argued that "the commute to Tempe ended a lot of people's college opportunities." As a result, she launched a campaign of fundraising and lobbying. Her husband, Sterling Ridge (a former Glendale mayor) also joined the crusade, getting elected into the state legislature. In 1984, the Ridges, seen here a few years later with Gov. Rose Mofford and former ASU West vice president Gerald McSheffrey (center), witnessed their success when ASU West was finally dedicated. The campus, pictured below, has become a point of pride and architectural beauty with over 12,000 students enrolled by 2011. (Right, courtesy of Sterling and Barbara Ridge; below, UAASUL.)

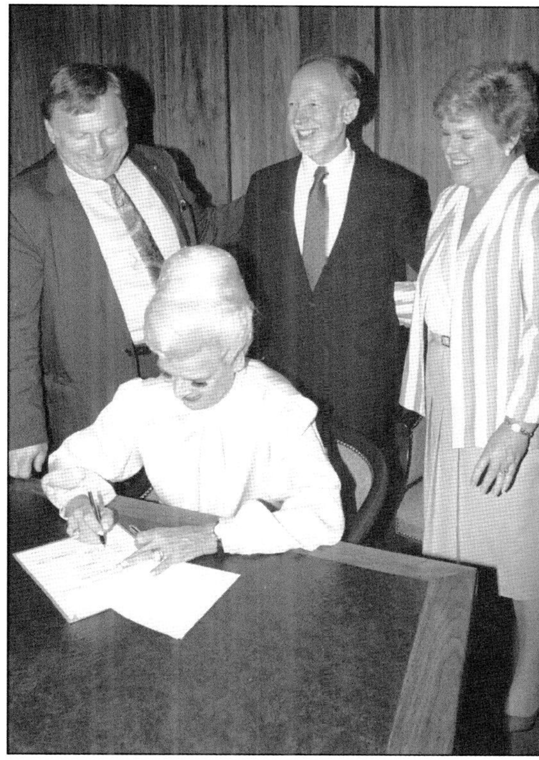

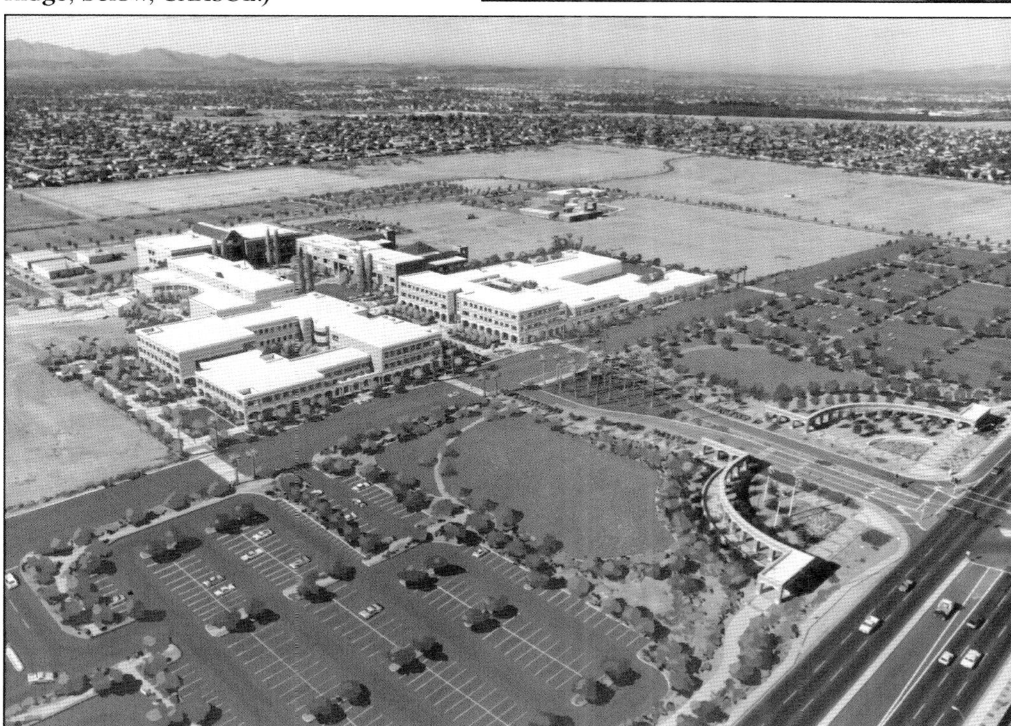

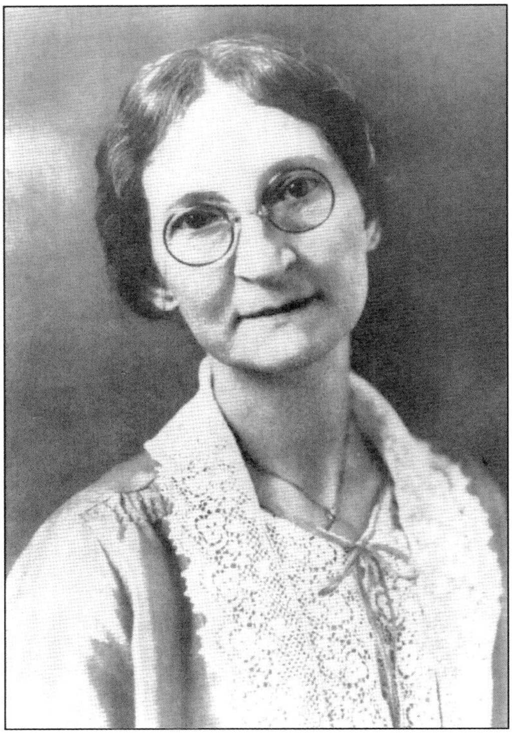

Besides the outreach programs and faculty, the libraries are also important resources for the wider community. Rebecca Cookson (left), assistant librarian from 1919 to 1941, and her librarian husband, C.J. Cookson, were so well loved that the students dedicated their 1925 yearbook to them, noting that "their willing service, untiring effort and deep sympathy have endeared themselves to the hearts of the students and proven their loyalty to Tempe Teacher's College." (Courtesy of THM.)

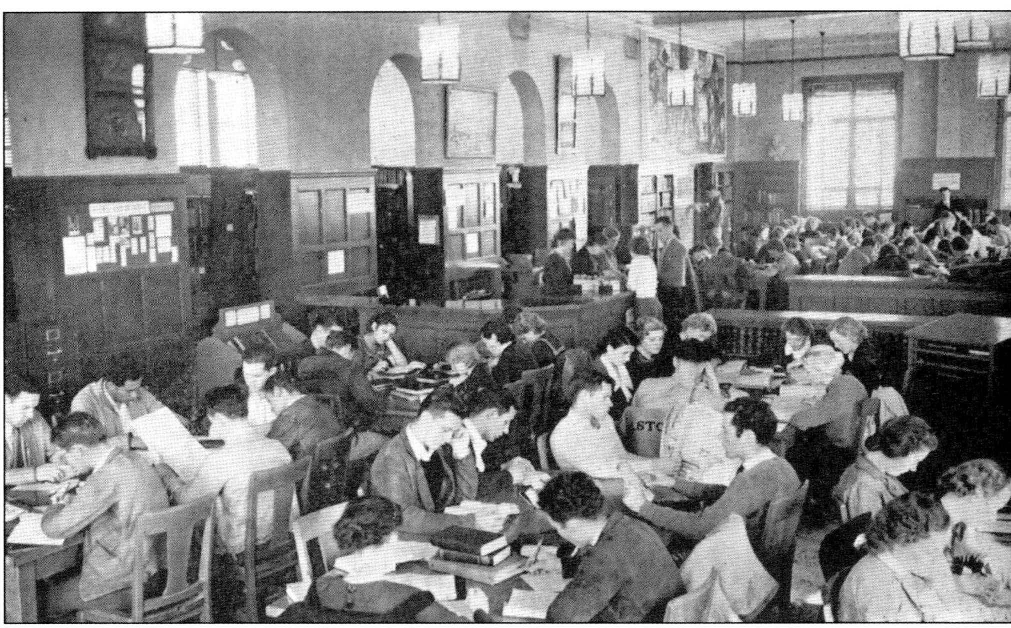

Libraries make everything else possible. After the first library of a single dictionary and globe in the first normal school building and the 700-volume library in Old Main, pictured on the cover, Matthews Library opened in 1930 with 14,000 books and was expanded in 1955. There used to be Sunday Teas at the library, drawing community members to campus. In 1966, Matthews closed, and 16 miles of books were moved. (Courtesy of THM.)

The Charles Trumbull Hayden Library opened in 1966, named after Tempe's founder, who "appreciated the benefits of a trained and concentrated intelligence." The five-floor building with keypunch checkout system, pictured here, could house one million volumes and seat 3,000 students. Other ASU libraries include the Howe Architecture Library (late 1960s), Music Library (1970), Noble Science and Engineering Library (1983), Fletcher Library (1988), and Ross-Blakley Law Library (1993). (Courtesy of UAASUL.)

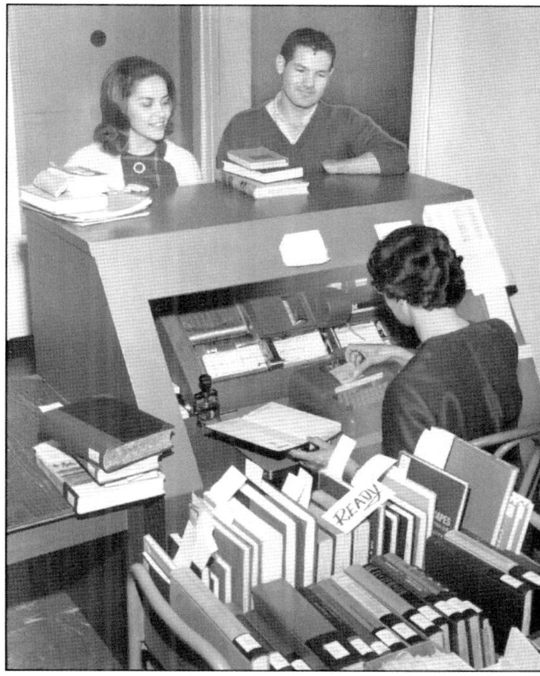

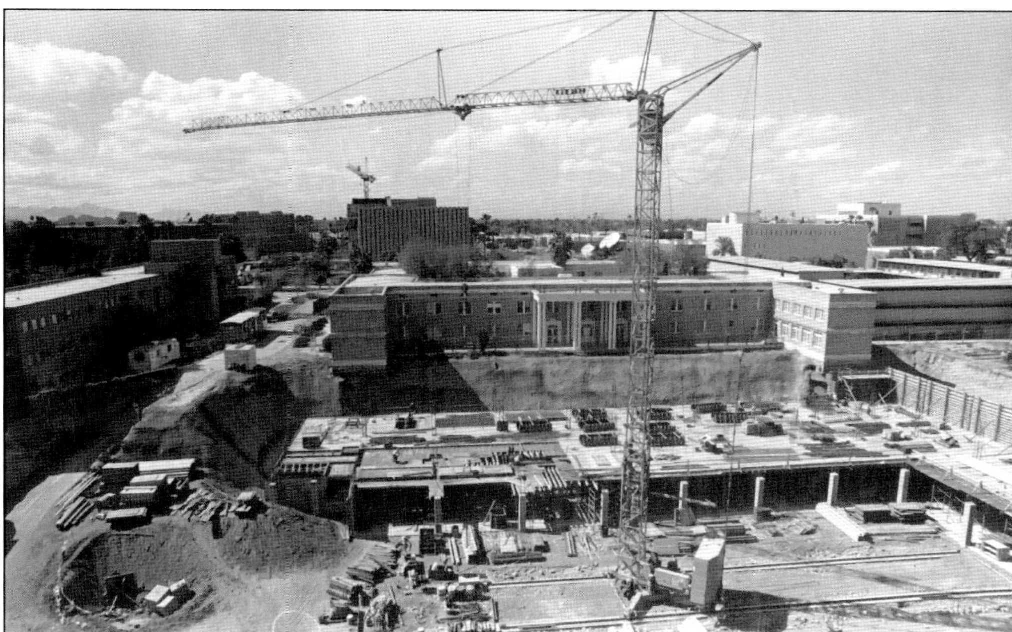

The Hayden Library, seen here during expansion, also houses the archives, founded in 1972 by the first university archivist, Alfred Thomas Jr. Archives and Special Collections cares for gems like Sri Lankan palm-leaf manuscripts and Sen. Carl Hayden's political papers. The original building (see page 118) expanded in 1989 to include space for 375,000 more volumes and 1,500 more seats. This entailed adding two floors underground, along with a dramatic new entrance. (Courtesy of the *State Press*.)

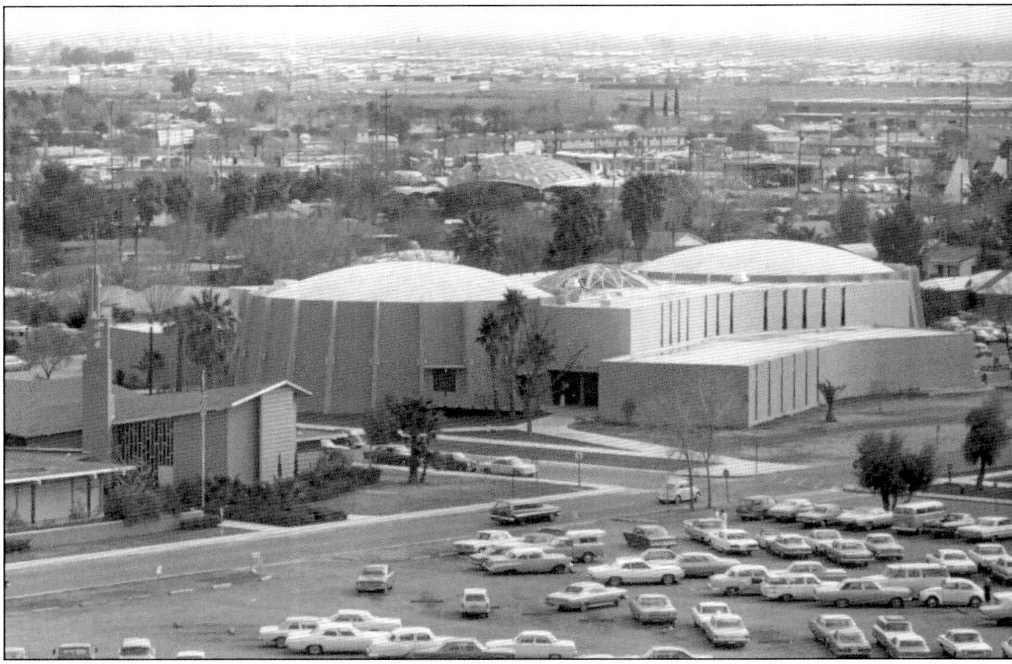

A different form of outreach involves guest speakers, invited to ASU to enhance students' learning opportunities. For example, Wilma Mankiller (below), the first female principal chief of the Cherokee Nation and recipient of the highest civilian honor, the Presidential Medal of Freedom, addressed students in the College of Law, whose premier Indian Legal Program, like other programs on campus, studies and serves tribal governments. Durham made the case for a law school in 1964. Founding dean Willard Pedrick welcomed the charter class into Matthews Library in 1967. Its new home, pictured above, was named John S. Armstrong Hall after ASU's founder and was dedicated in 1968 by US Supreme Court chief justice Earl Warren. In 2006, the school became the Sandra Day O'Connor College of Law after the Arizona legislator and first female US Supreme Court justice. (Above, courtesy of UAASUL; below, Jeorgetta Douglas, the *State Press*.)

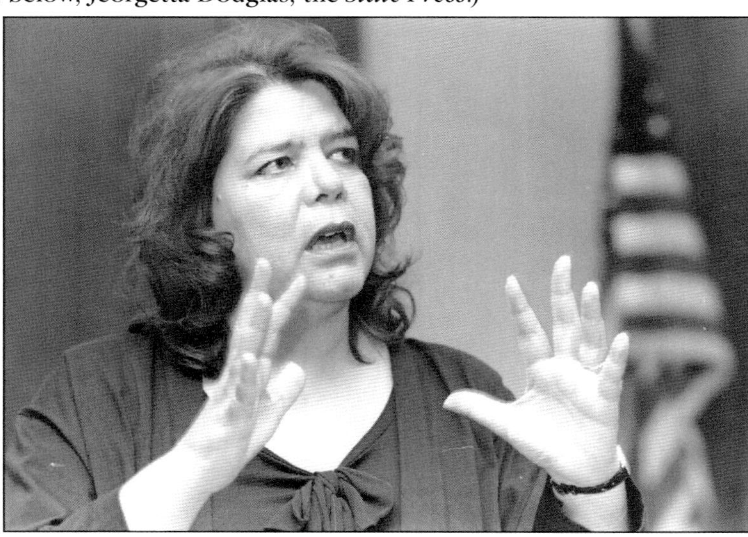

Students often build work experience with internships. For example, alumna Barbara McConnell Barrett, BS, MPA, JD, pictured at right with Don Dotts (center) at the Arizona State Capitol, was a legislative intern from 1971 to 1972, while Sandra Day O'Connor was a state senator. This inspired McConnell Barrett to include public service as part of her remarkable career history. She recalls, "ASU was the beginning of everything good that has happened to me." Later she was sworn in by Sandra Day O'Connor as ambassador to Finland in John S. Armstrong Hall in 2008, pictured below with her husband, Craig. The Barretts endowed the Honors College in 2000, changing the face of undergraduate education and building on foundations laid by early Honors Program director Richard Jacob and Honors College founding dean (1988–2003) Ted Humphrey. (Both courtesy of Barbara McConnell Barrett.)

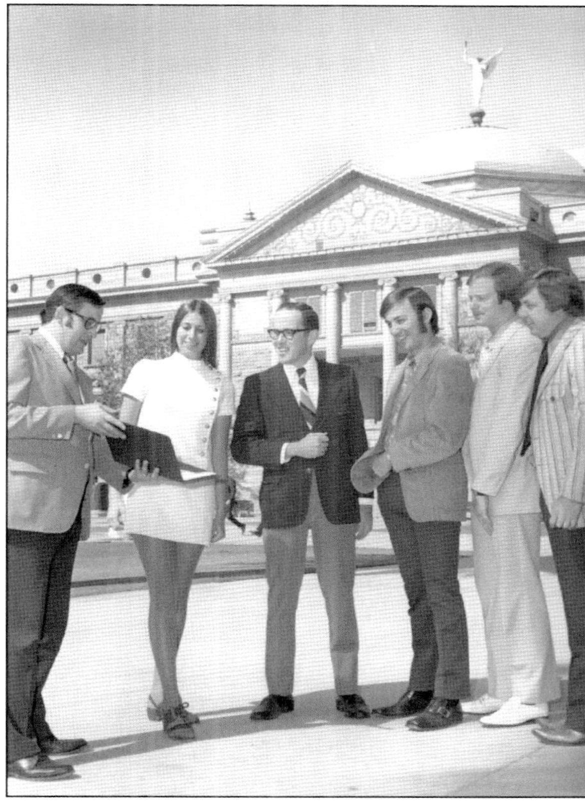

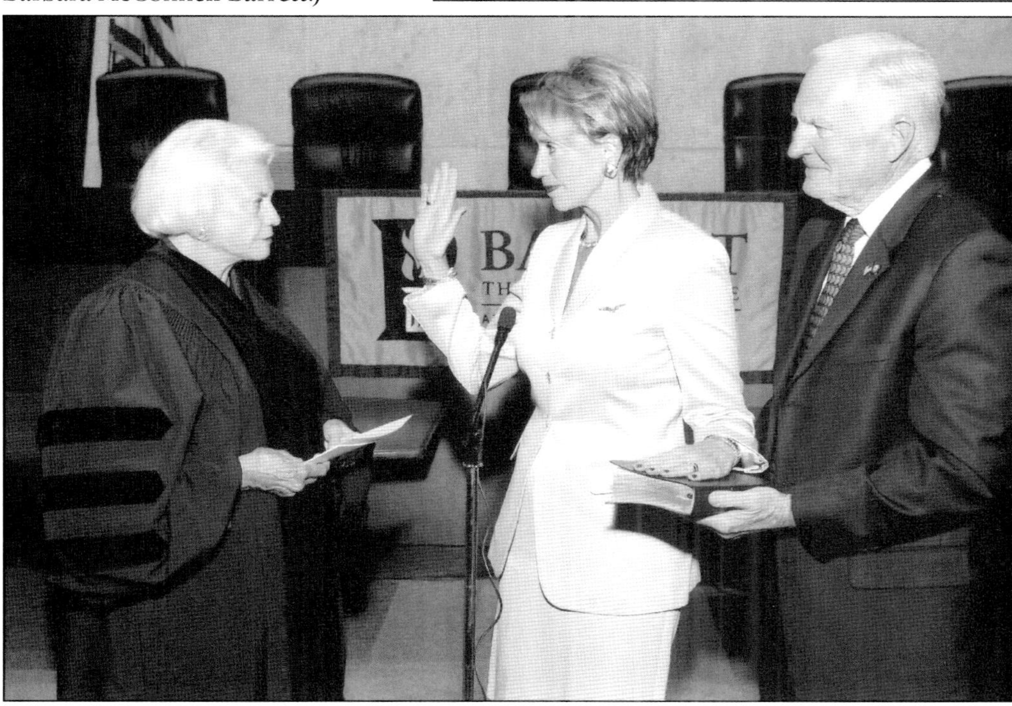

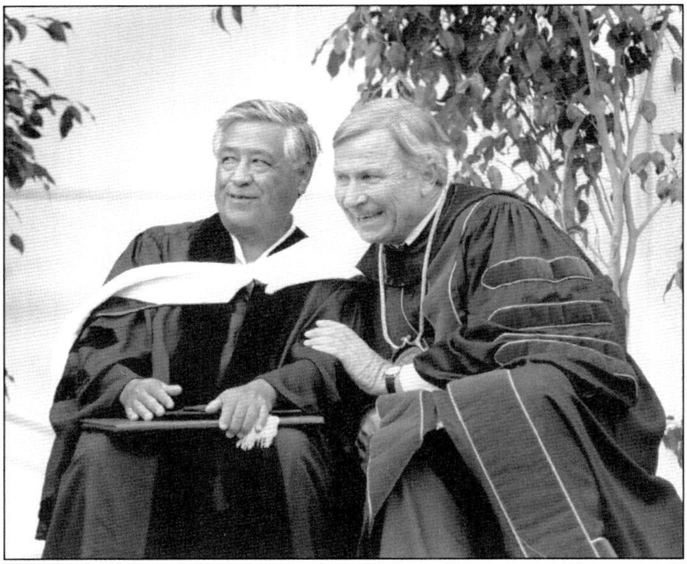

Barbara Barrett, and only 175 others between 1940 and May 2012, received an honorary degree from ASU. Such degrees are awarded to recognize contributions to society. The first honorary degree recipients were Frederick M. Irish and Pres. Arthur John Matthews in 1940, followed by Charles A. Stauffer 11 years later. Lattie Coor Jr. is pictured on the right with 1992 recipient Cesar Chavez, celebrated civil rights activist and Arizona native. (Courtesy of Lattie and Elva Coor.)

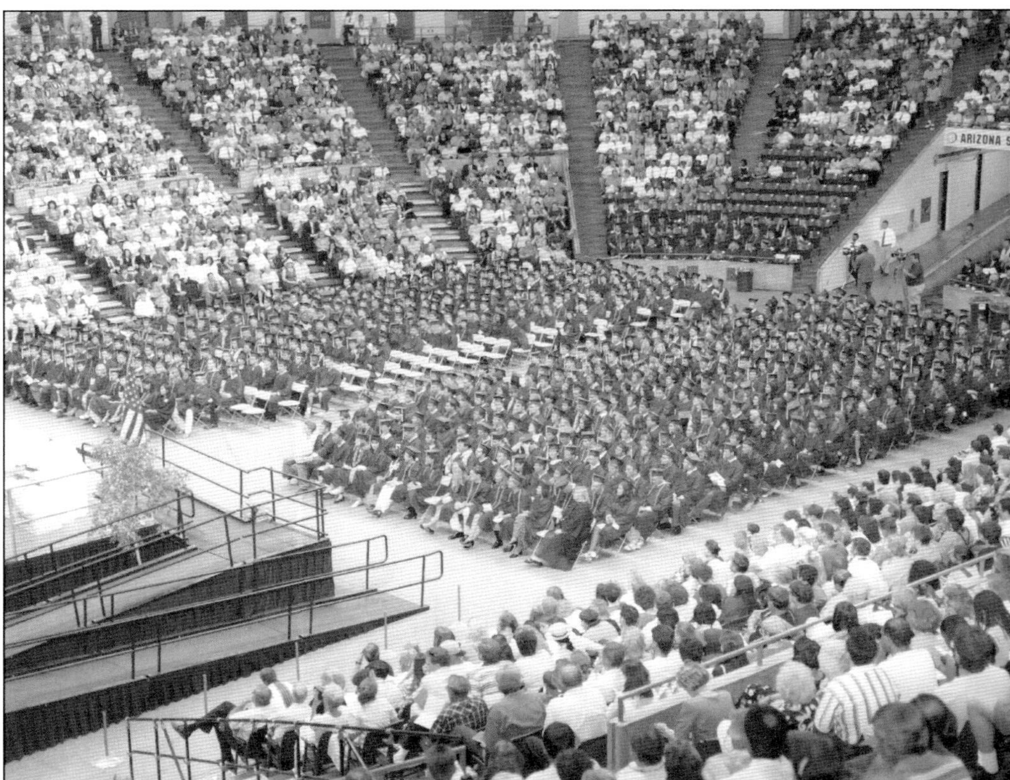

Honorary degrees are conferred at commencement ceremonies. Educating over 72,000 students is the key mission of the university, supported by the scholarship and teaching of the faculty glimpsed at in this chapter. Convocation, pictured here, is a smaller ceremony for a single group or college, whereas a commencement typically involves the whole university. (Courtesy of Gary Krahenbuhl.)

Three

MOMENTS IN ATHLETICS

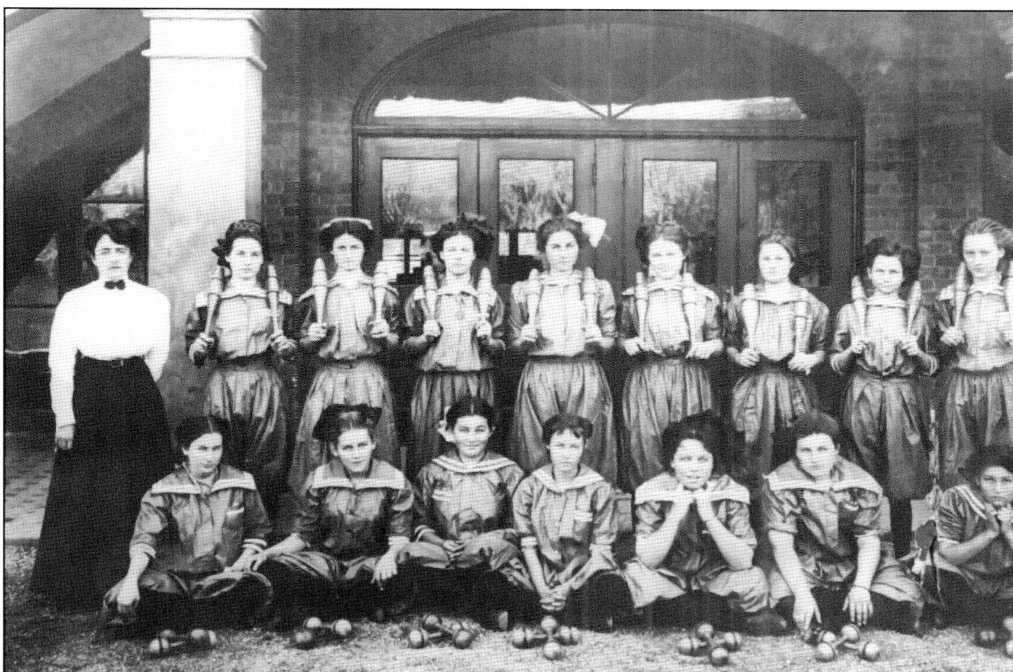

Daily activities were required for the well-being of the students, as exercise was, according to the student catalog, "essential to the best mental efforts of the health of body and mind." The experiences also prepared students to handle playground activities and to teach physical education. The first equipment was purchased for male students in 1891, and some equipment was acquired for women in 1895. Here, a women's gym class (1911–1912) poses with new dumbbells and clubs. (Courtesy of THM.)

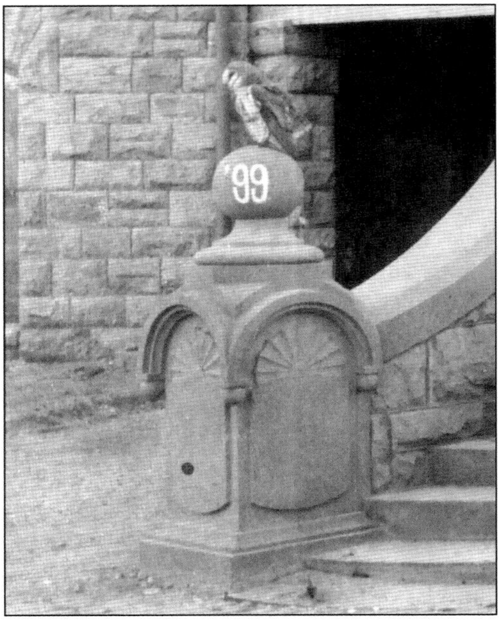

Beyond activities for balance and those pertaining to classes, extracurricular activities like organized sports began. The first mascot for the Normals, as the teams were commonly called, was an owl, appearing at least as early as 1889. The more natural landscape then, a mix of desert, pasture, and pecan groves, was rich with wildlife, so an owl on the newel post of Old Main, pictured here, would be a common sight. (Courtesy of THM.)

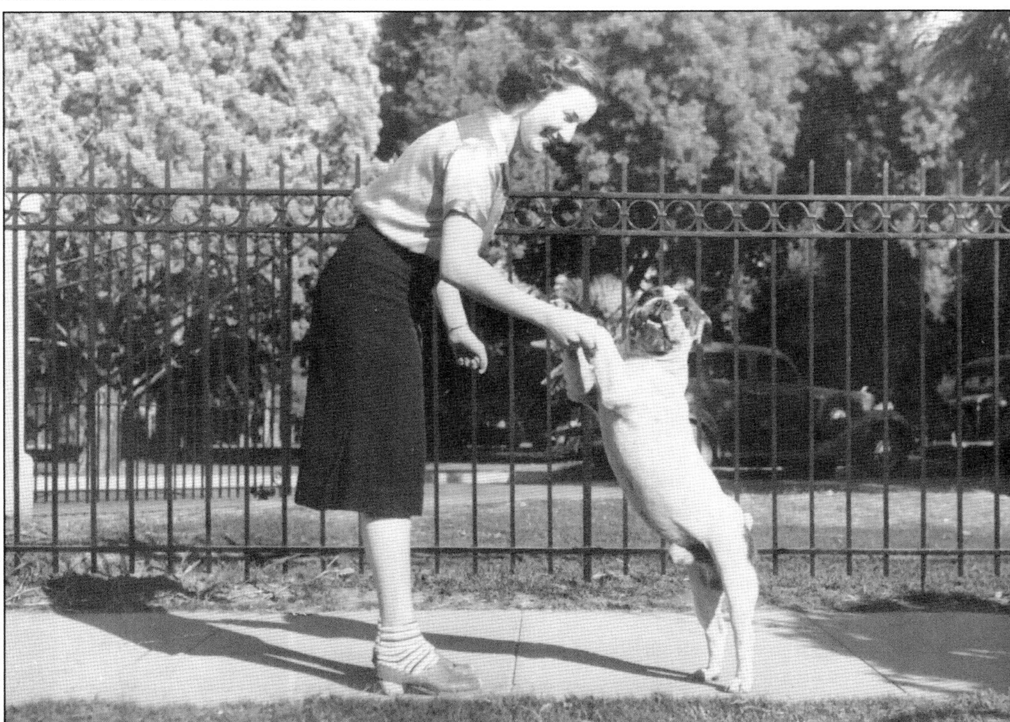

Owls became Bulldogs in 1922. Pete, above, one of the dogs who played mascot, greets Barbara Benson, secretary to Ira Payne, who influenced athletics as much as education. In 1946, the students voted 819 to 196 to become the Sun Devils. Shirley G. Schmitz, a 1949 alumna, reports having later met Walt Disney, who said to her that, in contrast to other reports, he had fun designing the devil himself. (Courtesy of UAASUL.)

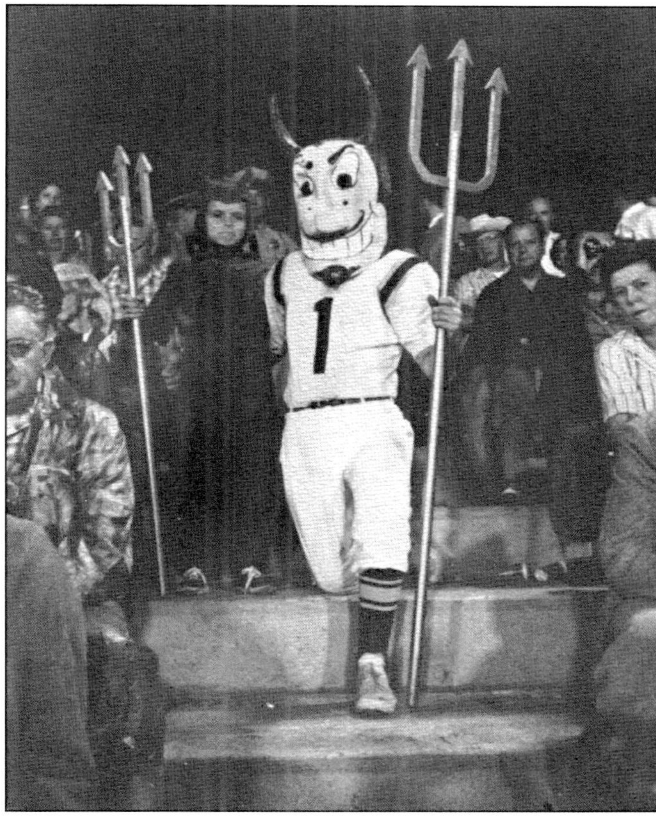

Joy Main (McLain), a flyer and tumbler, was the first Devilette (1953–1957), with partner Dick Jacobs. She wore tights, sequins, a devil headdress, and red cape. Alumnus Gary Richardson (left), a sixth-grader from the Payne Training School wearing red velvet, and student Bob Reynolds, in the mask, were the first mascots in 1959. Not yet "Sparky," they were called devil, imp, and Beelzebub. Richardson later became an Arizona legislator. (Courtesy of Gary Richardson.)

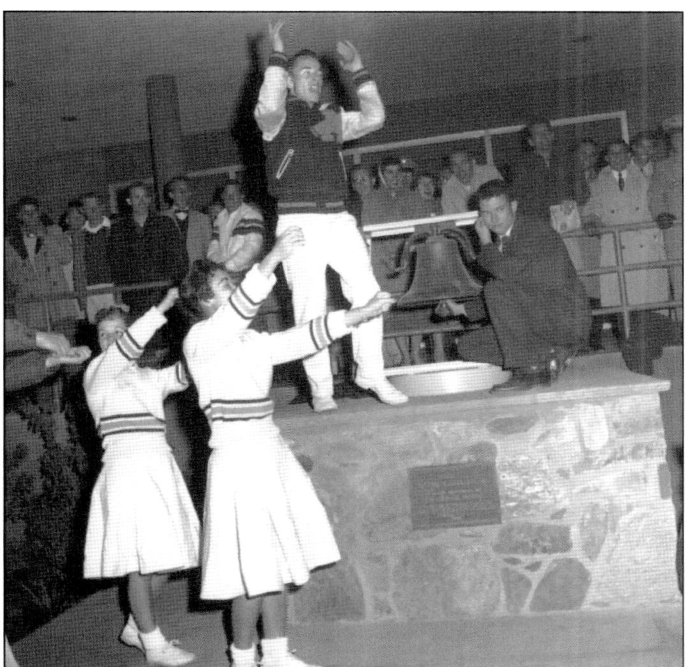

The original victory bell called students to meals and celebrated victories as early as the 1930s. Its history was honored when it was installed on the Memorial Union's west patio in 1956 on sandstone from the original White House, donated by Sen. Carl Hayden. Misplaced during a remodel in the 1970s, it has yet to be found. A 2,000-pound victory bell, donated in the late 1960s, still rings outside Sun Devil Stadium. (Courtesy of UAASUL.)

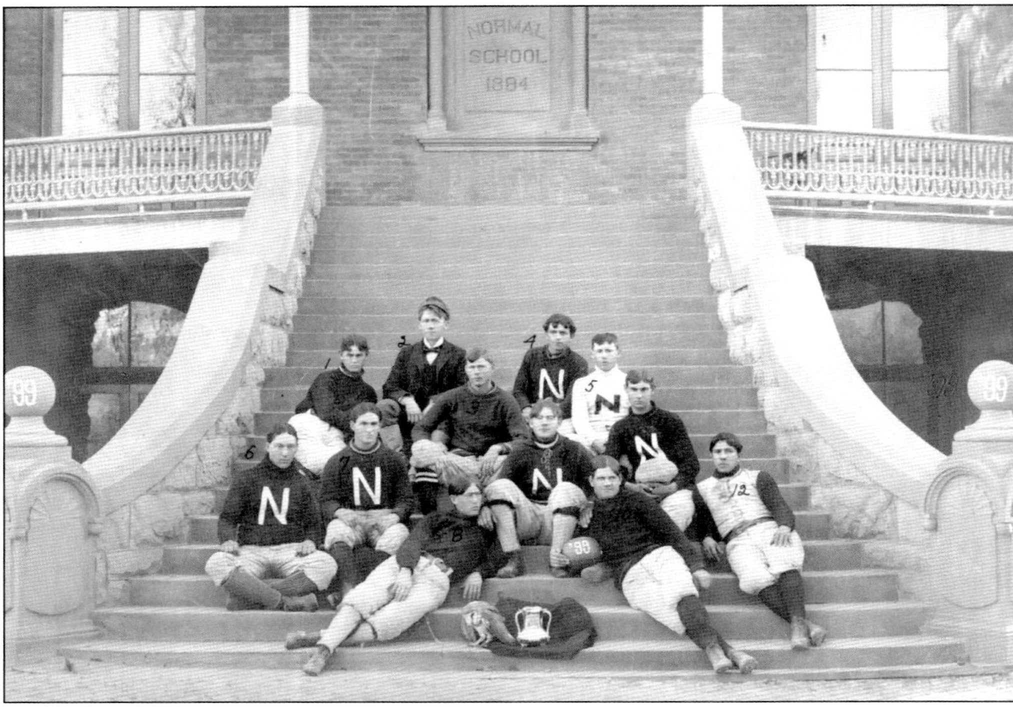

Among other traditions, like stealing the Flagstaff Lumberjacks' axe, the rivalry with the University of Arizona (UofA) Wildcats for the Territorial Cup persists. Above, the 1899 Normal football team poses with the trophy and owl mascot after winning the Arizona Territorial Championship against the UofA in their first match, with 300 audience members. Famed Charlie Haigler (far left) and Garfield Goodwin (at right in the last row) were among players coached by Frederick Irish. Initially, the rivalry was gentlemanly. There were no special facilities then, so eager students played on a dirt field and made their own uniforms. When teams traveled for road games, by horse or train, the host team members and community housed the players. Friendliness and sportsmanship were expected. Later, the rise of homecoming floats, as pictured below in 1940, reflected tensions between the schools that went beyond sports. (Above, courtesy of UAASUL; below, THM.)

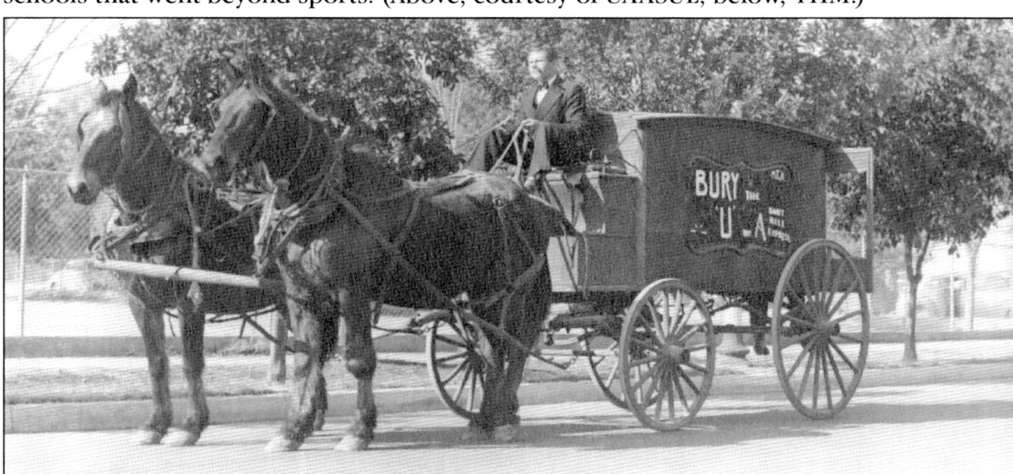

The first activities or sports on campus were throwing horseshoes, horseback riding, and rodeo-related events, as horses were the main method of transportation at the time. In 1949, the students voted to form a rodeo association, and over 100 athletes competed in the first intercollegiate contests. Rodeo activities continued under different sponsors until the last recorded events in 1981. At right, students gather in front of Matthews Library in the 1950s. (Courtesy of UAASUL.)

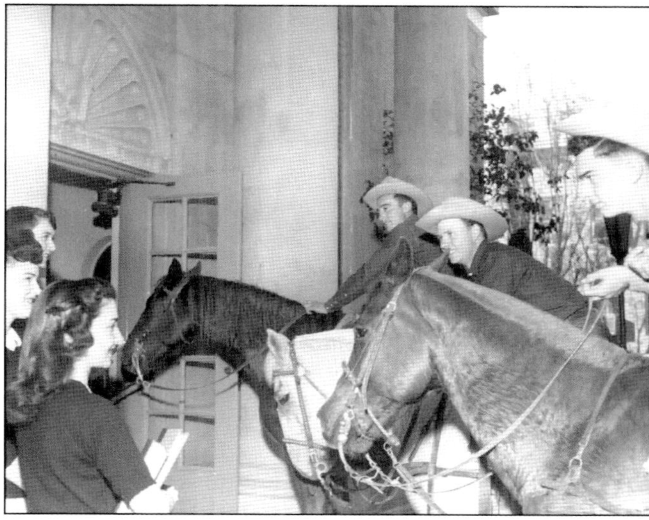

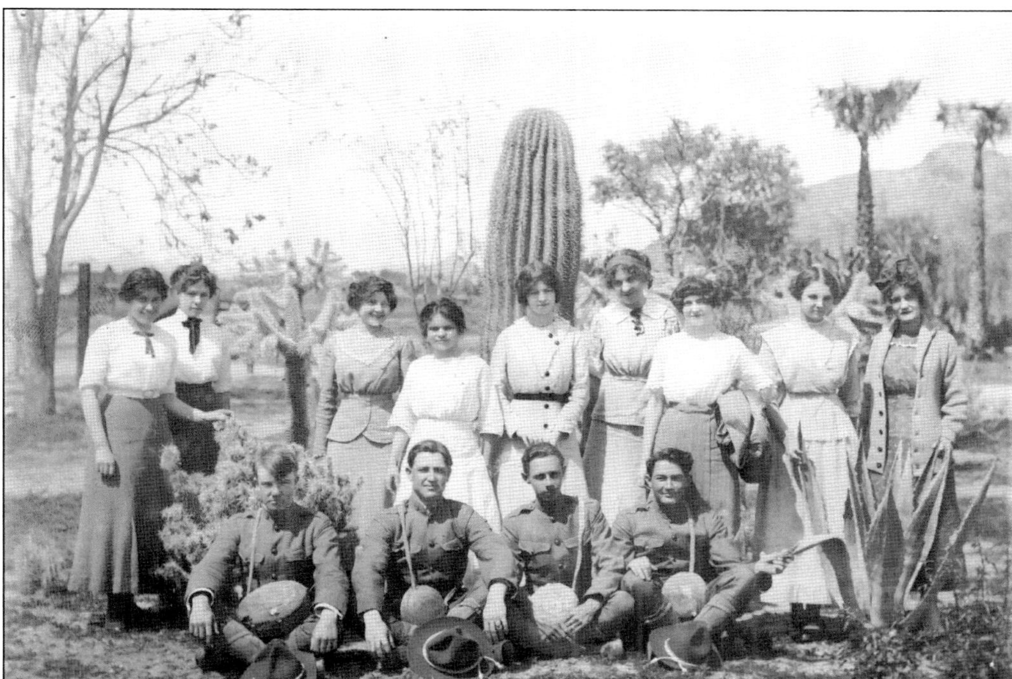

Hiking was popular from the start and continued to grow even as horse-related activities waned. Hikes and picnics in the desert were daily affairs, with longer hikes or camping on the weekends under the watch of Fred Irish or Ira Payne or, later, perhaps President Matthews himself. One of the best and earliest hiking/camping clubs was the Cactus Walking Club, which developed as early as 1914. (Courtesy of UAASUL.)

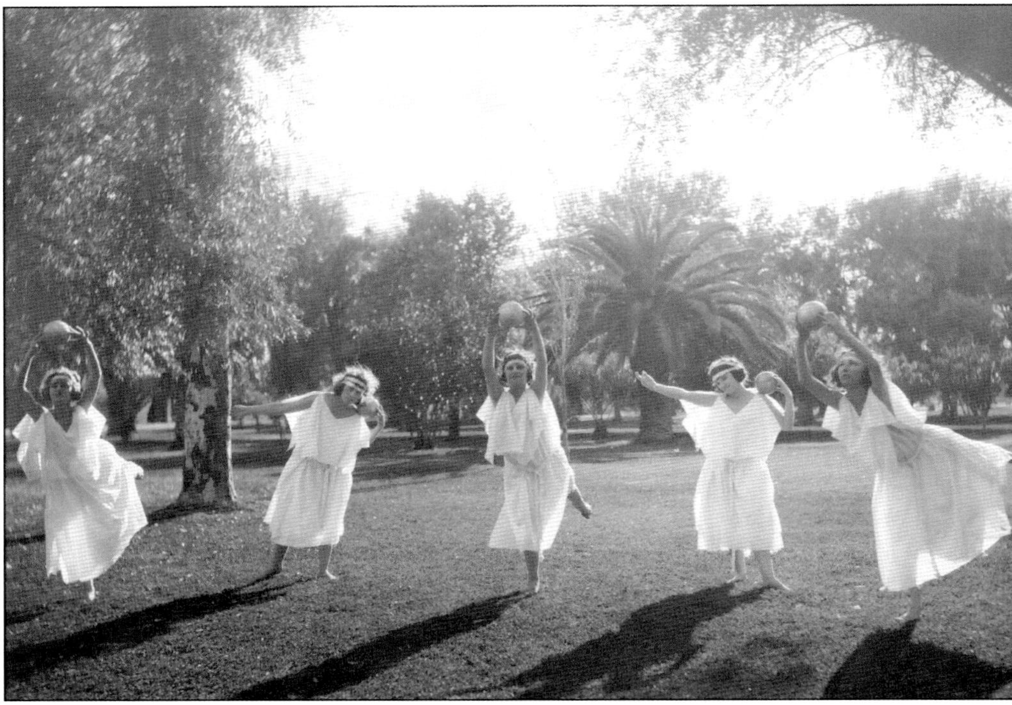

Physical education initially involved formal drills and marches. By 1911, folk dancing, aesthetic dancing, and more "fancy drills with scarfs" were introduced, leading to public performances of increasing complexity over the years. Dorothy Gillanders's arrival (1937–1938) enriched dance offerings. The male students could learn dance too, and later, they might be sent to dance class by coaches to help improve their footwork for sports. (Courtesy of THM.)

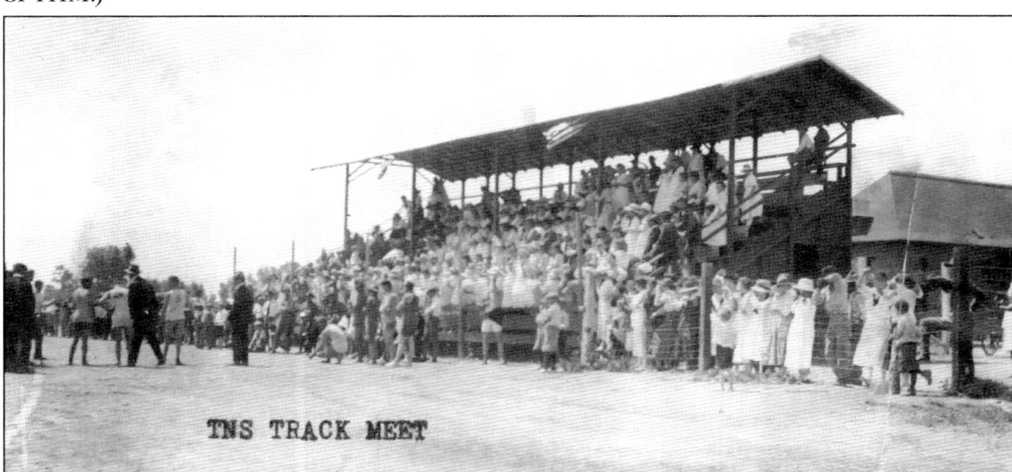

The track team at the Normal Field was going strong by 1911 with the fastest man in the territory, Joe Sheldon. It frequently won, including the Track Championship of the Salt River Valley in 1912 and 1913. Dismantled for World War I, track and field was resurrected in 1919, producing greats like "the fastest human alive" Henry Carr (1962–1964) and Olympic gold-medalist Maicel Malone (1989–1992). (Courtesy of the Chandler Museum.)

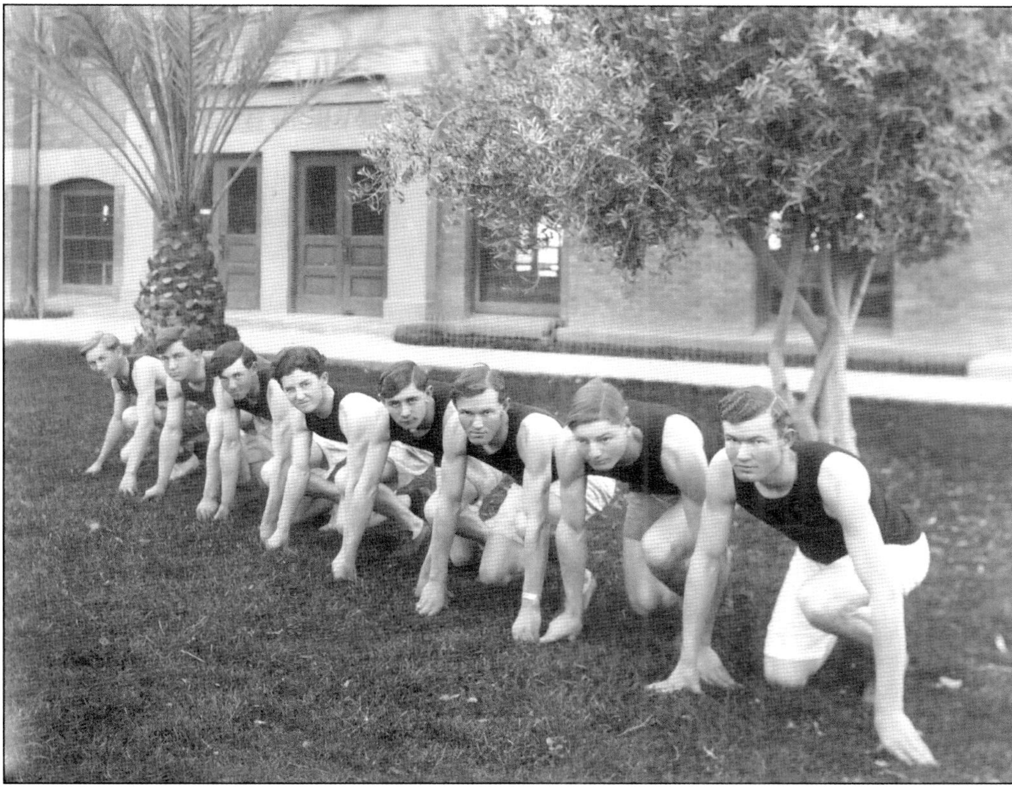

Above, the 1914 track team poses in front of the two-story auditorium-gymnasium that Matthews had built in 1909 on the quad. The structure had a 1,000-seat auditorium on top and a hardwood floor gymnasium, running track, 200-seat spectator gallery, and male and female changing rooms in the semi-basement. The Durham Language and Literature Building now stands at the former site. Track and field's long history of success includes Benny Garcia (right), the Border Conference javelin champion all four years (1953–1956) who also competed in the 1956 Olympic preliminaries. Senon "Baldy" Castillo, coach from 1953 to 1980, built on Donn Kinzle's work to lead the track and field team to national status, including a 1977 NCAA team championship and with 13 Olympians. (Both courtesy of UAASUL.)

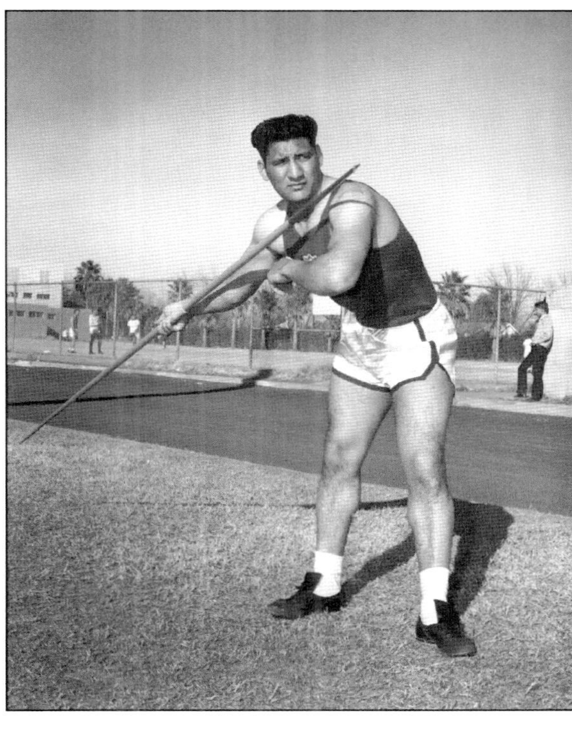

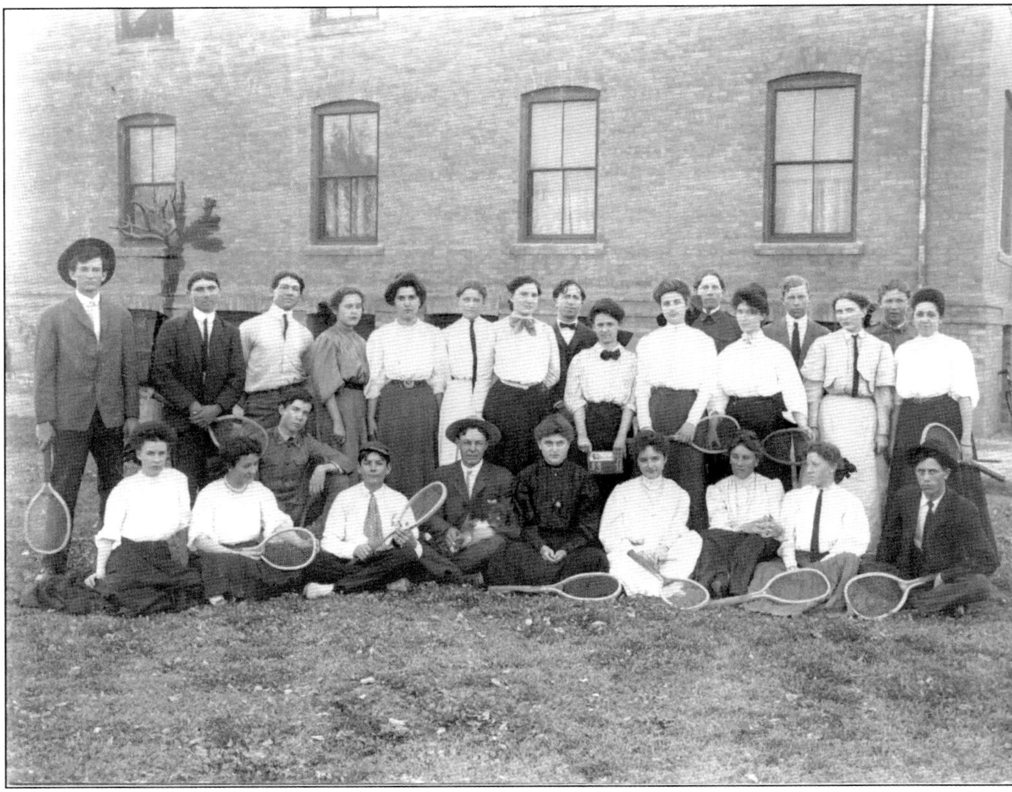

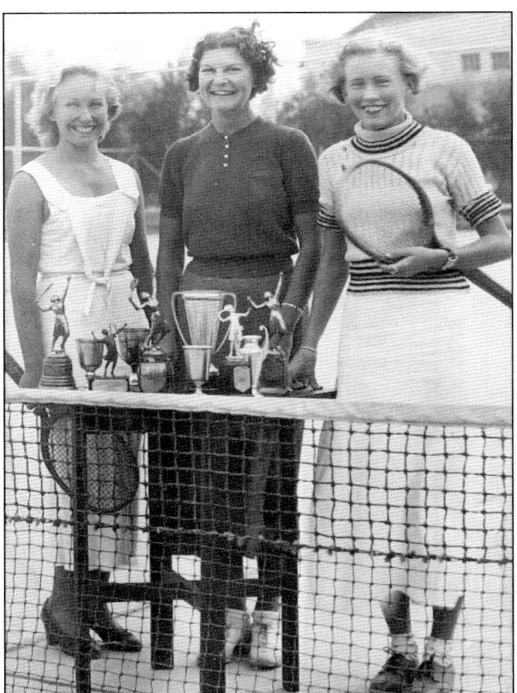

Tennis started as early as 1898 and has been played continuously since. The Normal School Tennis Club, pictured above in 1907, began with a dirt court that Irish laid out. It had seven courts by 1912 and 12 by 1918. For years, the common understanding was that any varsity woman who could beat Ira Payne in two out of three sets would be treated to fine dining in Phoenix accompanied by a women's physical education teacher. As women's tennis developed, every coach played a part, as did Bettse Marten, center, with players Catherine Tomlinson, left, and Evelyn Tomlinson. Under Anne Pittman's coaching (1954–1984), especially when the sport was supported by the university, tennis gained national recognition with, among other accomplishments, four conference titles (1974–1976 and 1978) and three national championships (1971, 1972, and 1974). (Both courtesy of UAASUL.)

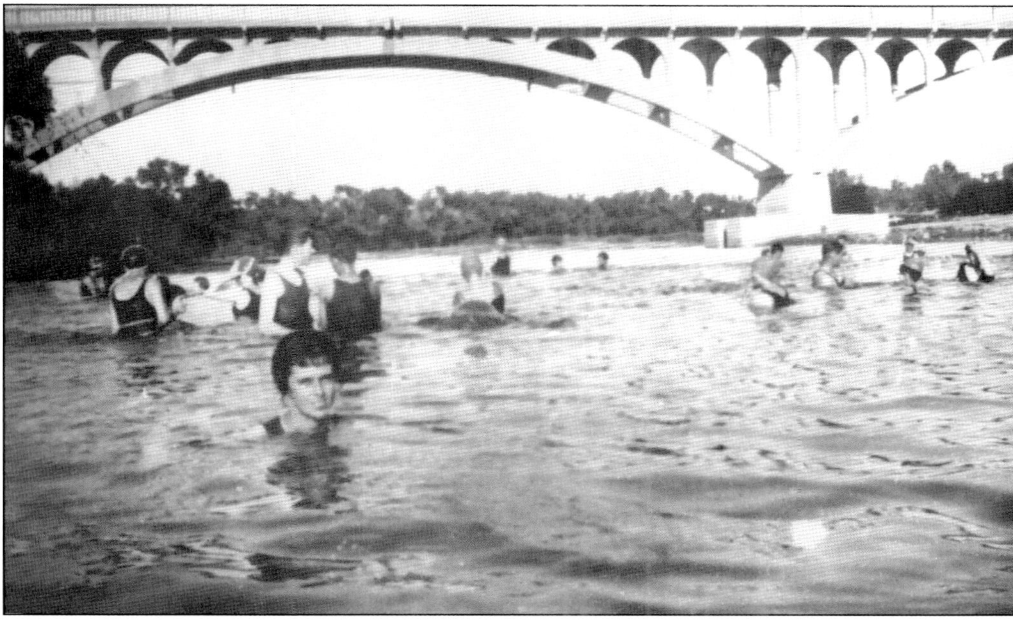

Swimming was an enjoyable activity during the hot months. In the early years, male students kept their distance when the women hiked to the swimming hole at the Salt River, between the buttes. Due to a lack of dams at the time, water flowed continuously, so plenty of large native trees and shrubs provided shade and privacy. Later, repeat national-championship swim and diving teams developed under Ramona "Mona" Plummer, coach from 1957 to 1978, for whom the aquatic center is named. She is pictured here in the far lower right with the 1978 winning team. In addition to nine Olympians, the 1960s Naiads, an honorary women's water ballet club, are remembered for elaborately themed shows with, for instance, 11 acts, including some men's swim team (also a winning team) members as clowns and exhibitions by diving champion and Olympian Patsy Willard. (Above, courtesy of THM; right, UAASUL.)

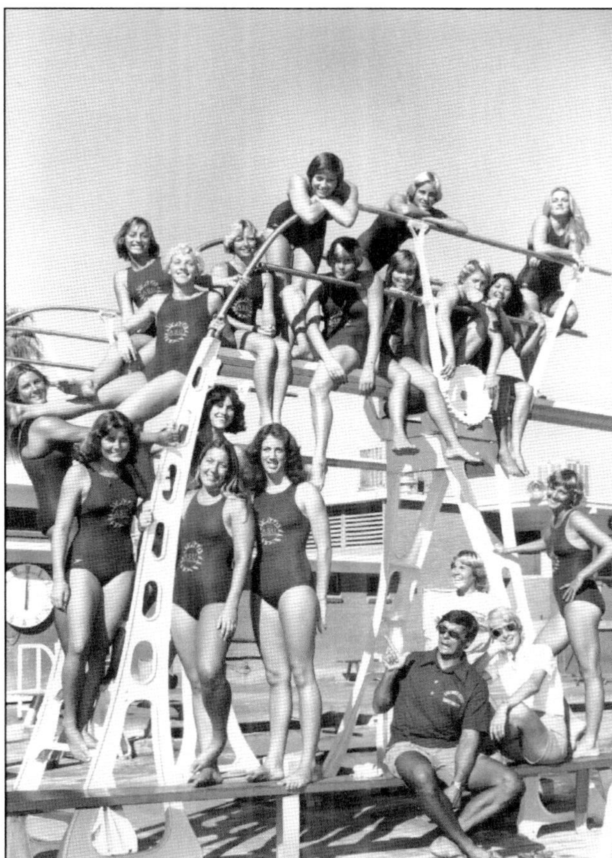

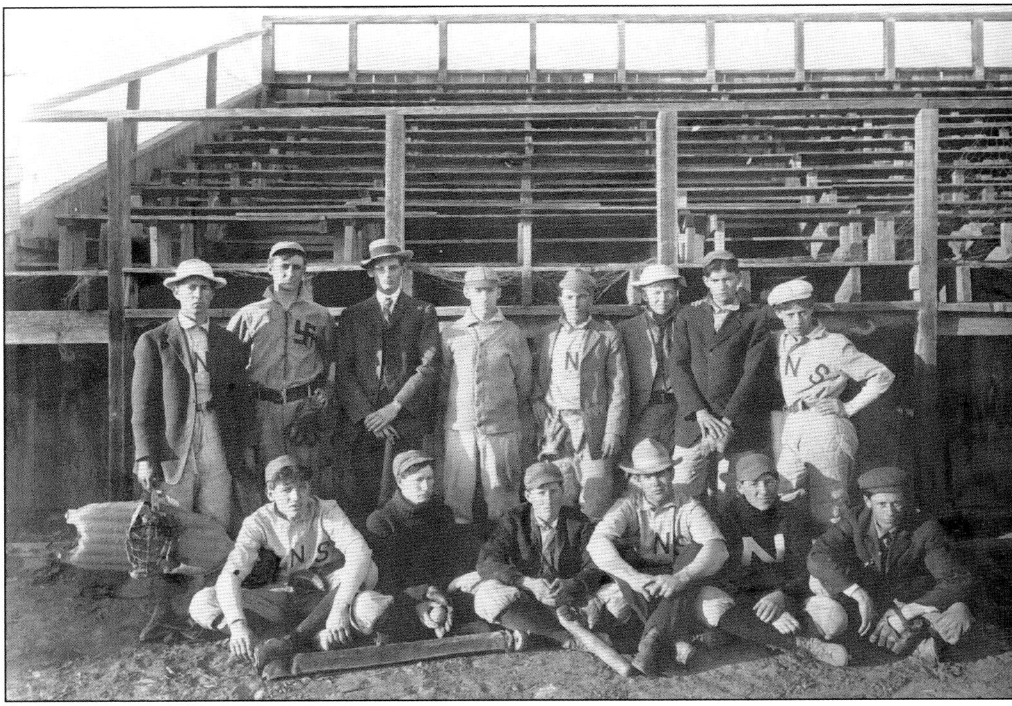

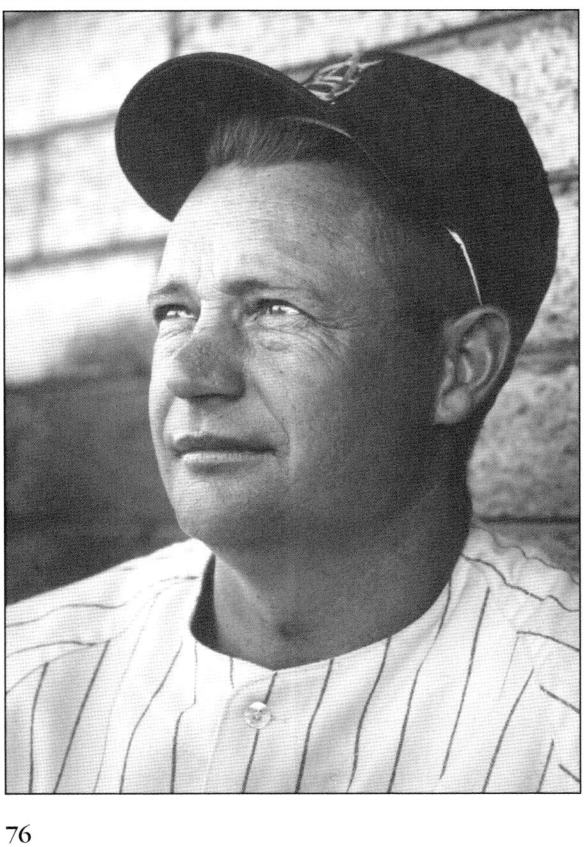

An 1891 baseball game with the Mormon settlement Stringtown is the first recorded external sports match. The baseball team went on to win the Arizona Territory Championship against Prescott High (1905–1906) and against the UofA in 1906–1907. The pre-1908 photograph above shows the team prior to them getting new uniforms. Note the swastika on the jersey before Hitler co-opted the symbol. Early coaches included Fred Ayer and John R. Murdock, for whom Murdock Hall is named, the 1920s history professor-turned-dean-turned-Congressman from Arizona. Best known were Bobby Winkles (1958–1971), left, and Jim Brock (1972–1994). Winkles's efforts to rebuild the disbanded sport led to the school's first College World Series wins in 1965, 1967, and 1969. Brock's amazing record included two more in 1977 and 1981. These two sent more players to the major leagues than any other college. (Both courtesy of UAASUL.)

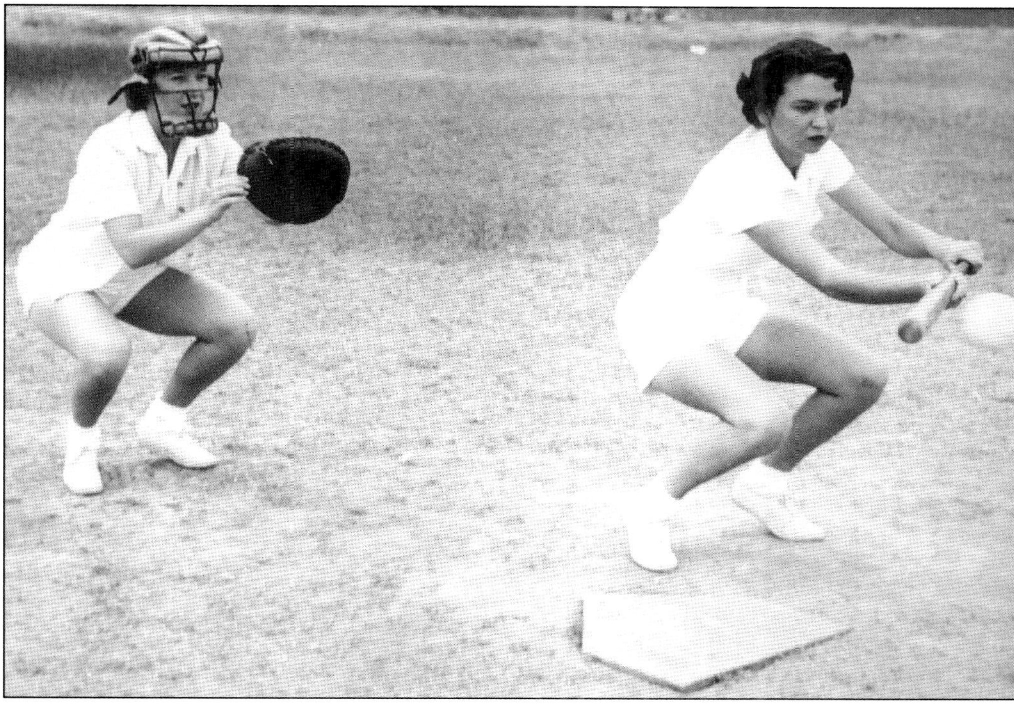

Women played baseball as early as the 1920s, including winning against the UofA (1924–1925), until softball, above in the 1960s, became popular. Mary Littlewood coached volleyball (1965–1974), basketball (1967–1974), and softball (1967–1989). Her softball teams won two College World Series titles in 1972 and 1973, her basketball record was 49-18, and her volleyball record was 59-14. Littlewood, who built on the start that Sallie Hayden (daughter of Charles) gave volleyball in 1921, is pictured below with the team in 1969–1970, including Cassie Hays (no. 28) and Phyllis Wilkins (no. 32). Wilkins recalls that before Title IX, players bought their own shoes and shorts. Shirts were kept in a locker for use by other teams, and they usually drove personal vehicles to away games as they "paved the way for the girls" like three-time Olympic volleyball player Tammy Webb. (Above, courtesy of UAASUL; below, Phyllis Wilkins Ruoho.)

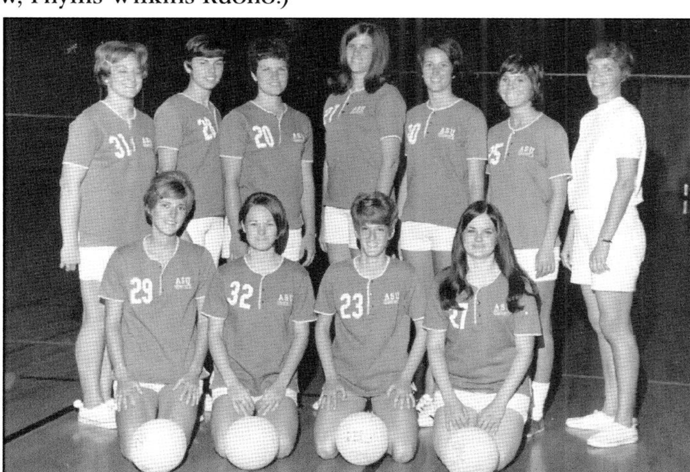

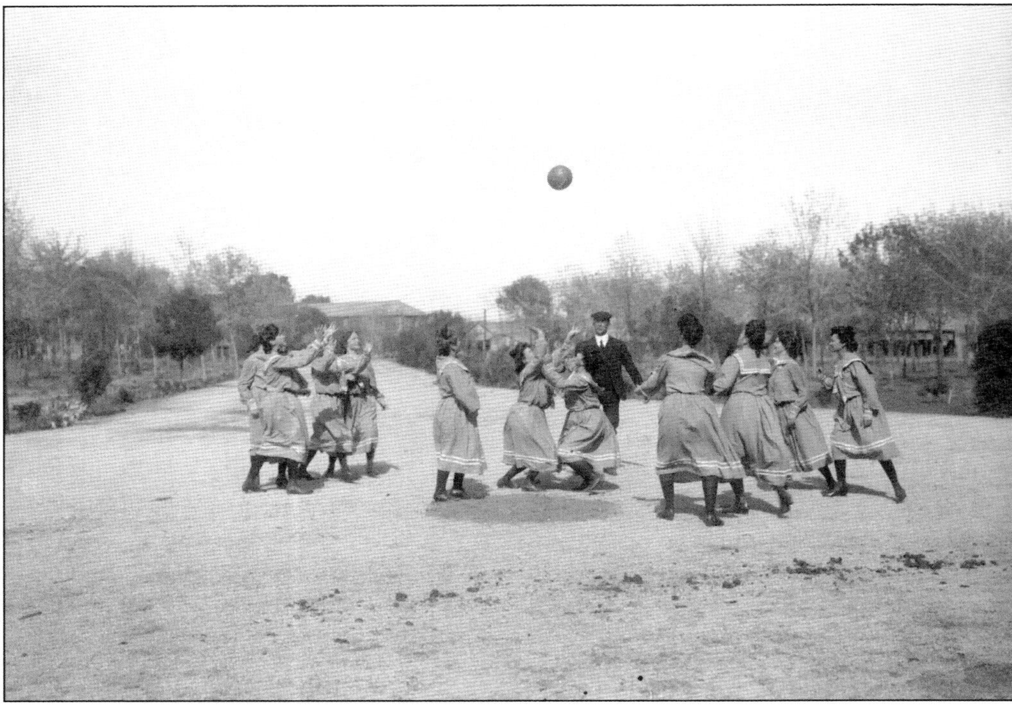

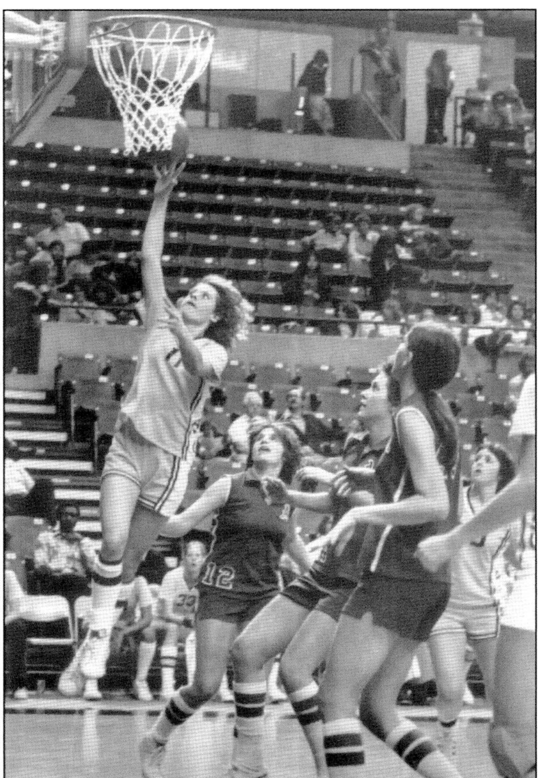

Starting before 1900 and coached by Irish until 1925, the first inter-school and inter-class basketball competitions had divisions for Brownies, the smaller students, and Regulars. The motto was "defeat is only a stepping stone to success." The first official women's basketball uniforms, pictured above in 1907, were sailor suits of medium-blue cashmere trimmed with white braids. In 1909, the new bloomer uniform, with over four yards of material per outfit, was instituted; a few years later, the amount of yardage was reduced to three. The students usually made their own uniforms. From those roots, 1970s intercollegiate teams formed. The sport would produce star players like Kym Hampton in the 1980s and rack up an impressive list of successes under coaches like Charli Turner Thorne, whose reign began in 1996. (Both courtesy of CC, UAASUL.)

Teams were small for the first recorded season of men's basketball (1911–1912), which stopped in 1916, during the war years. The sport was revived in 1920 by coach George Cooper, to the left in the photograph below, with the help of Wilfred G. Austin, pictured holding the ball. Austin, also a track star and baseball player, later became the superintendent of public schools in Chandler, his birthplace, where he coached winning teams. From the humble beginnings of the Tempe Normal School basketball court, pictured at right, came much grander facilities like the 14,198-seat University Activity Center, built in 1974. The floor there is called Ned Wulk Court after the winning coach (1957–1982) who led the Sun Devils to nine NCAA Tournaments, among other fine achievements. He helped design the facility, now Wells Fargo Arena, which is used for many events besides basketball. (Both courtesy of Chandler Museum.)

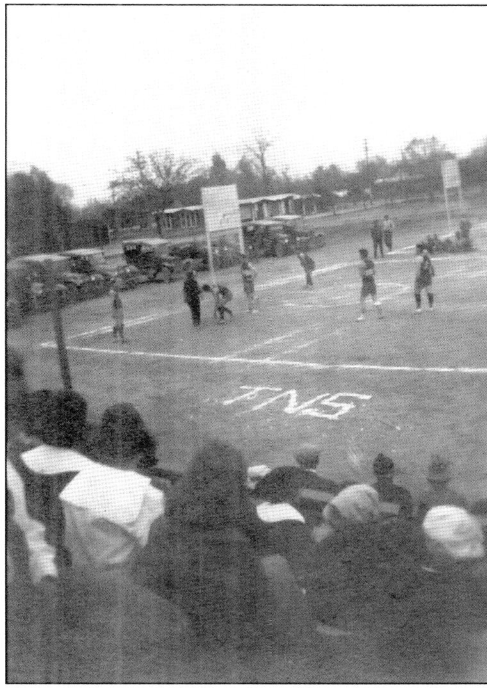

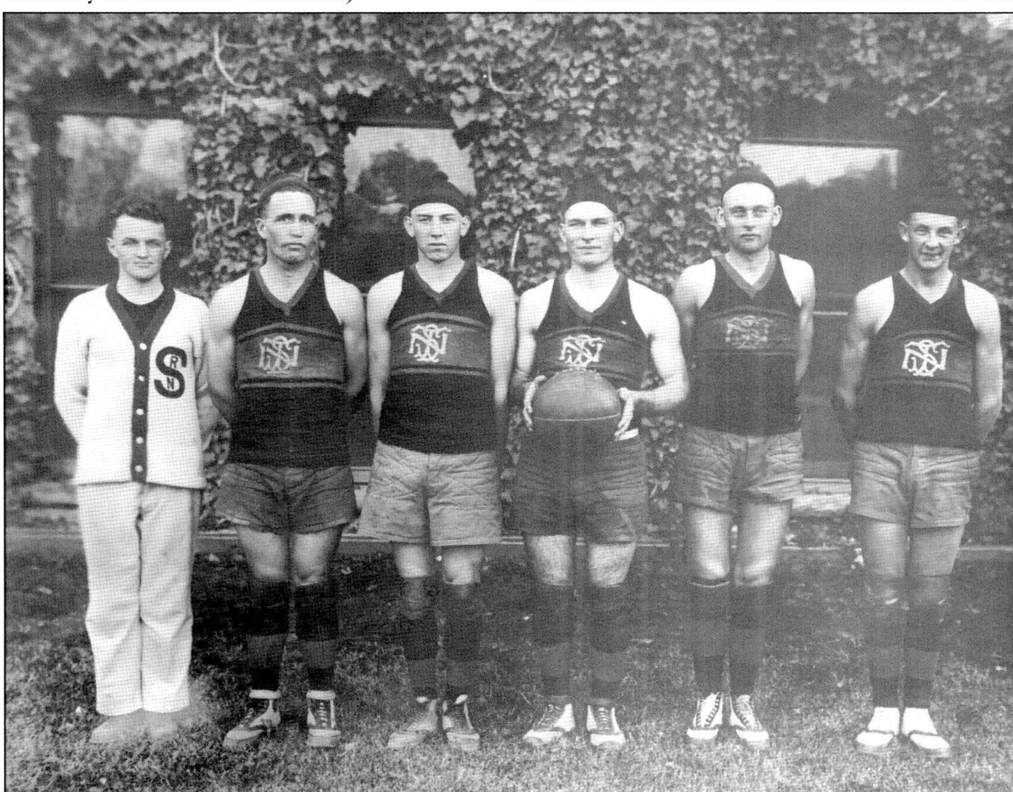

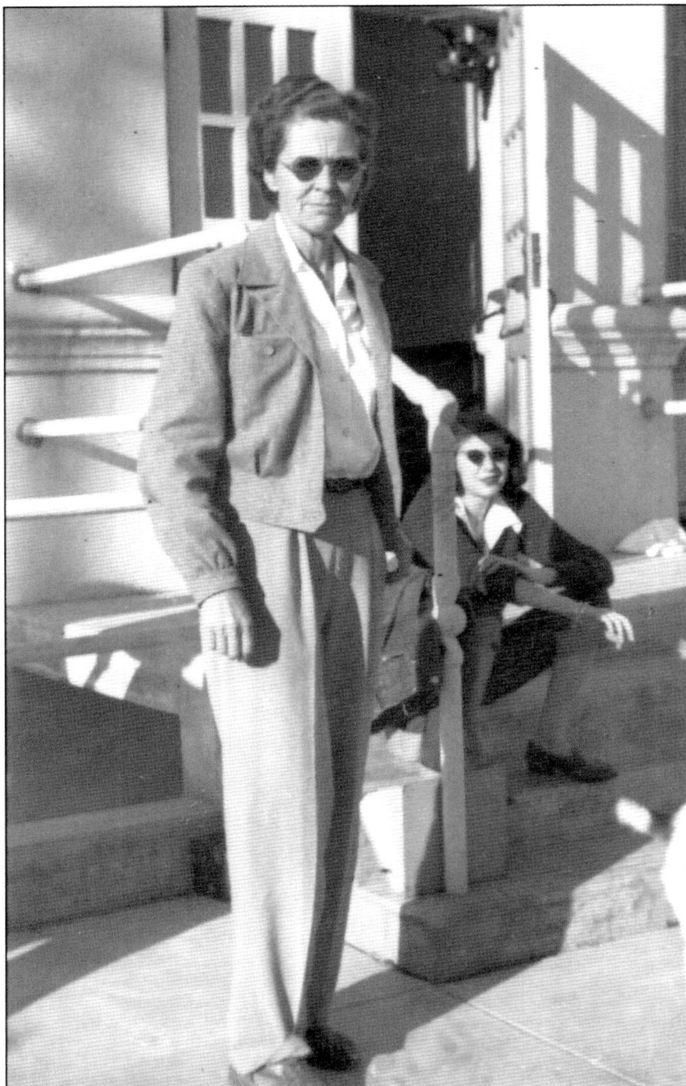

Nina Murphy's impact in her long career (1924–1969) was monumental. As head of Women's Physical Education (1934–1964), she looked out for the girls, from wrangling with the coaches of men's teams for field time and space to supervising their camping trips, complete with the occasional broken-down bus, as seen below in 1935. In 1967, the new Women's PE building and athletic field finally offered more of the space they deserved. Beside Murphy, pictured at left in the late 1940s, is the wagging tail of Suzie, a wire-haired terrier who became the unofficial mascot of the women's teams from 1935 to 1952. Suzie attended every camping trip and was part of classes and events, raising morale through dedication and devotion. Fondly remembered, former students and athletes who call themselves "Murphy's Girls" still meet annually at ASU in her honor. (Left, courtesy of Shirley G. Schmitz; below, THM.)

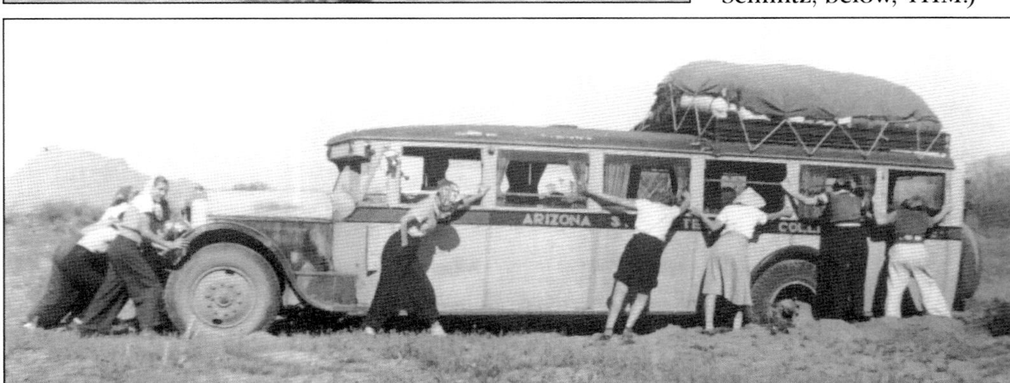

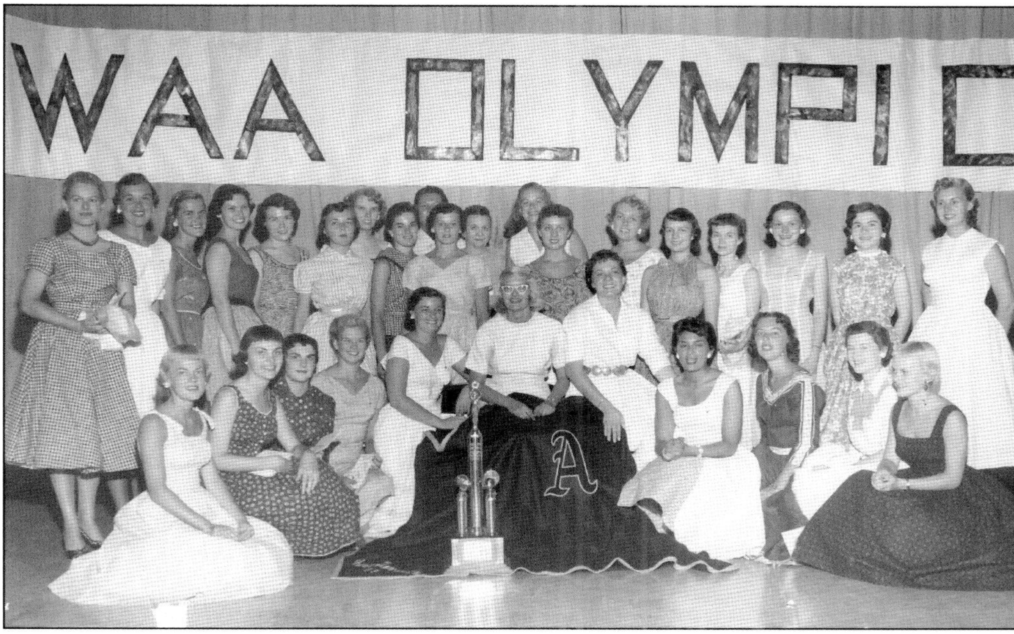

The Murphy's Girls could rough it, but they also cleaned up well. PE became the second major (1929–1930), and by 1931, Murphy founded the Women's Athletic Association for female students, which sponsored extensive intramurals and participation via a point system for awards. Group awards included a participation trophy, won by Alpha Delta Pi in 1955, as seen above with Sherry Stevenson under the coveted "A" blanket and Marsha Hatch just to the right. The Pemm Club (Physical Education Majors and Minors) formed for the women going into health, PE, or recreation professions. They were supervised on this 1958 camping trip to Camp Tontozona by teacher and tennis coach Anne Pittman, below, second from left in the back row. Some trips were class-related so that future teachers could learn to supervise all kinds of physical activities. Other trips were just for fun. (Above, courtesy of Marsha Hatch Coleman; below, Jo Wilson West.)

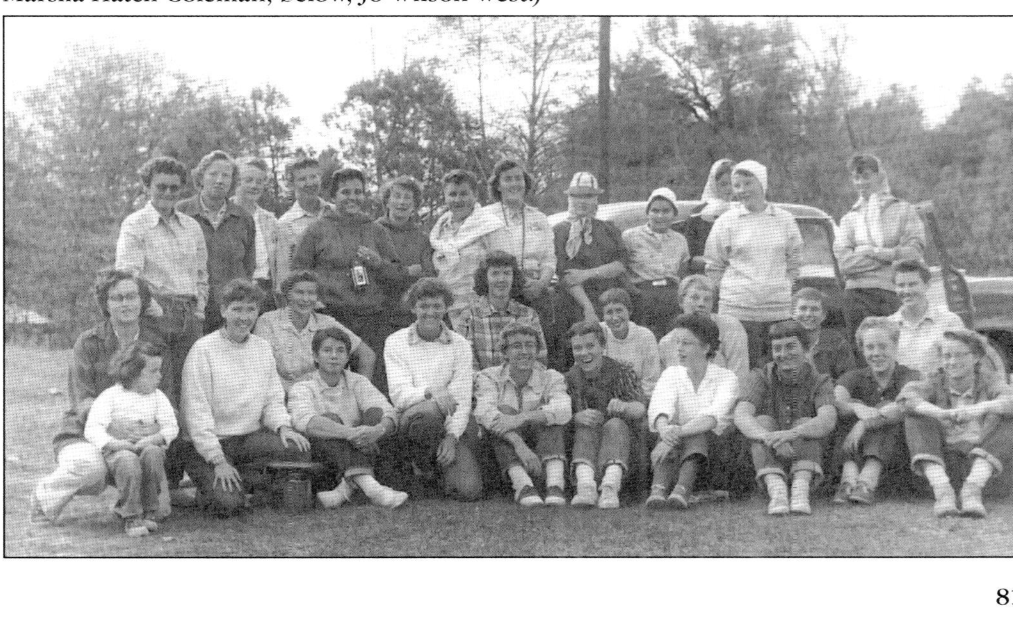

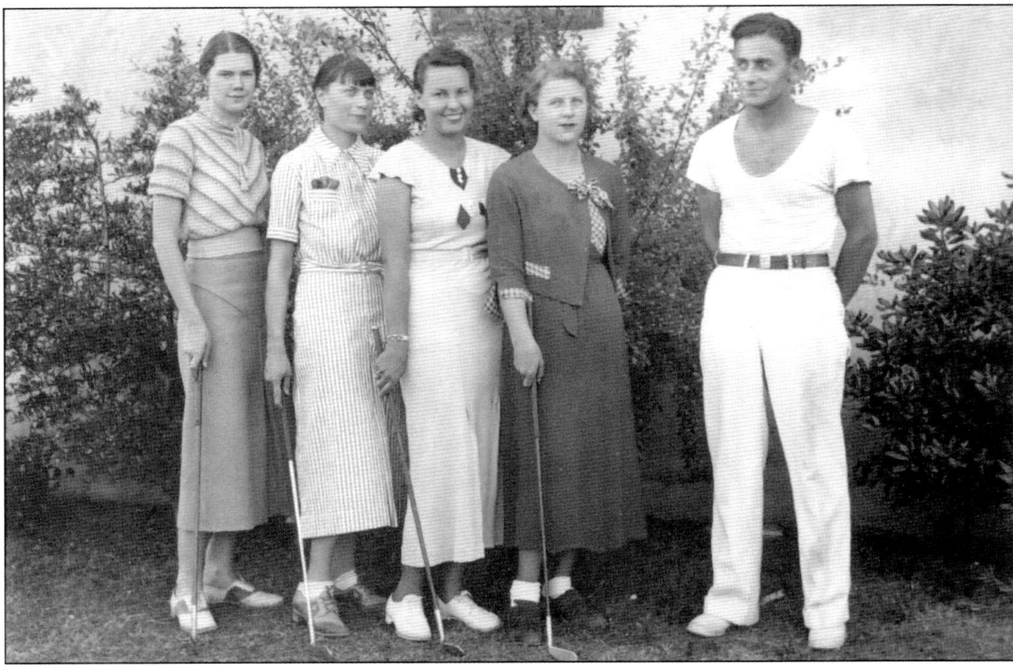

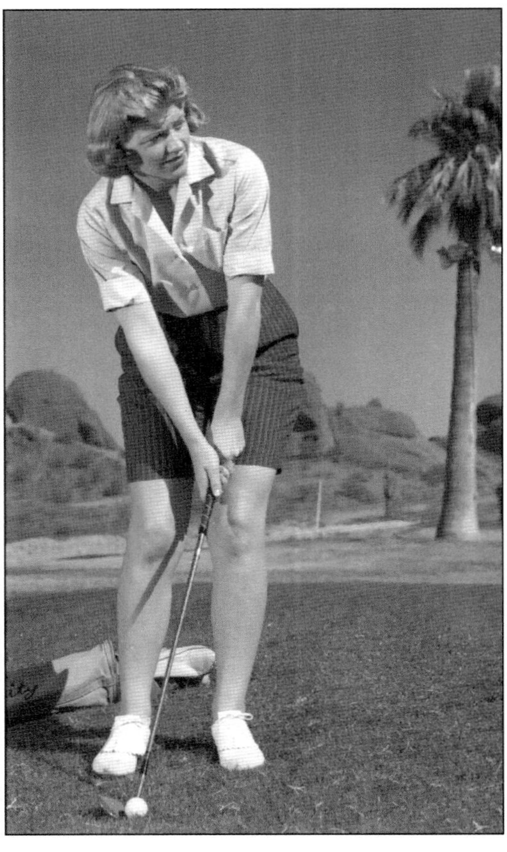

Though women's golf started in 1931, and alum/coach Joe Sellah (above right) did a great job coaching, it was not until the mid-1950s that coaches like Betty Graham and players like JoAnne Gunderson (Carner), left, brought it to institutional prominence. Gunderson's amateur career, including winning the 1960 National Collegiate Championship, and three-decade professional career are legendary. Her talent was nurtured, as she was the first woman in the United States to receive a golf scholarship. Later, former ASU golfer Linda Vollstedt (1964–1968) returned to coach golf in 1980 for 21 years with an impressive string of individual titles and six team national championships. Unsurprisingly, she was named coach of the year five times. Men's golf has produced greats too, like player Phil Mickelson (1988–1992), who was a three-time NCAA champion and four-time All-American, among other international recognitions. (Both courtesy of UAASUL.)

Archery started in 1931, becoming intercollegiate in the 1950s. Margaret Klann coached from 1955 to 1976, making the coed teams among the nation's best, with 16 national team titles and seven individual champions, such as Steve Lieberman, the first ASU male athlete to win All-American four years in a row (1971–1974), among many other US and World championships, as well as Marcia Nygaard (1957–1961), the first ASU woman archer to compete nationally. At right, an ASC archer takes aim in 1953. (Courtesy of Robert Ellis.)

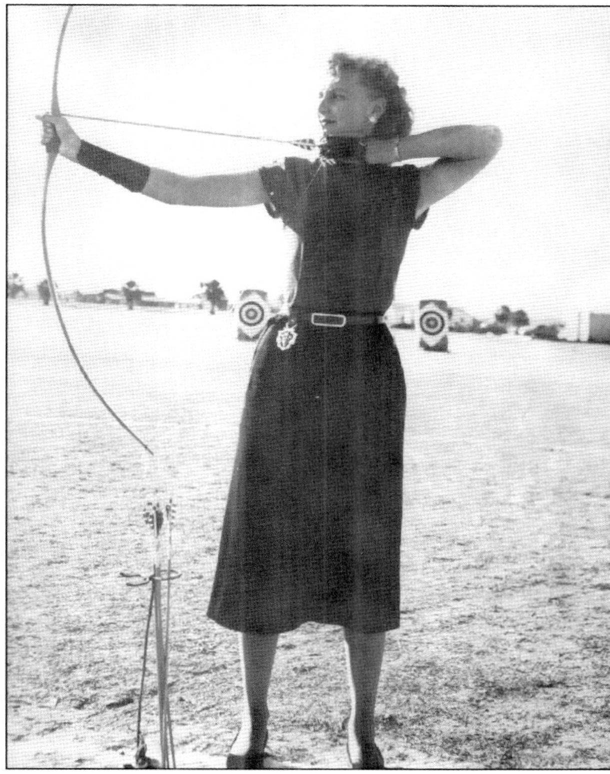

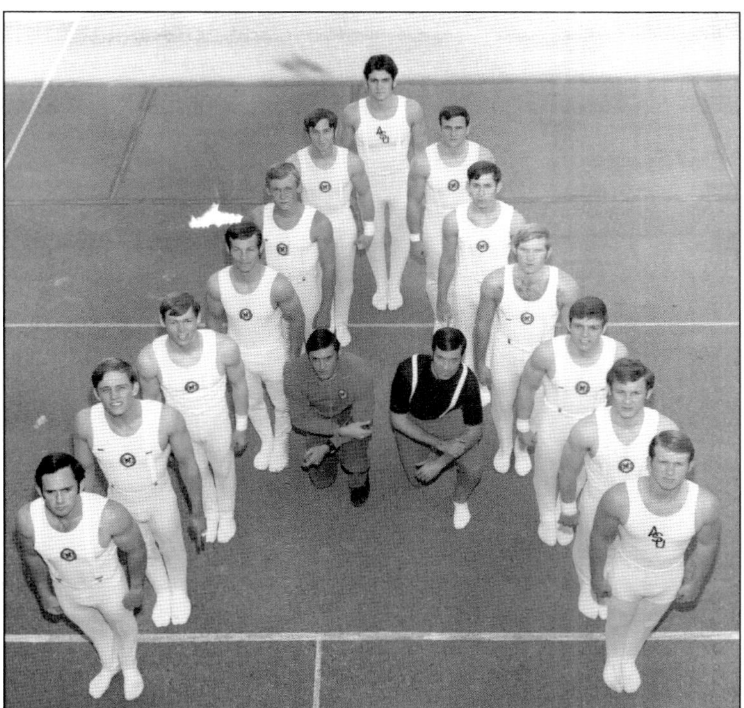

Archery, men's gymnastics (seen here), and badminton lost ASU funding in 1993. Athletes within these sports tried valiantly to save them, but short of an endowment, there was no hope at the time, even though badminton's success under coach Merle Packer from 1967 to 1984 included 56 All-Americans and 13 national team titles. While women's gymnastics is going strong, many sports continue with a club status, like the strong ice hockey team. (Courtesy of UAASUL.)

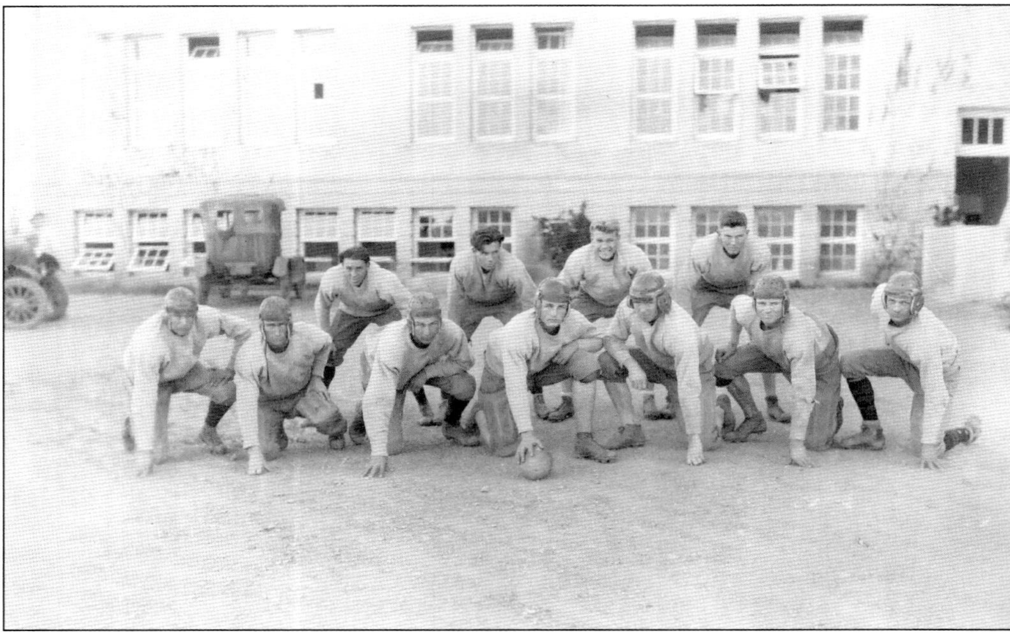

While football started in the 1890s, it was 1928 before the school had a road game to California, when Lattie Coor Sr. (far right) was on the team. He also pitched on the baseball team, including a demonstration game against the Detroit Tigers in 1929. Coor's life as an educator led to Avondale, Arizona, where a school was named in his honor. His son Lattie Coor Jr. became the 15th president of ASU. (Courtesy of Lattie and Elva Coor.)

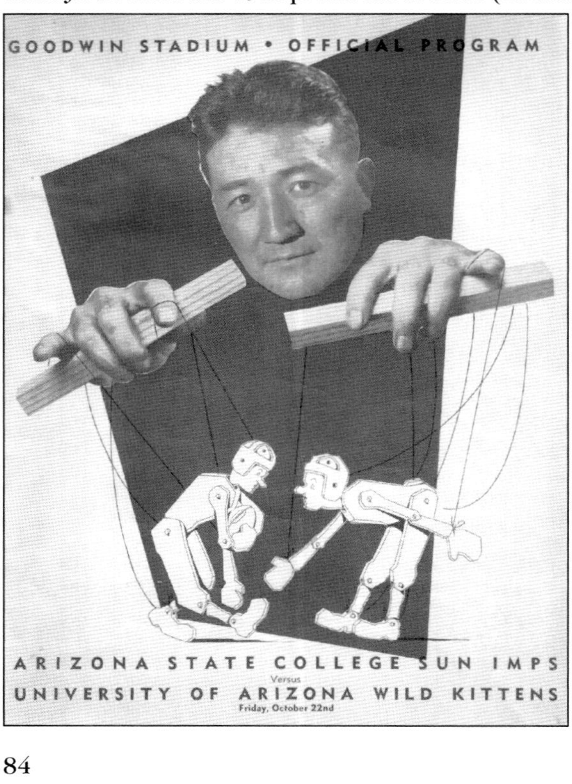

Bill Kajikawa played basketball, baseball, and football at Arizona State starting in 1933. He later coached these sports, including a run with the freshman football team known as the Sun Imps in 1948. Except for military service, he was at ASU until retiring in 1978, winning numerous honors. His daughter Christine, a born Sun Devil, also served ASU in many roles in her successful ongoing career. (Courtesy of Christine Kajikawa Wilkinson.)

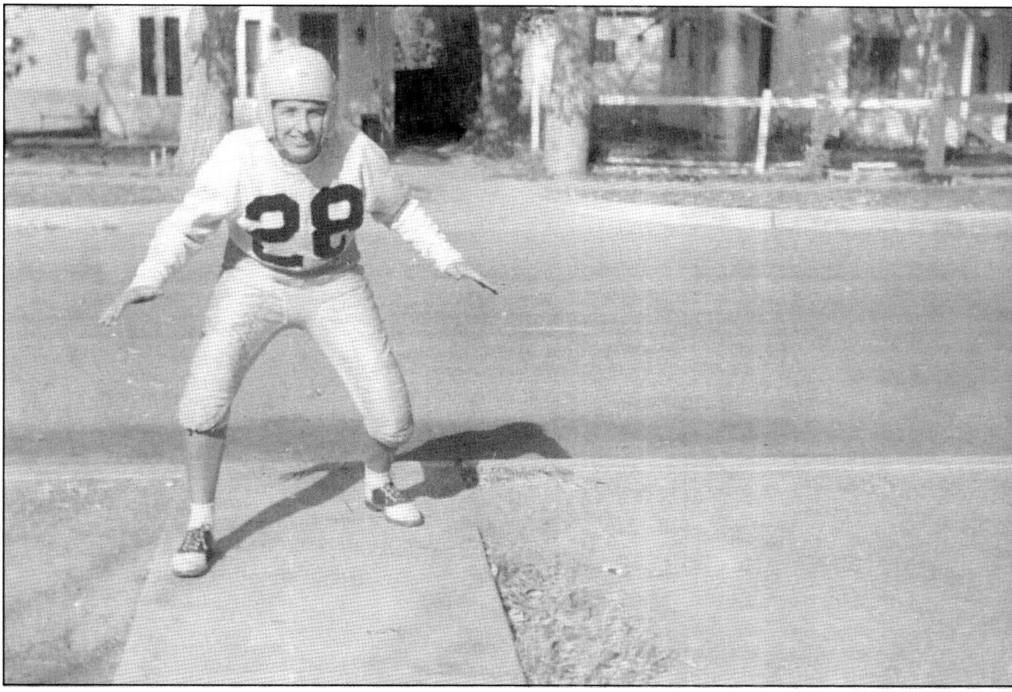

Football was interrupted by the start of World War II. Upon its return, there were women's football demonstration games at half time, including 1949 PE alumna Shirley G. Schmitz, above. Later, Schmitz earned many business awards, including one as an outstanding international businesswoman, and in 1995, she was founder and charter funder for ASU's Center for the Advancement of Small Business, now the Spirit of Enterprise Center. (Courtesy of Shirley G. Schmitz.)

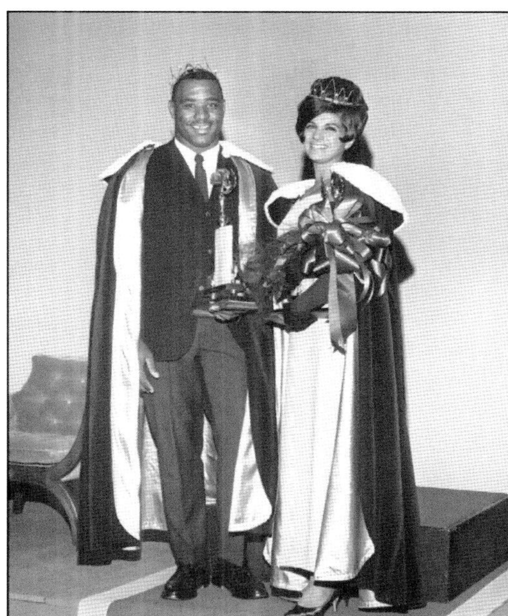

In earlier times, athletes commonly played in multiple sports, like Wilford "Whizzer" White (track and football), his son Danny (baseball and football), and many others. Well-loved Curly Culp was a four-time Western Athletic Conference champion wrestler and a first-team All-American football player. Culp, pictured as 1967 homecoming king with queen Carolyn Griez, went on to play professional football with both the Kansas City Chiefs and the Houston Oilers. (Courtesy of THM.)

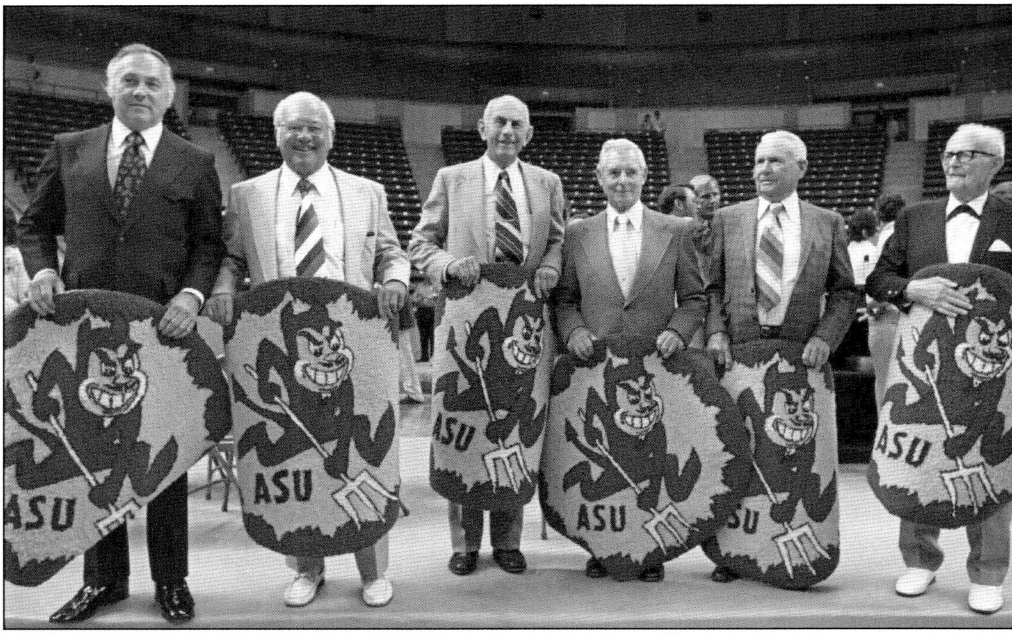

There is a great deal of behind-the-scenes work that goes into creating successful sports programs, with groundskeepers, medical crews, equipment managers, and more. Behind it all, however, are the athletic directors. Past directors were honored at the 1974 dedication of the Activity Center. From left to right are Donn Kinzle (1949–1952), Tom Lillico (early 1930s), Rudy Lavik (1933–1949), Clyde Smith (1954–1971), Aaron McCreary (1923–1929), and D.R. VanPetten (1952–1954). (Courtesy of THM.)

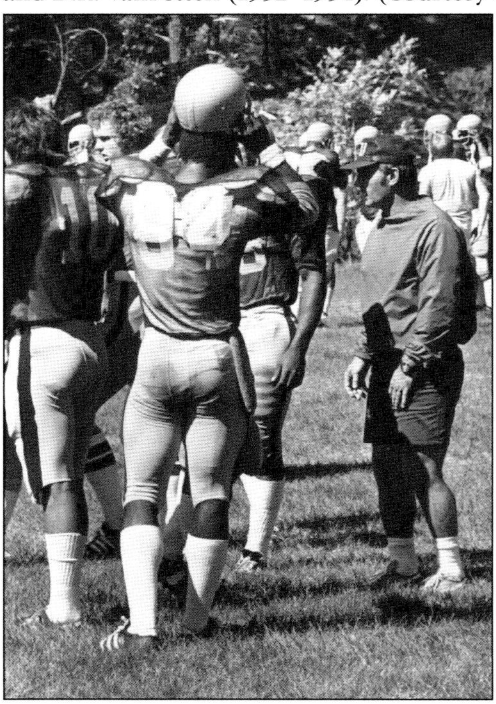

ASC acquired land near Payson in 1951 that science professor Martin Mortensen and a bevy of Sun Devil volunteers initially developed. The creek, rocks, and plants were subjects of study; many groups used the land. Yet Camp Tontozona is best known for the 10-day, high-elevation, distraction-free, pre-season training that football coach Frank Kush began in 1960. Love it or hate it, the hardcore boot camp helped produce winning teams. (Courtesy of UAASUL.)

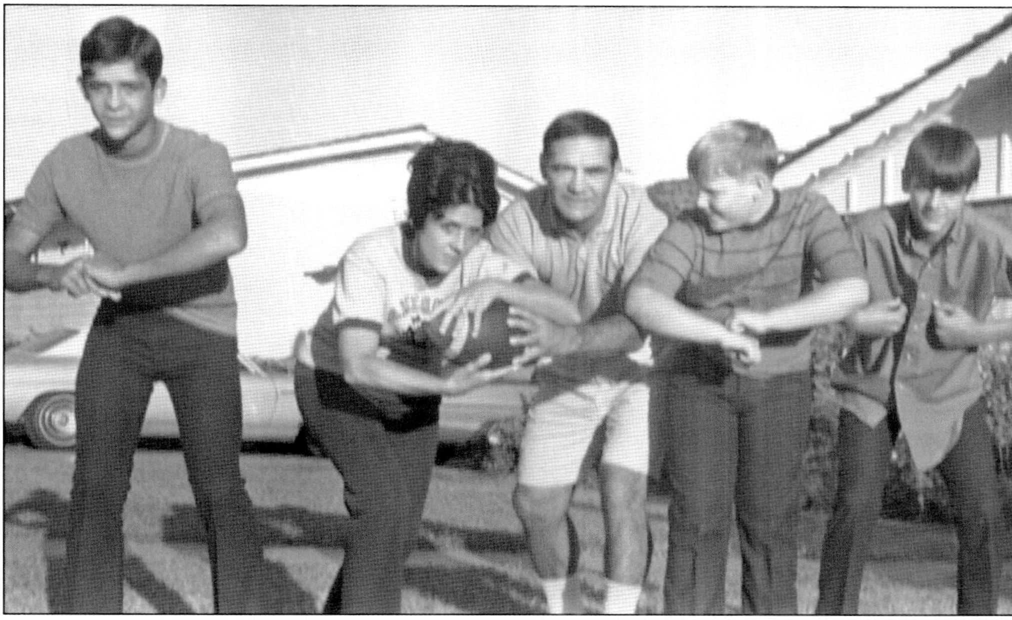

Many strong football coaches came before and after Frank Kush, but his winning 22-year record is the most legendary. He was tough, yes, but also a persuasive gentleman while recruiting. His wife, Francis, enjoyed meeting recruits when Frank brought them by the house, and she would later remember their names at games, offering a friendly face. Francis is pictured here in the 1960s with Frank, holding the ball, and sons (from left to right) Daniel, Damian, and David—all alumni. (Courtesy of Frank Kush.)

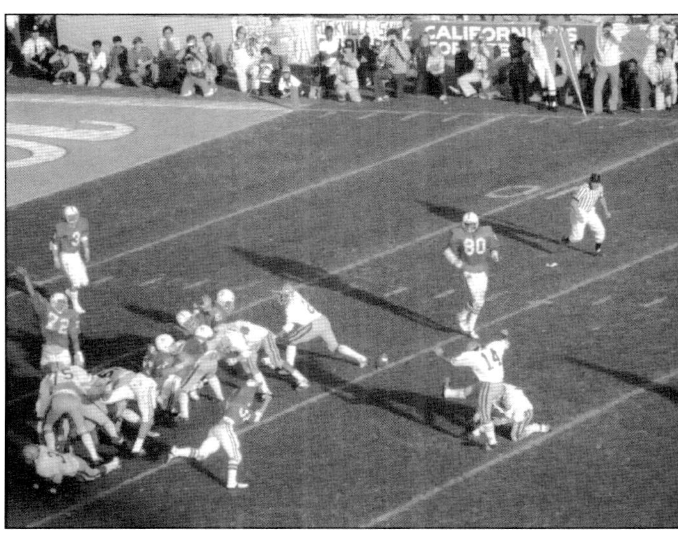

Along with the 1970 Peach Bowl (whipping North Carolina in the snow) and the 1987 Rose Bowl (beating Michigan), the 1975 Fiesta Bowl game against Nebraska is hailed as the best game in ASU history. It was a nail-biter, but the undefeated Sun Devils beat the Cornhuskers with plays like "The Catch" by John Jefferson and the winning 29-yard field goal kicked by Danny Kush, right, for a 17-14 win. (Courtesy of Gary Krahenbuhl.)

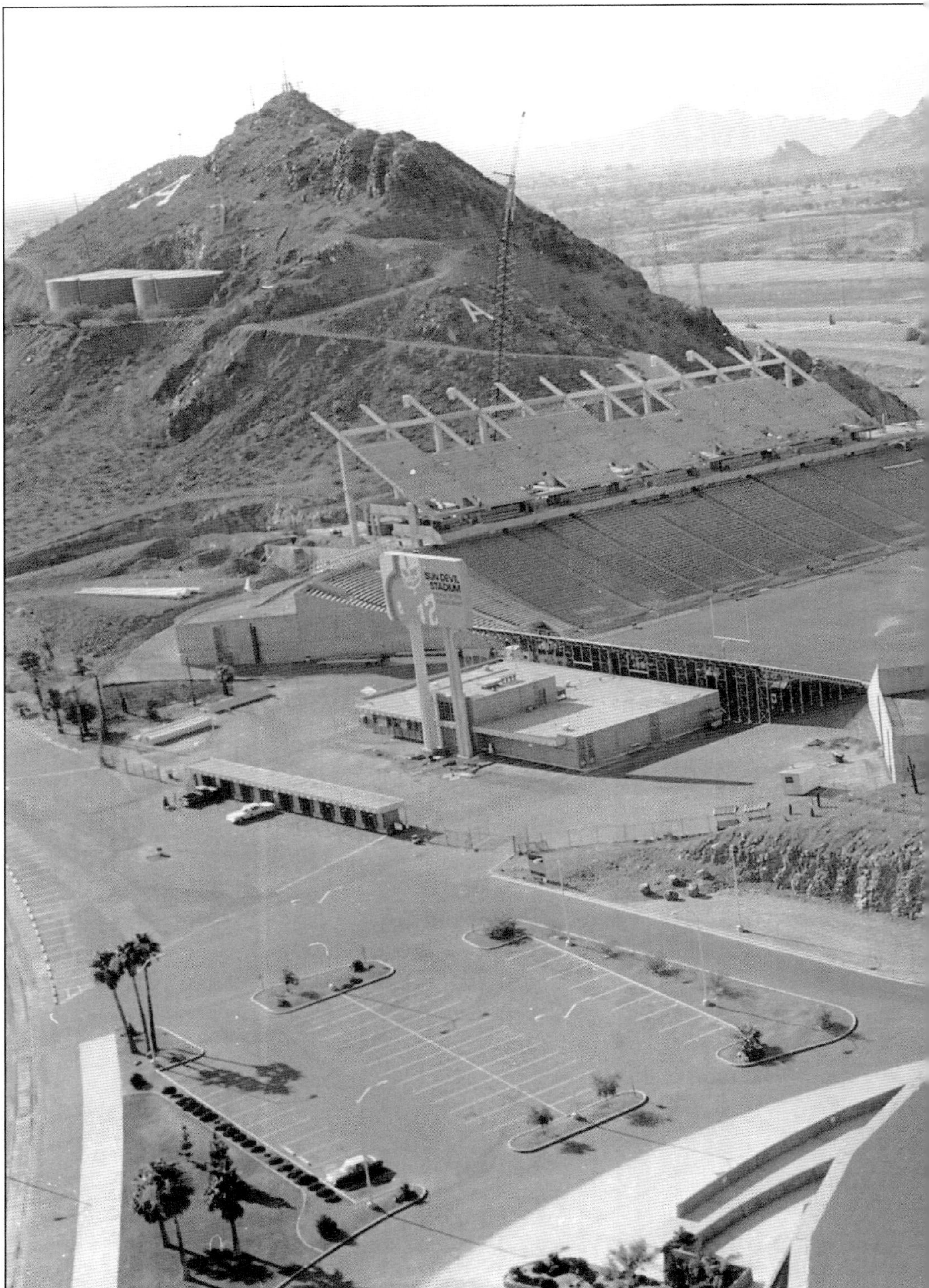
SUN DEVIL STADIUM

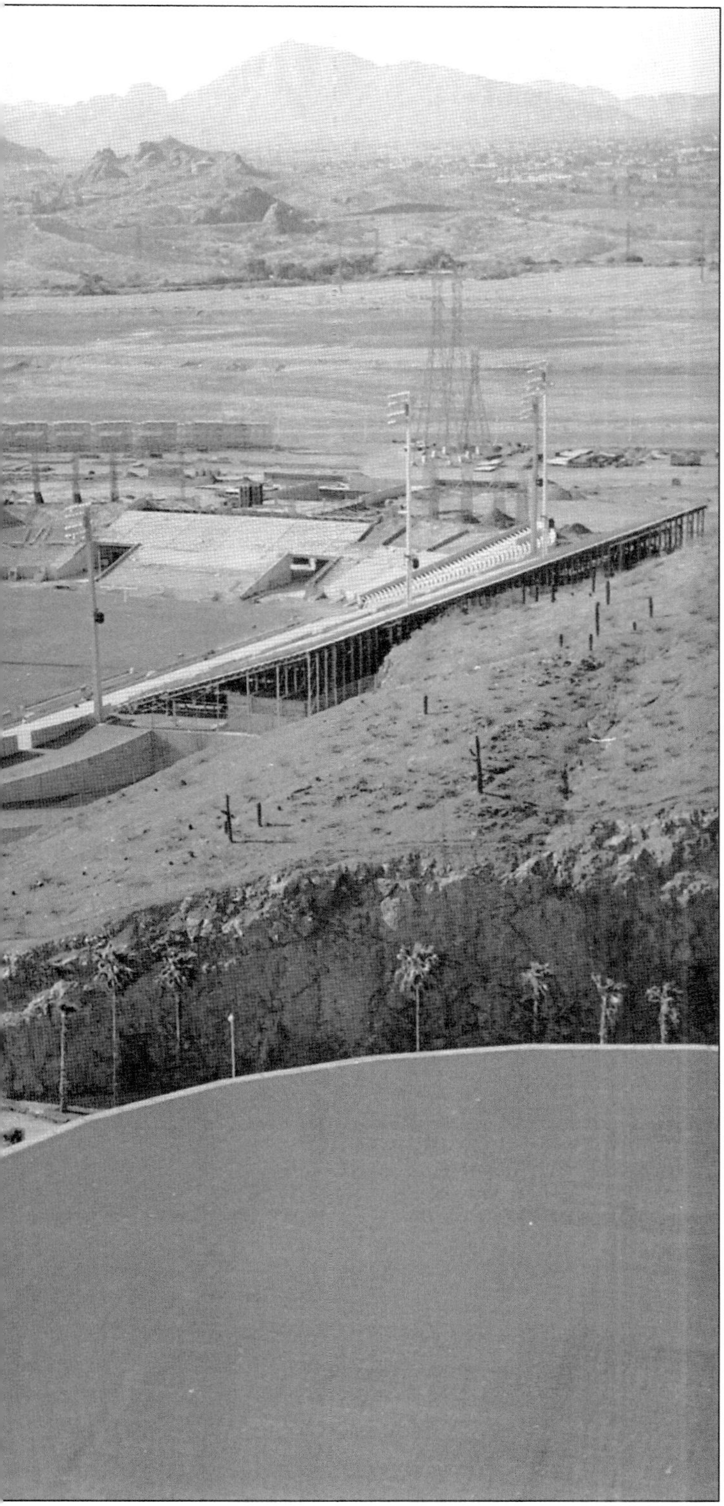

Completed in 1958, Sun Devil Stadium was expanded in 1977 to seat 57,700 fans. It grew to over 71,700 seats by 1988, which is also when the Ed and Nadine Carson Student-Athlete Center was added. In 1996, the gridiron within was named the Frank Kush Field. The earliest games were played on the 1896 Normal Field, with its 1914 wood grandstand, which was replaced by Irish Field in 1928 (with lighting added in 1930). Then the concrete Goodwin Stadium, complete with a grass field, was built in 1936 to seat over 5,000. The team played in the Border Conference beginning in 1931 (champions in 1931, 1939, 1940, 1952, 1957, 1959, and 1961), then in the Western Athletic Conference beginning in 1962 (champions in 1969–1973, 1975, 1977), then in the Pac-10 beginning in 1978 (champions in 1986, 1996, 2007), and as of 2011 in the Pac-12. (Courtesy of Neil Miller.)

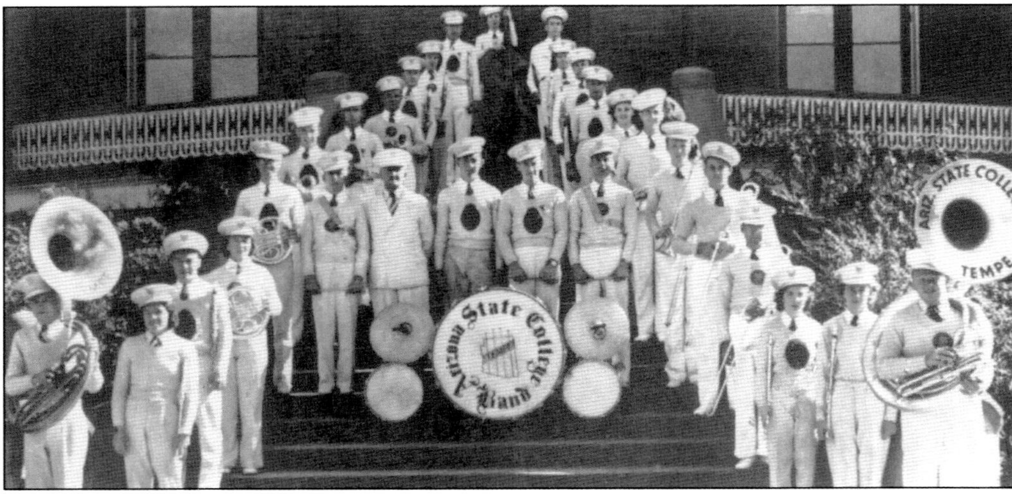

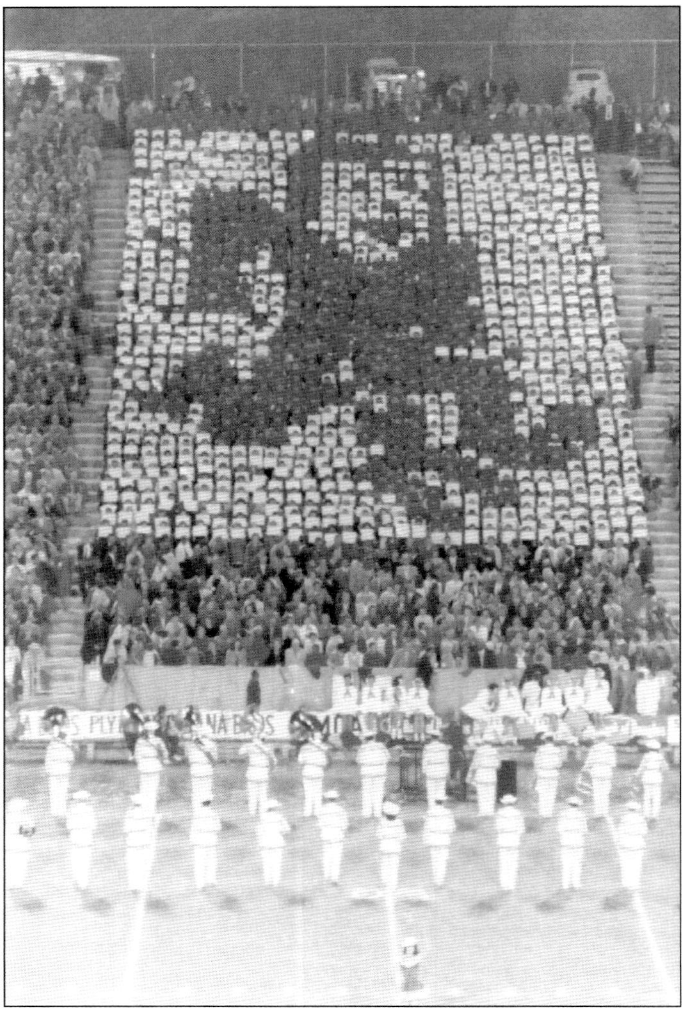

Gracing games and other events at ASU and in the community, the Tempe Bulldogs Marching Band, above at Old Main in 1937 and left in 1940, became the "Pride of the Southwest" Sun Devil Marching Band. Directors like Felix McKernan (1946–1951) and Harold Hines (1952–1965) led the band to honors including the Sudler Trophy in 1991, awarded to one band a year for impressive standards in music and marching routines. Al Davis, director in the 1940s, wrote the first school fight song, "Go, Go Sun Devils," and McKernan wrote the current "Maroon & Gold." Hazel Quaid (music) and Kathryn Gammage (lyrics) wrote the first alma mater in 1937; the current song by Miles A. Dresskell and Ernest Hopkins was adopted in 1955. Skilled cheerleaders, dancers, twirlers, and, as of 1975, the color guard also add spirit to the games. (Both courtesy of THM.)

Four

Snapshots of Student Life

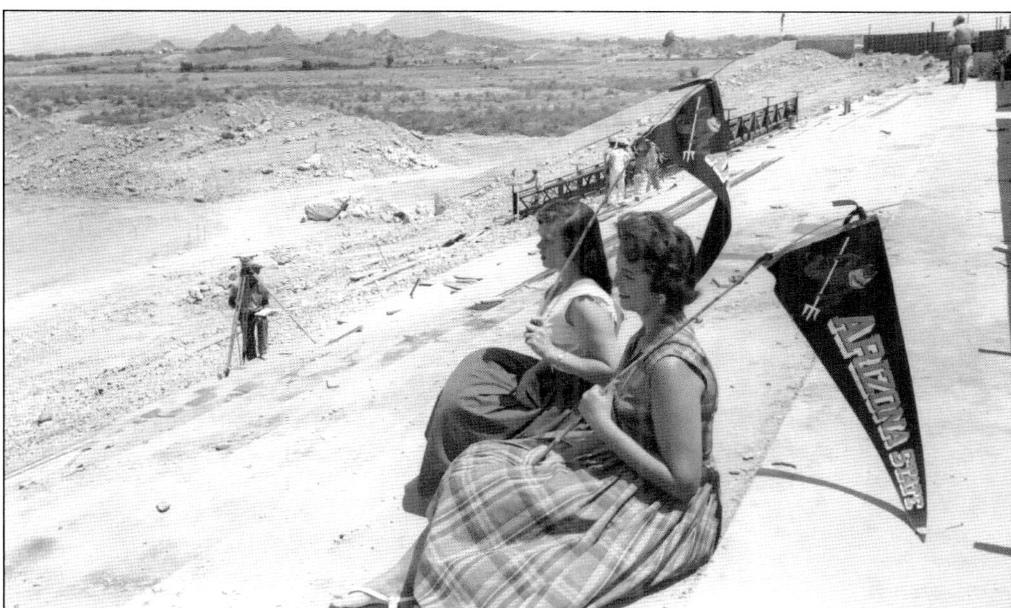

The college years are for building memories. Whether students choose to spend their time playing or watching sports, being in a club or campus ministry, pledging a fraternity or sorority, running the student government, or any number of other possibilities, their experiences are certain to leave an impression. These two students anticipate the memories to come as they await the completion of Sun Devil Stadium in 1958. (Courtesy of THM.)

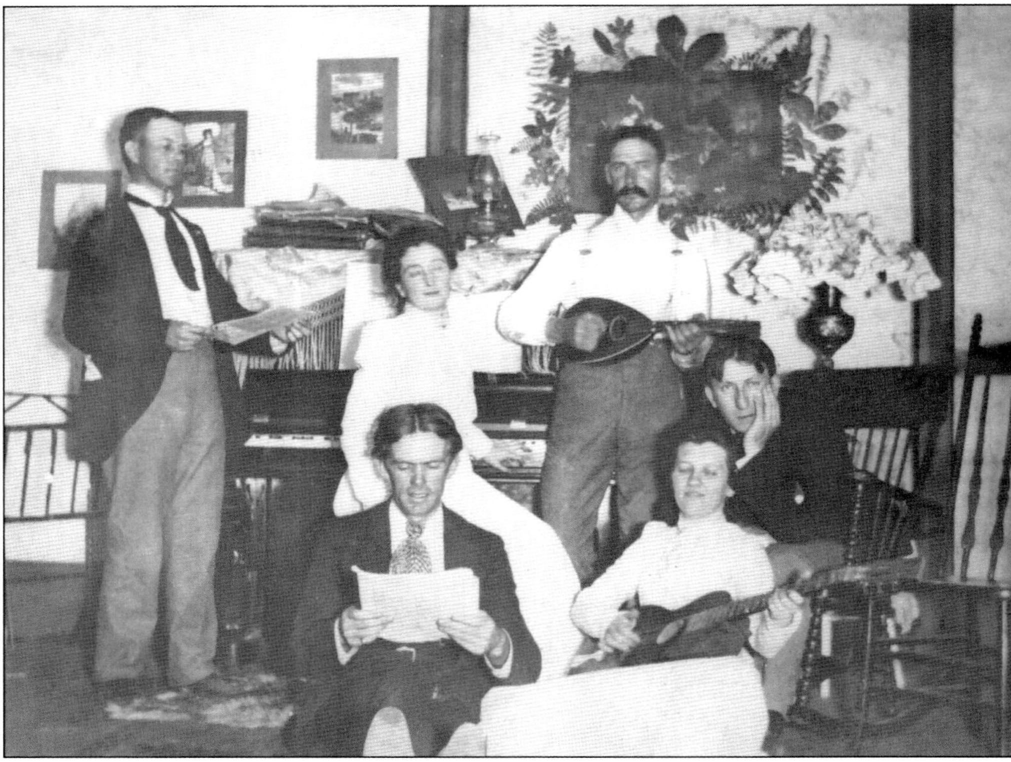

The lives of early normal school students were filled with a variety of fun and lively activities. While many spent their free time horseback riding, hiking, and desert picnicking, others preferred to engage in some indoor fun. The 1890s was known as the "singing period," when students came together, such as these students in the Alpha Boarding Club, to play popular pieces or to compose tunes of their own. (Courtesy of THM.)

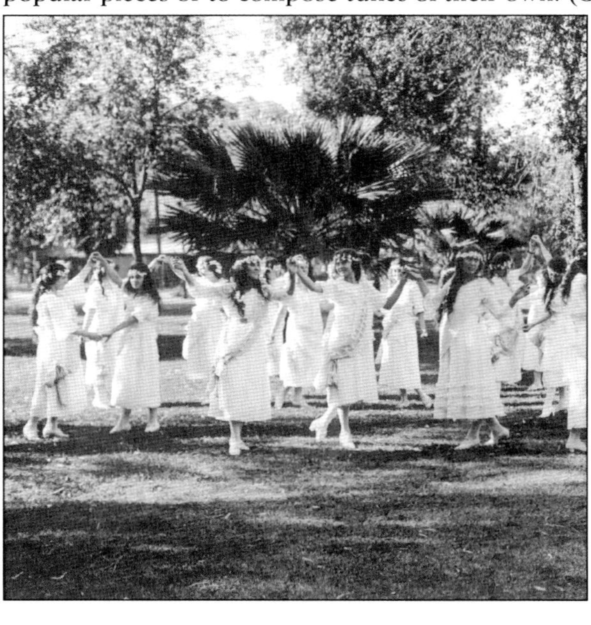

As a small town, Tempe offered few forms of entertainment. Arizona Territorial Normal School students seized the opportunity to organize elaborate pageants, such as a May Day pageant seen here in the 1920s, as well as programs that local residents turned out in large numbers to attend. The programs involved theatrical productions, singing, dance, recitations, and displays of elocution. Many of the pageants even involved children from the training schools. (Courtesy of UAASUL.)

From the start, students were expected to develop their intellectual capacities in much the same way as university students. This is of no surprise given the succession of normal school principals with an affinity for language, logic, and the classics. Chess tournaments, such as the one seen here in 1894, were part of students' training outside of the classroom. When President Matthews arrived in 1900, he intended to further elevate the school's prestige by creating the Philomathian, Alpha, and Olympian Literary Societies. Membership was mandatory until 1911, when they were disbanded. In 1921, the Philomathian Society was resurrected as an all-female group (the precursor to Alpha Delta Pi). A bench the society built near Old Main in the 1920s with assistance from the alumni association still stands. (Right, courtesy of THM; below, UAASUL.)

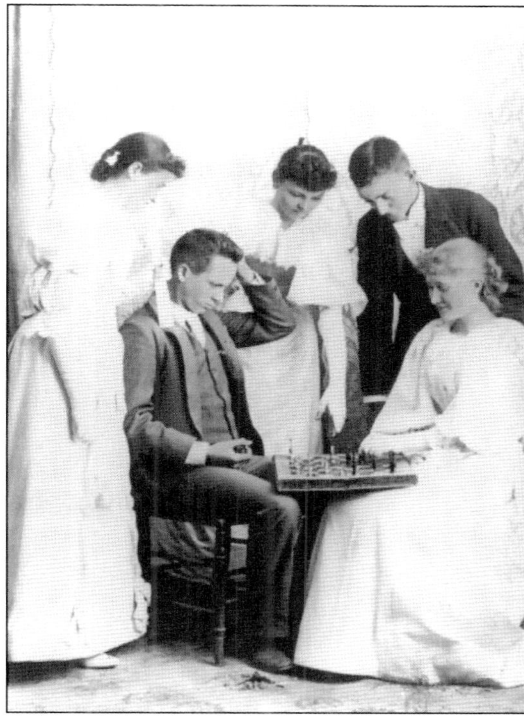

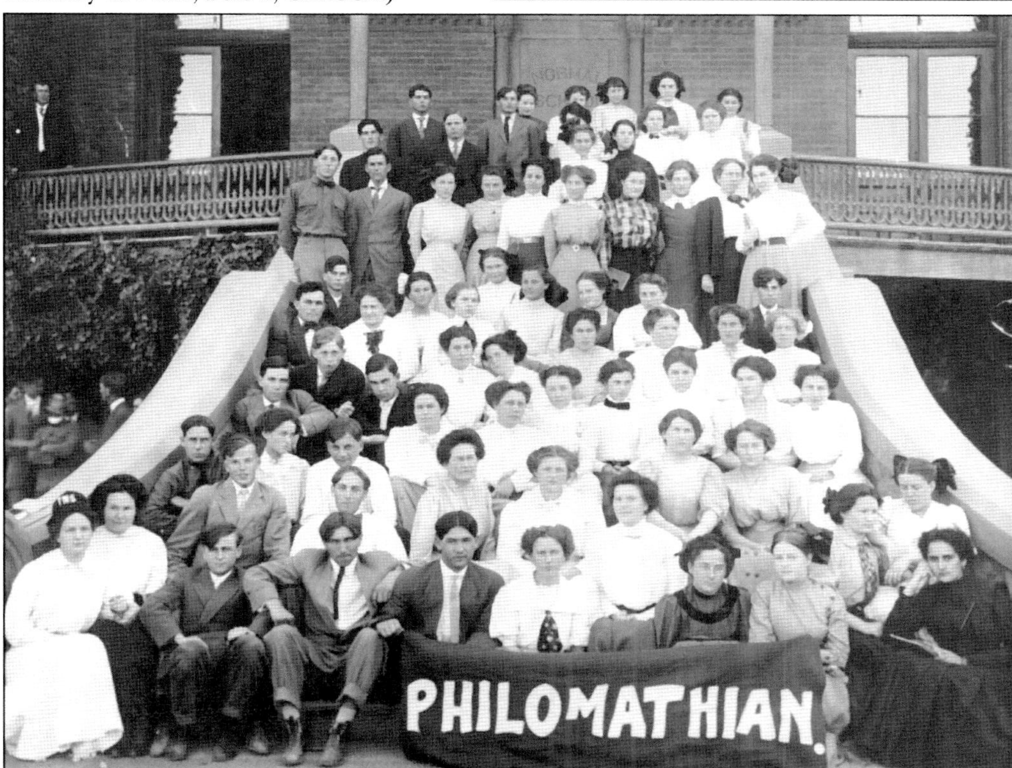

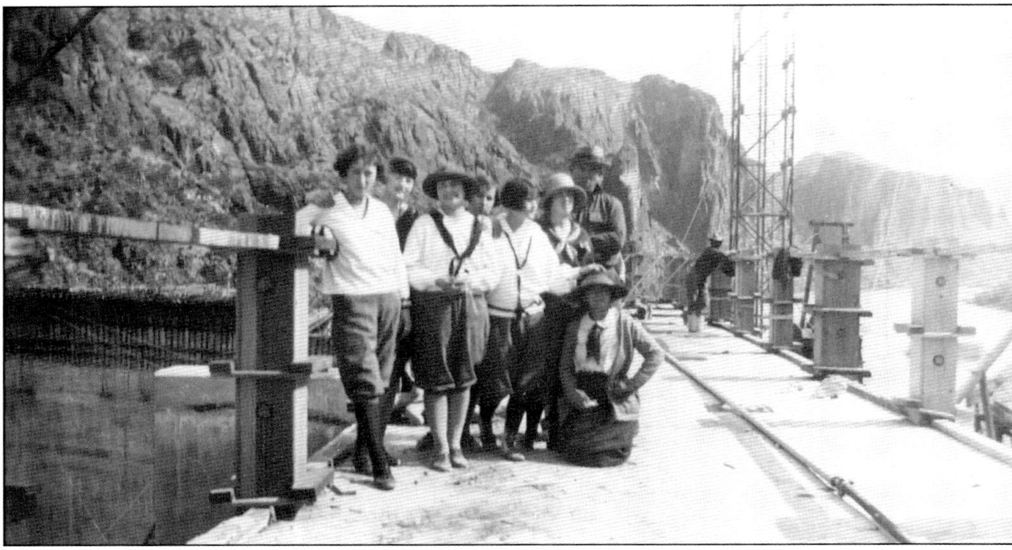

By 1912, students were no longer required to be members of a literary society, but there was still a strong interest in them. As a result, multiple literary societies formed or reformed. For example, the Kalakagathia Society, which is considered to be one of ASU's first sororities, studied literature and eventually became associated with the Camp Fire Girls. Also, the Zetetic Society, above, reorganized from what had been a debate society in 1895. In 1912, the group focused on music and world literature; however, when the membership grew too large, the male students broke away and created the Athenian Debating Club, pictured below in 1907. Members of the Zetetic Society, also called Zeta Sigmas, were a close-knit group who worked together to send supplies to World War I soldiers and went on frequent camping trips. (Both courtesy of UAASUL.)

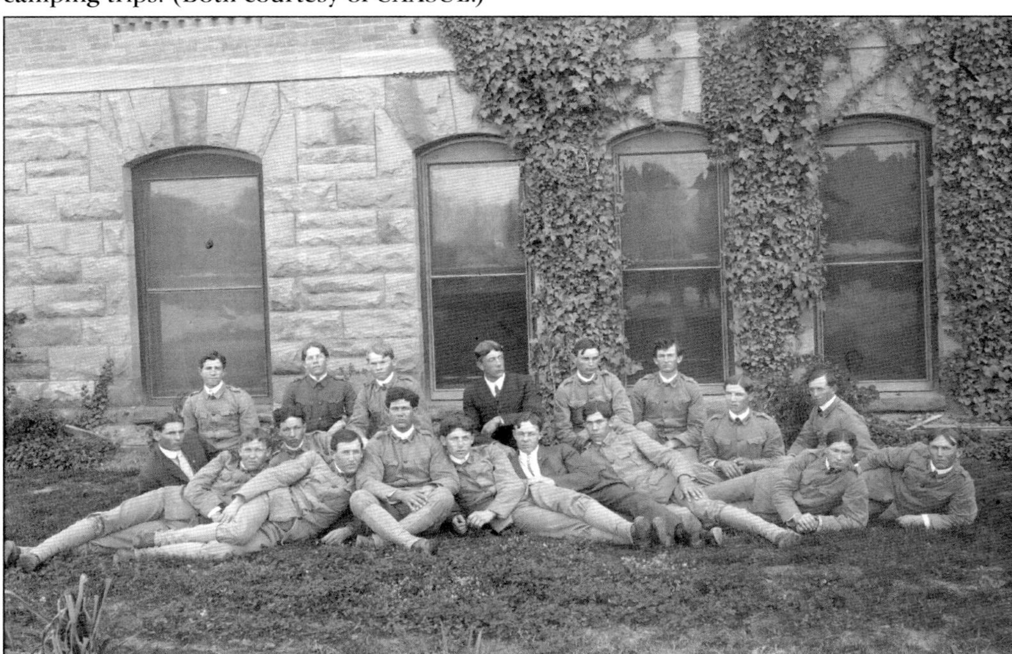

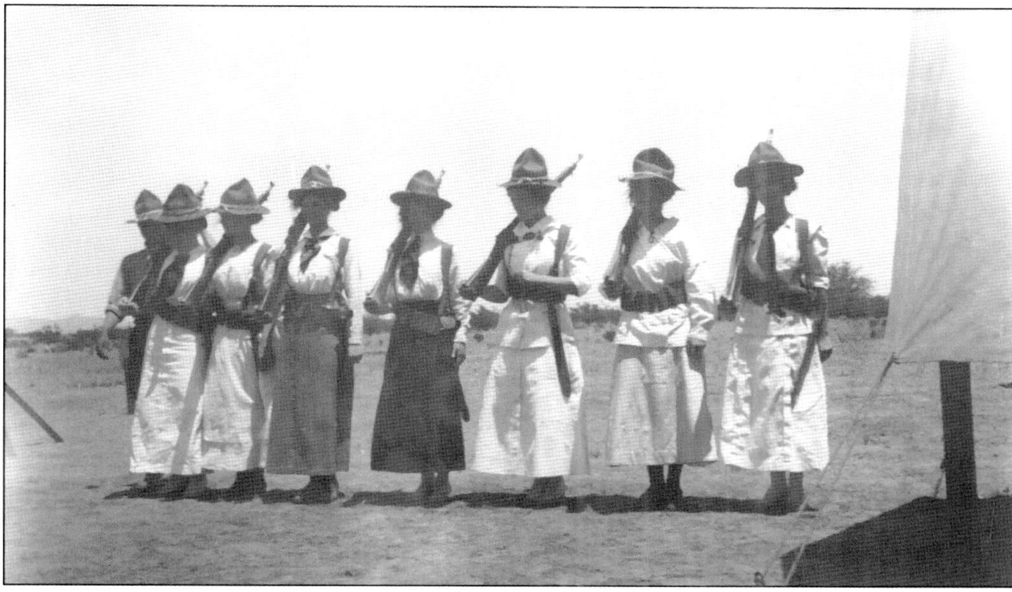

Formed in the 1890s, the Normal School Cadet Company spent the next several decades building a strong reputation, a point of pride for the school. As a result, some female students formed their own cadet company in the 1910s as a symbol of solidarity and support for the military program. (Courtesy of UAASUL.)

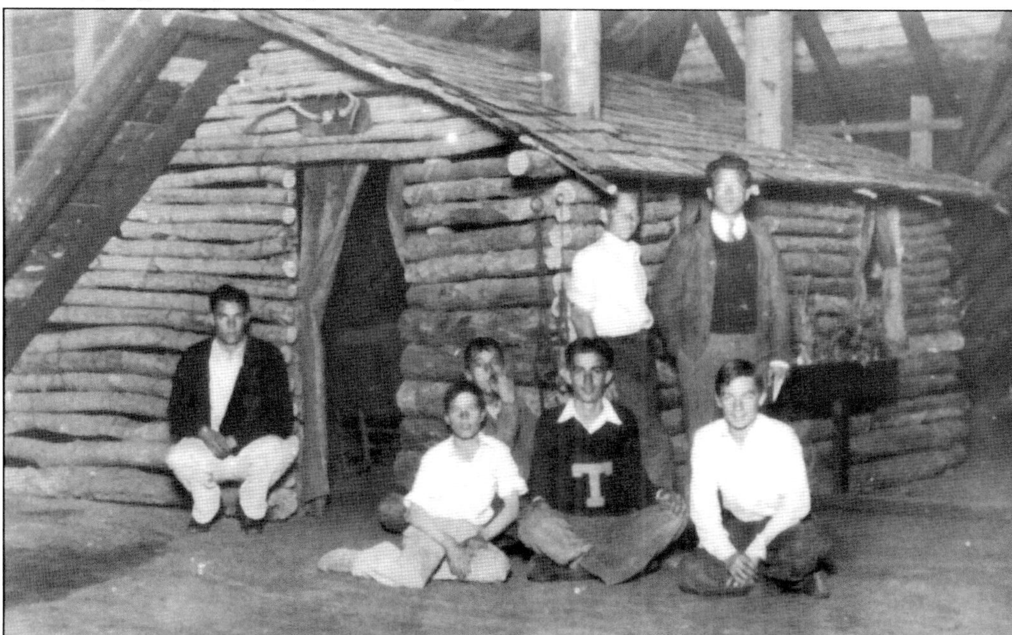

Boy Scouts, Cub Scouts, and Camp Fire Girls had a strong presence on campus by the mid-1920s. Students participated in leadership trainings and retreats, preparing them to lead their own groups. The Boy Scouts used the attic of Old Main to build replicas of a hogan, kiva, and log cabin. Some students and a teacher are pictured here in front of the cabin in 1931. (Courtesy of UAASUL.)

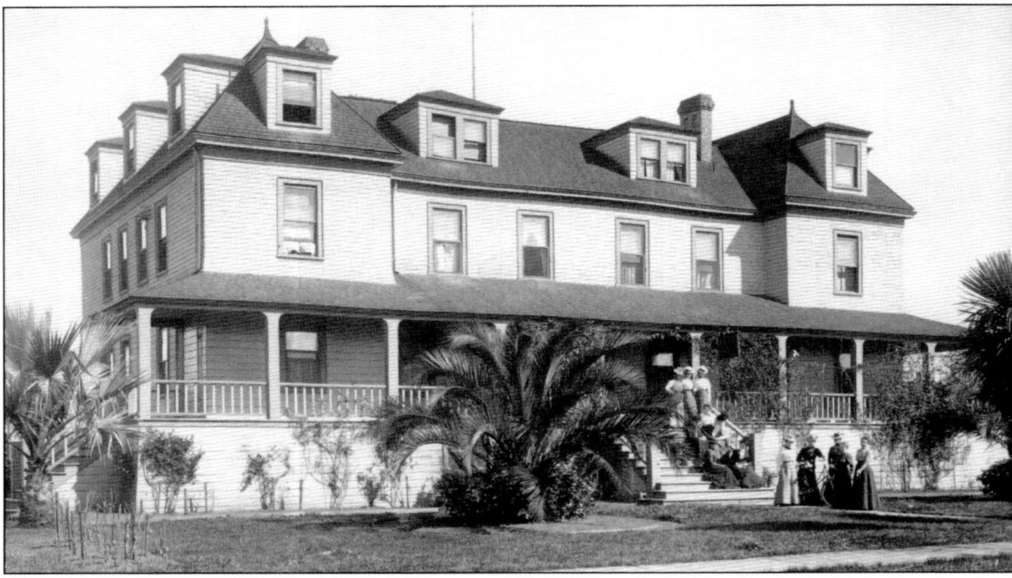

Residence halls, such as this women's hall, became a home away from home. Following the opening of Alpha Hall in 1902, a long line of other residence halls and dormitories followed. A great deal of effort was placed into making them comfortable, with the most up-to-date amenities of their time; some of them even had sleeping porches for hot Arizona nights. (Courtesy of THM.)

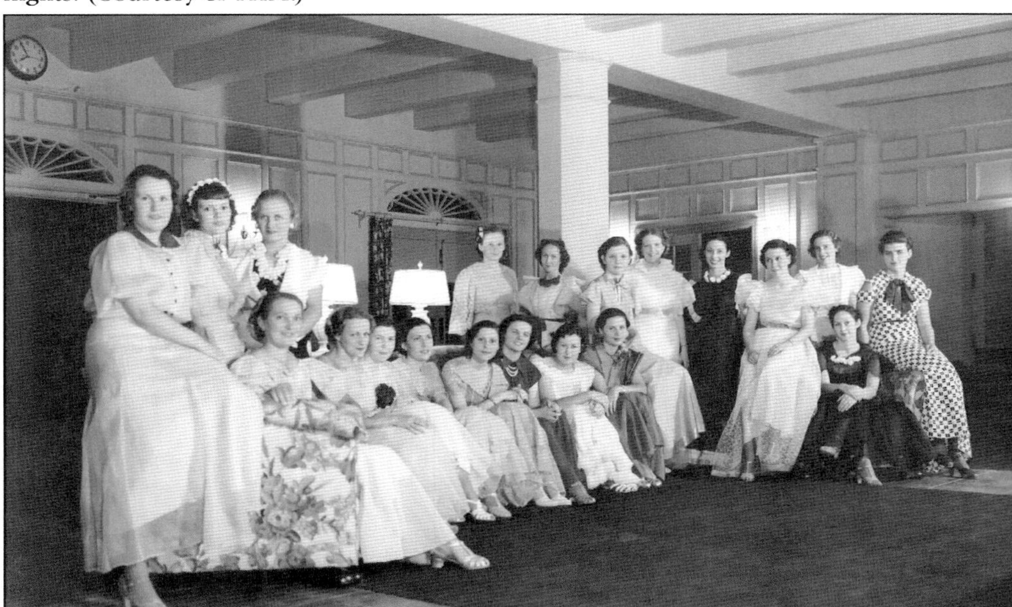

Each hall had its own traditions. For example, the women of West Hall, seen here posing in the parlor, had a Daisy Ring Ceremony that began in 1938. Halls often hosted campus-wide parties, formal dances, picnics, and intramural sporting events. Their early scrapbooks are treasures full of "Hall Songs," poems, drawings, and copies of letters to parents inviting them to visit. (Courtesy of THM.)

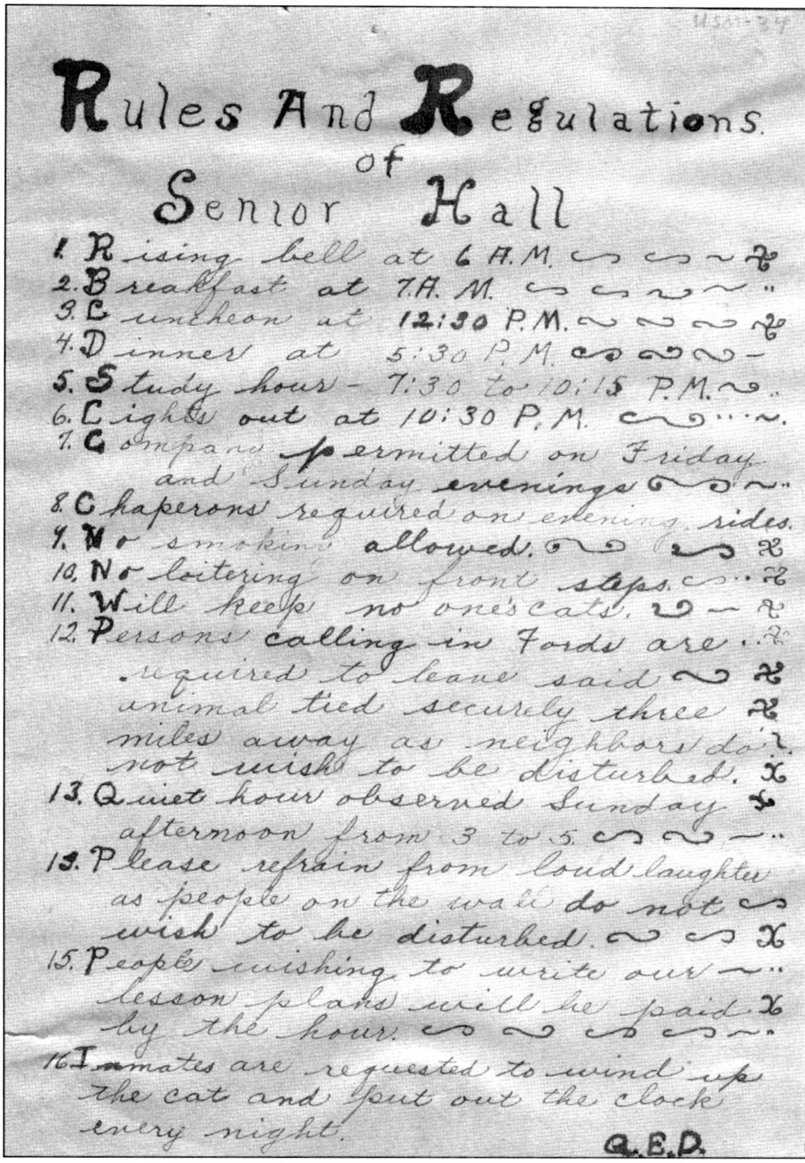

Rules And Regulations
of
Senior Hall

1. Rising bell at 6 A.M.
2. Breakfast at 7 A.M.
3. Luncheon at 12:30 P.M.
4. Dinner at 5:30 P.M.
5. Study hour - 7:30 to 10:15 P.M.
6. Lights out at 10:30 P.M.
7. Company permitted on Friday and Sunday evenings
8. Chaperons required on evening rides.
9. No smoking allowed.
10. No loitering on front steps.
11. Will keep no one's cats.
12. Persons calling in Fords are required to leave said animal tied securely three miles away as neighbors do not wish to be disturbed.
13. Quiet hour observed Sunday afternoon from 3 to 5.
14. Please refrain from loud laughter as people on the wall do not wish to be disturbed.
15. People wishing to write our lesson plans will be paid by the hour.
16. Inmates are requested to wind up the cat and put out the clock every night.

Q.E.D.

Residence halls have rules and expected codes of conduct. This early example offers some insight into those rules. In particular, item no. 12 requests that students leave their horses (or Fords) tied three miles away "as neighbors do not wish to be disturbed." Although there were some attempts to designate areas for horses to be boarded in 1896, charging students $1 a month for use of the pasture, further campus expansion and the increase of automobile usage forced the campus to deal with the "parking problem" in other ways. Not all students lived on campus; there has always been a substantial population of commuter students as well. The 1926 annual reveals that the Timakaeena Society and the Village Collegians were organized to support students "who drive to school from various places in the valley" and to promote "a stronger relationship and fellowship between those girls residing on the campus and those who live off the campus." (Courtesy of Cora Beardsley Collection, UAASUL.)

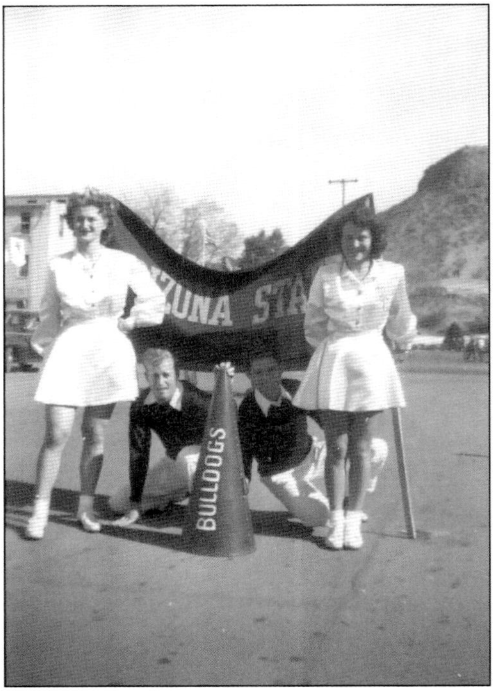

The first homecoming parade was held in 1926, and students have since shown their school spirit by building floats, running for homecoming court, or marching in the procession, as these cheerleaders did in the 1940s. The Lantern Walk, a campus tradition beginning in 1917, involves passing the symbolic torch from seniors to juniors atop "A" mountain and has also become part of the homecoming observance. (Courtesy of Shirley G. Schmitz.)

"In our midst we have beautiful women of every type," proclaims the 1923 school annual. In fact, campus beauties were acknowledged through numerous titles, including Homecoming Queen, Rodeo Queen, Military Queen, Cotton Queen, and others. The school was also attended by the only two Arizona recipients of the Miss America title: Jacque Mercer won in 1949 and Vonda Kay Van Dyke in 1965, congratulated here by President Durham at homecoming. (Courtesy of THM.)

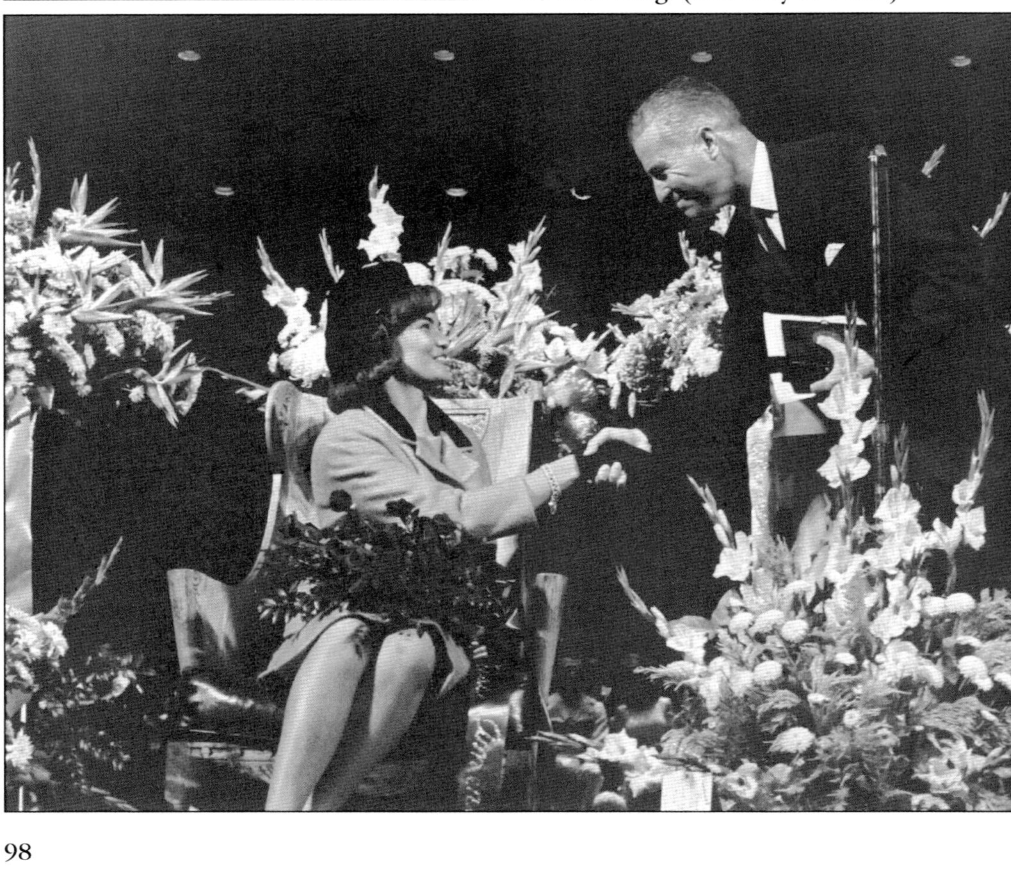

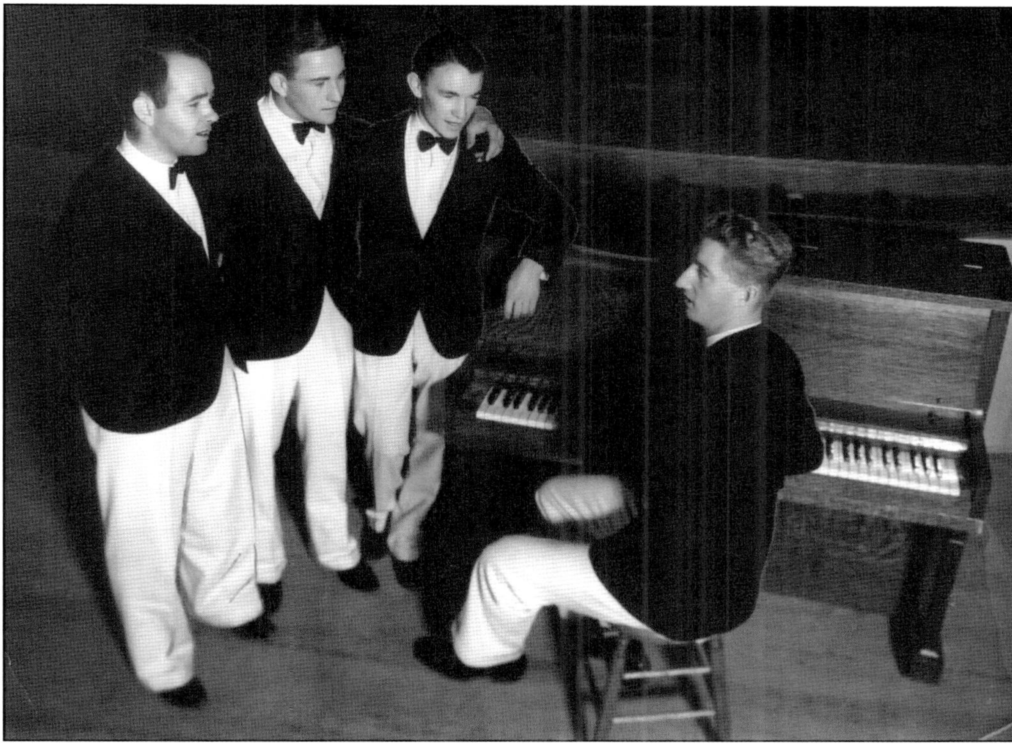

By the 1920s, students began to move beyond the literary societies and debate clubs that once defined their extracurricular activities and develop clubs that allowed them to focus on other interests. For example, in 1922, the boys' glee club was formed, and it became quite popular, opening membership to "anyone who sang well." The club performed regularly in various venues around Arizona. By 1926, the all-female glee club was established. (Courtesy of UAASUL.)

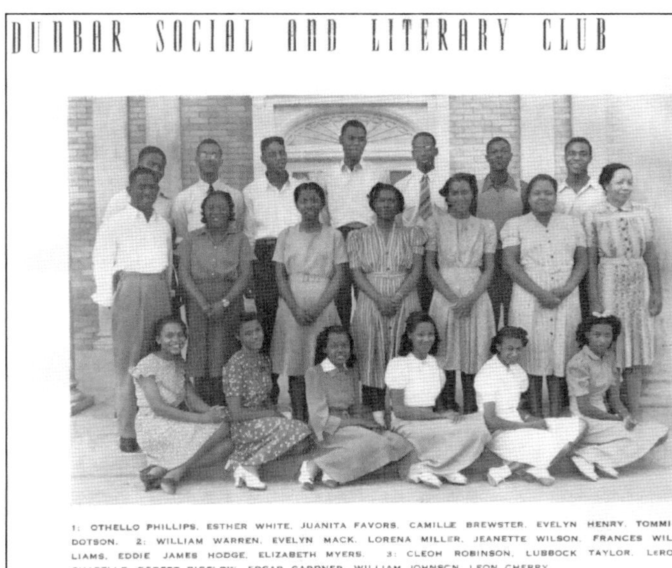

The Dunbar Social and Literary Club, organized in 1936, was the first African American student group on campus. Its purpose was to promote "leadership and scholastic attainment for the purpose of promoting good will and understanding." The group hosted dances and various other activities. Prior to 1930, eight African Americans attended the institution, with the first to graduate in 1924. (Courtesy of UAASUL.)

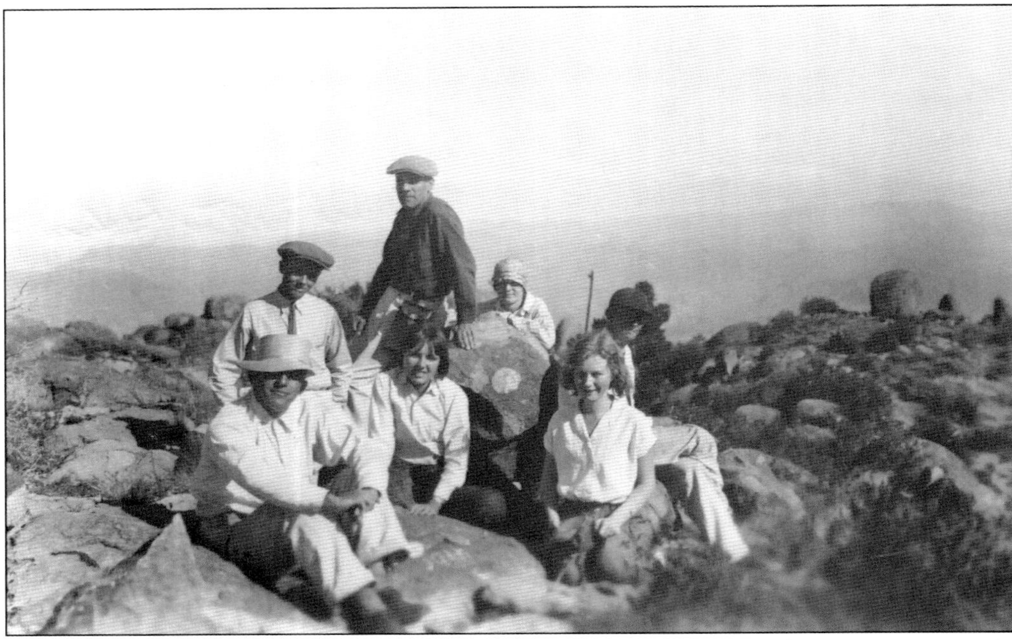

The Geographic Society was organized in 1924 to promote the study of Arizona's geography. As captured in this 1928 image of club members hiking in the Superstition Mountains, the group took frequent field trips around the state to improve its understanding of the local landscape. Other discipline-specific clubs formed around this same time, including the Pasteur Society, Art and Psychology Clubs, and the Associations for Architects and Engineers. (Courtesy of UAASUL.)

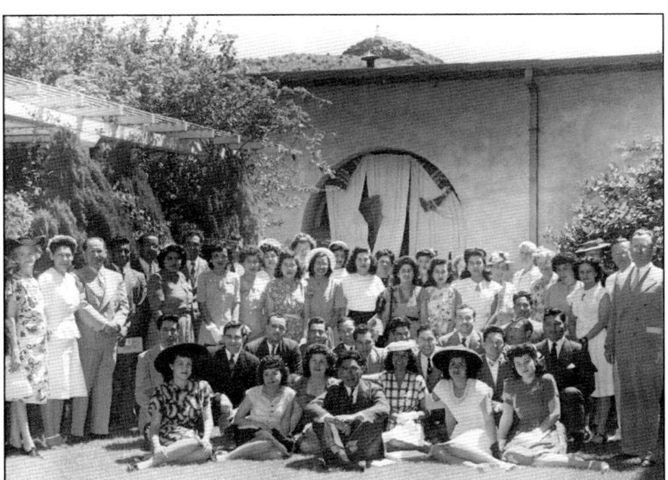

Los Conquistadores was a social club organized by Latino students in 1937. Members developed strong friendships, raised funds for scholarships, and collaborated with other campus groups to host parties. Although there is no evidence of a similar type of club to serve the 151 Latino students who attended prior to 1930, the Hispanico Club (1916) and El Club Espanol (1921) were organized for students studying Spanish. (Courtesy of UAASUL.)

Honorary clubs recognize student achievement in leadership, academics, or athletics. Groups like the Blue Keys, a scholastic fraternity founded in the 1940s, developed their own traditions and even raised money for campus improvements. In 1955, the Lariats formed, aiming to join the national Spurs organization, a women's honorary group limited to select sophomores from different departments. At right, Kathryn Gammage congratulates members on attaining Spurs status. (Courtesy of Grady Gammage Jr.)

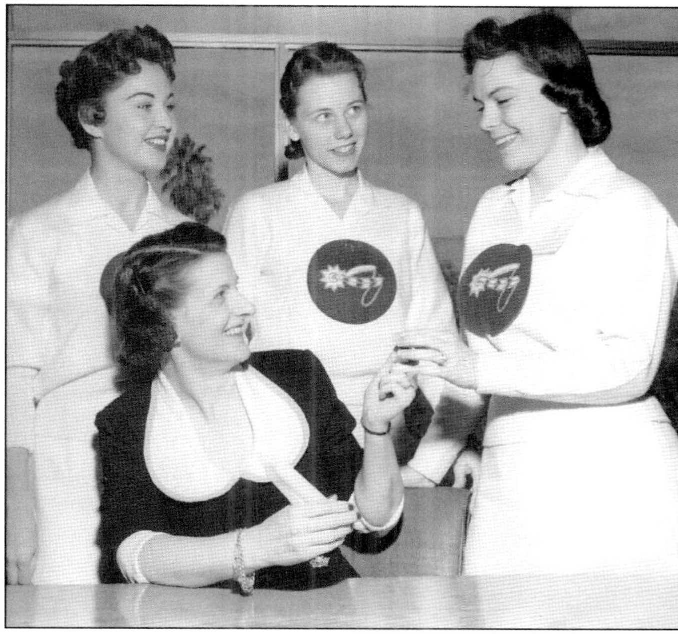

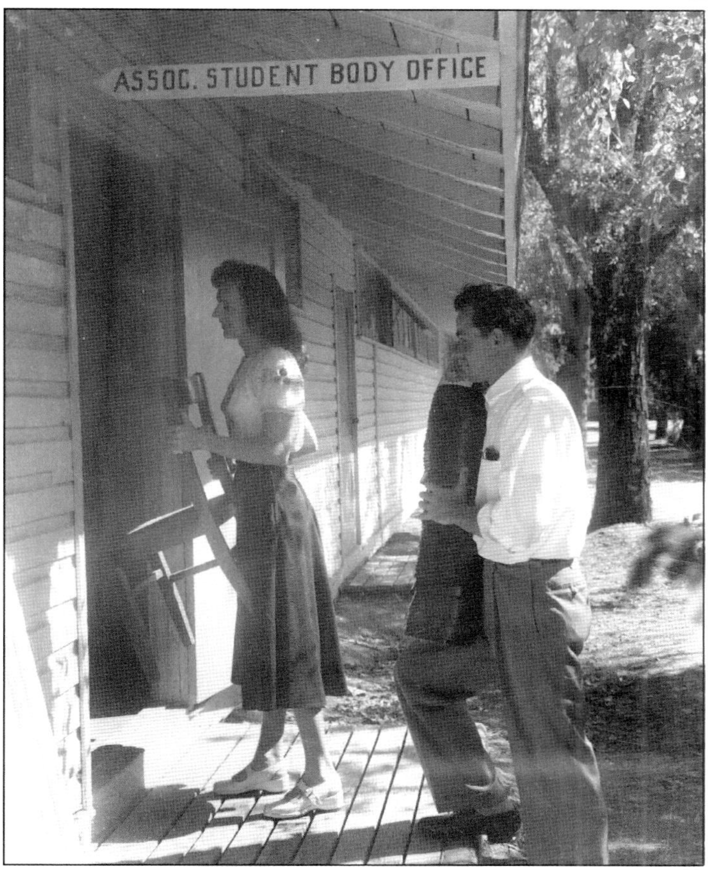

The first student government, established in the 1890s, had a social and disciplinary function. As the school's status changed over time, so did the organization of student leadership that, among other things, sent representatives to administrative meetings and raised funds for such things as sports, library books, and even the purchase of a carillon (1966). In 1948, the Associated Student Body officers, seen here, moved into an office in converted Army barracks. (Courtesy of UAASUL.)

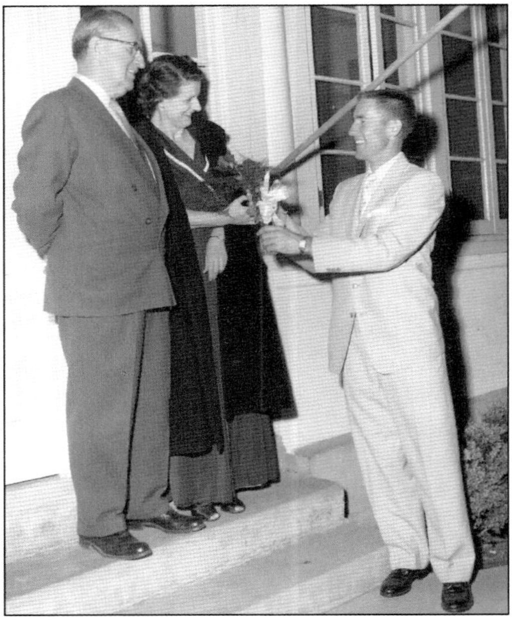

Greek organizations at ASU can trace their histories to the first sorority (1911) and the first fraternity (1924). Often tied to national Greek orders, each group developed its own unique set of activities and traditions. Pictured here is a representative of the Alpha Tau Omega fraternity delivering flowers to President Gammage and his wife, Kathryn, in celebration of their wedding anniversary in 1956. (Courtesy of Grady Gammage Jr.)

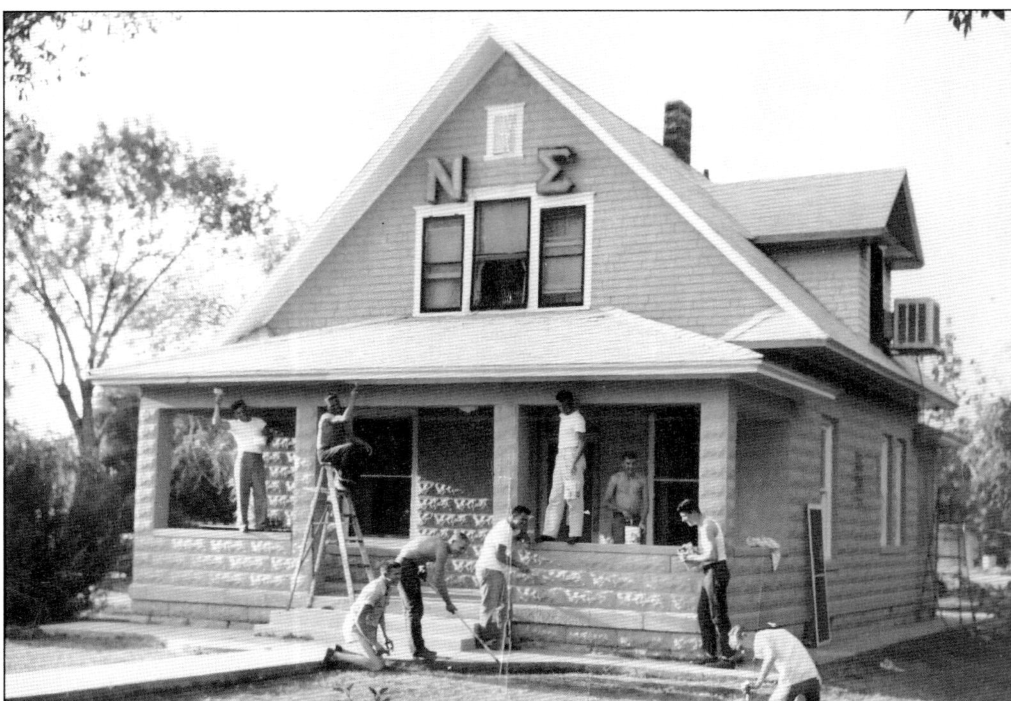

The first fraternity house was occupied by Lambda Phi Sigma on Normal Avenue in 1932, with many more to follow around campus. Sigma Nu, seen here cleaning and painting its house in 1955, relocated to fraternity row on Alpha Drive in 1962 along with nine other fraternities to accommodate their growth. The number of fraternities tripled from seven in 1950 to 21 in 1965. (Courtesy of Sigma Nu.)

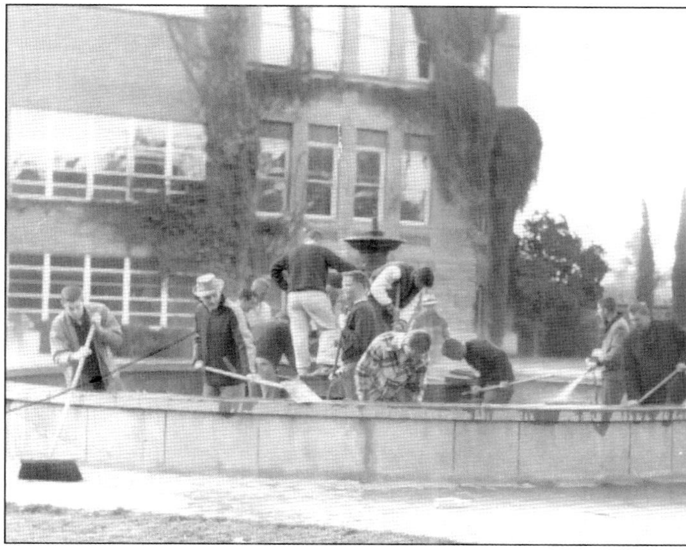

Many student traditions involved maintaining the beauty of the campus. The class of 1901, for example, started an annual tree-planting tradition and even planted English Ivy at Old Main, as seen in the background when Old Main had a front addition. Fraternities and sororities also helped with campus maintenance, such as the cleaning of the fountain at the old quad, seen here in the 1950s, or various other chores delegated to pledges. (Courtesy of Sigma Nu.)

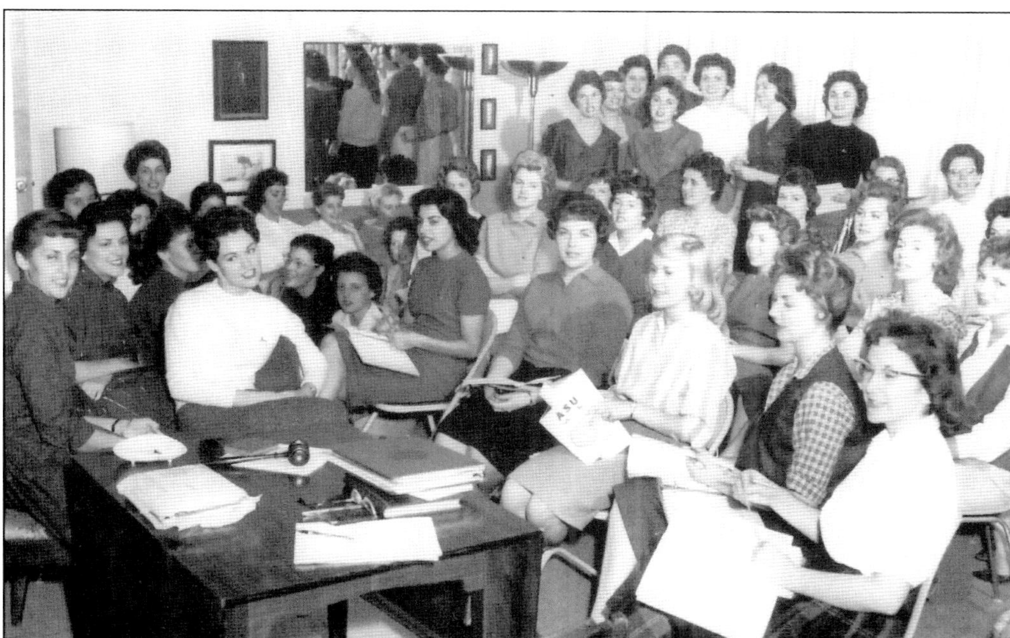

Sororities also saw rapid growth, with their numbers jumping from five groups in 1950 to 11 by 1965. This photograph was taken during a 1959 Chi Omega meeting in Palo Verde Hall. The Intersorority and Panhellenic Councils act as mediators between all the sororities on campus, allowing them to collaborate on event planning. In this case, they offered representation in the Associated Women of Arizona State College (AWS) Council. (Courtesy of Lynn Steinko Smith.)

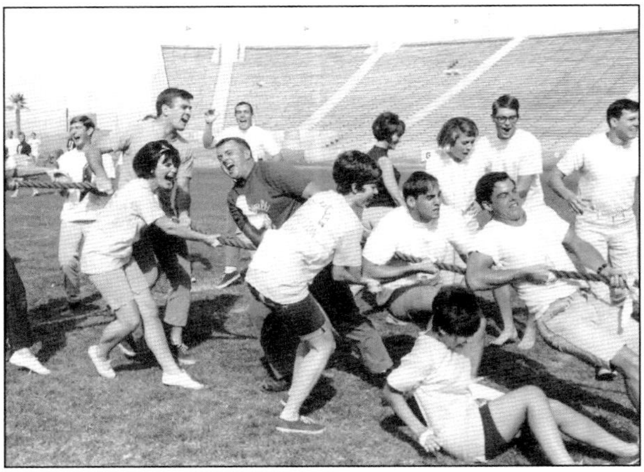

Fraternities and sororities enjoy full social calendars rife with rushing, dances, picnics, talent shows, camping, homecoming activities, service projects, and intramural competitions, such as this 1960s tug-of-war involving some Alpha Delta Pi sorority sisters inside Sun Devil Stadium. Greek organizations also engage in philanthropic activities by helping to raise money for charitable organizations such as the Ronald McDonald House or Childhelp. (Courtesy of Susan Hibler.)

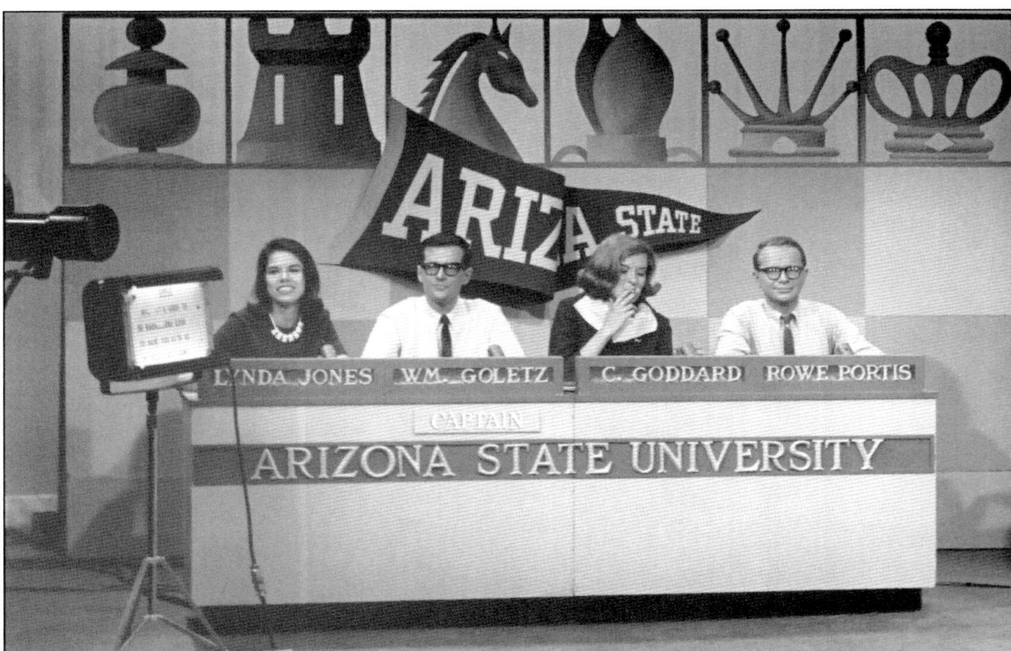

In 1964, Arizona State University matched wits with other universities on the televised General Electric College Bowl. The four-person team was carefully selected and coached by English professor Nicholas Salerno. It won four times before losing to Loyola University by 15 points. In 2006, the ASU Academic Bowl was instituted using the College Bowl model to promote healthy intellectual competition between the undergraduate colleges on campus. (Courtesy of THM.)

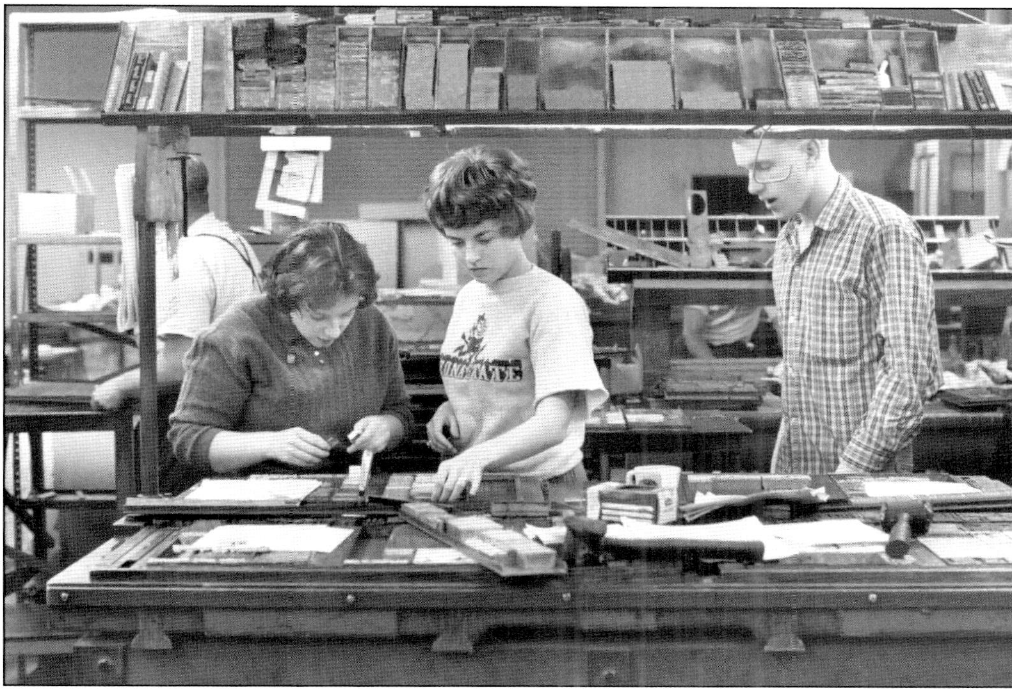

Since the *Normal Echo* was first published in 1890, there have been a succession of student publications. In addition to the series of campus papers that went through multiple name changes until becoming the *State Press*, whose 1960s staff is pictured above, students also contributed to the publication of school annuals from 1905 to the mid-1990s, literary journals, academic proceedings, and the 1970s counterculture publication that eventually became the *New Times*. (Courtesy of UAASUL.)

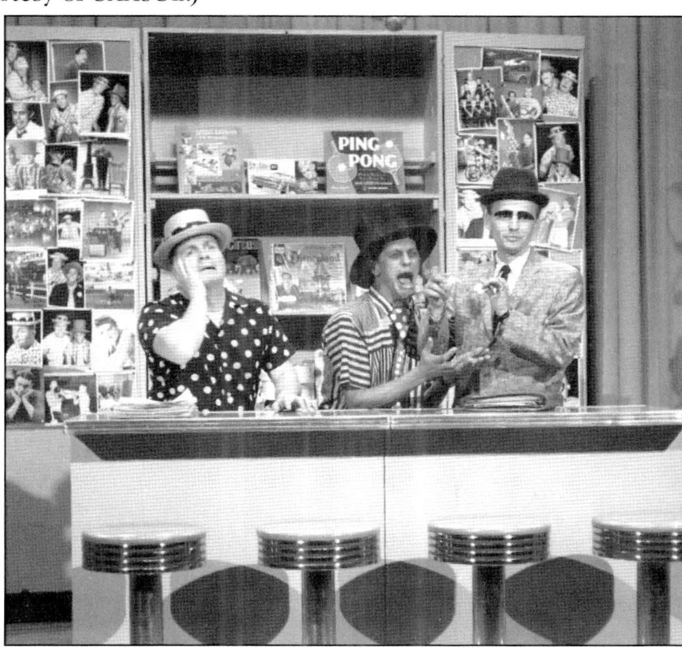

Arizona State College student Ladimir "Ladd" Kwiatkowski is an example of an involved student. Arriving in 1949, he played varsity baseball, captaining the team in 1952, and wrote a *State Press* column called "Kwiat's Kwikies." Finishing his journalism degree, he then entertained local children from 1954 to 1989 as cohost of what became the beloved *Wallace and Ladmo Show*. From left to right are Bill "Wallace" Thompson, Ladd Kwiatkowski, and Pat McMahon. (Courtesy of the Kwiatkowski family.)

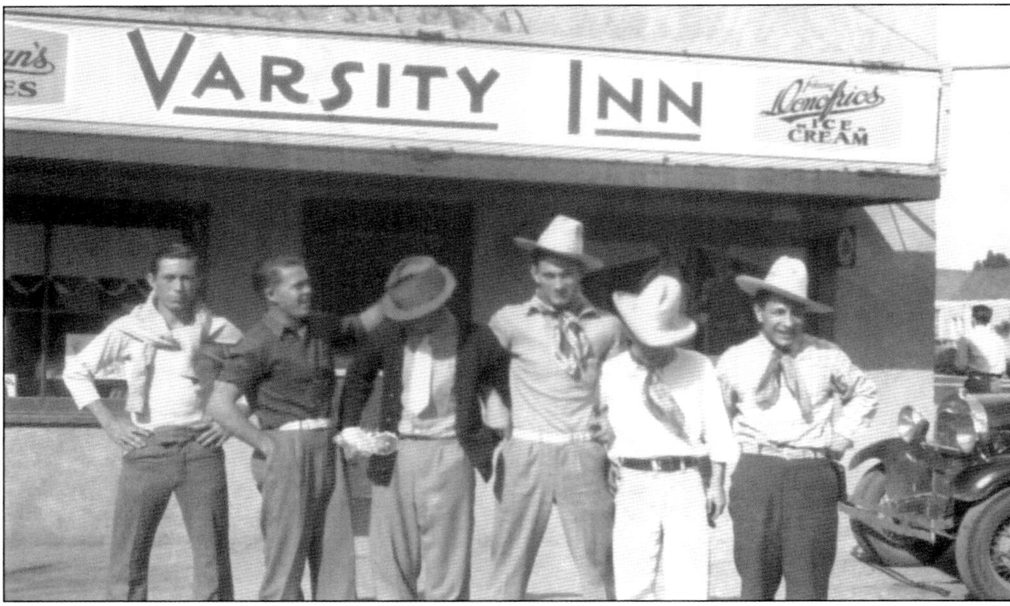

Popular hangouts are the settings for many fond memories. Alumni recall good times at meeting places on campus, such as one of the fountains or the "Secret Garden," as well as several off-campus hangouts, including the Campus Inn and the Varsity Inn. Above, students pose in front of the Varsity Inn, open from the late 1920s to 1964. (Courtesy of THM.)

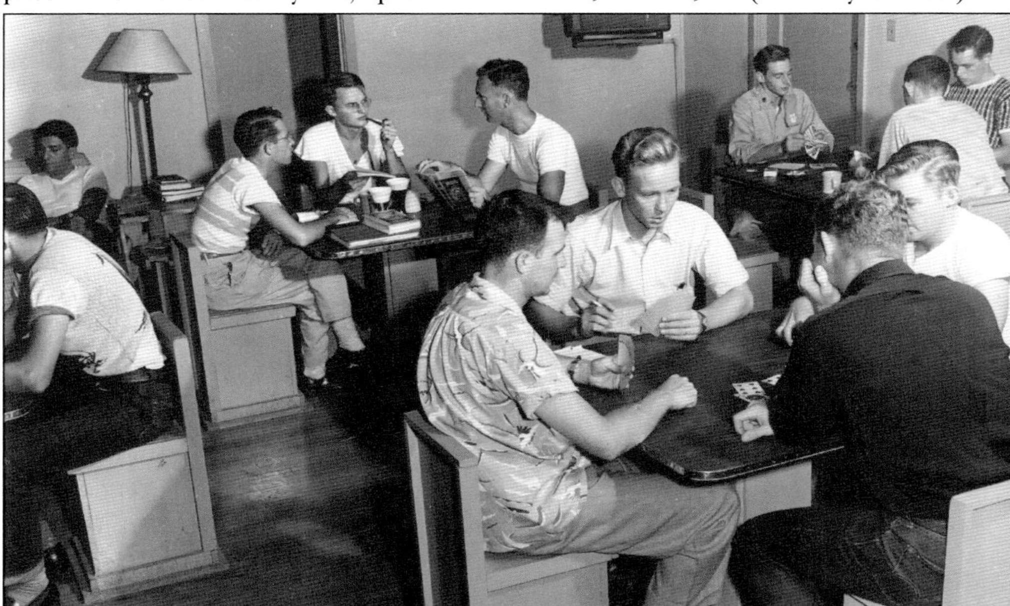

Before the Memorial Union was built, the Devil's Den, created from a barracks-type building, served as the on-campus student hangout. As this 1950s photograph demonstrates, this is where students went for a cup of coffee, a sandwich, or a quick game of cards between classes. Live radio shows were also broadcast from the location, showcasing student talent. (Courtesy of UAASUL.)

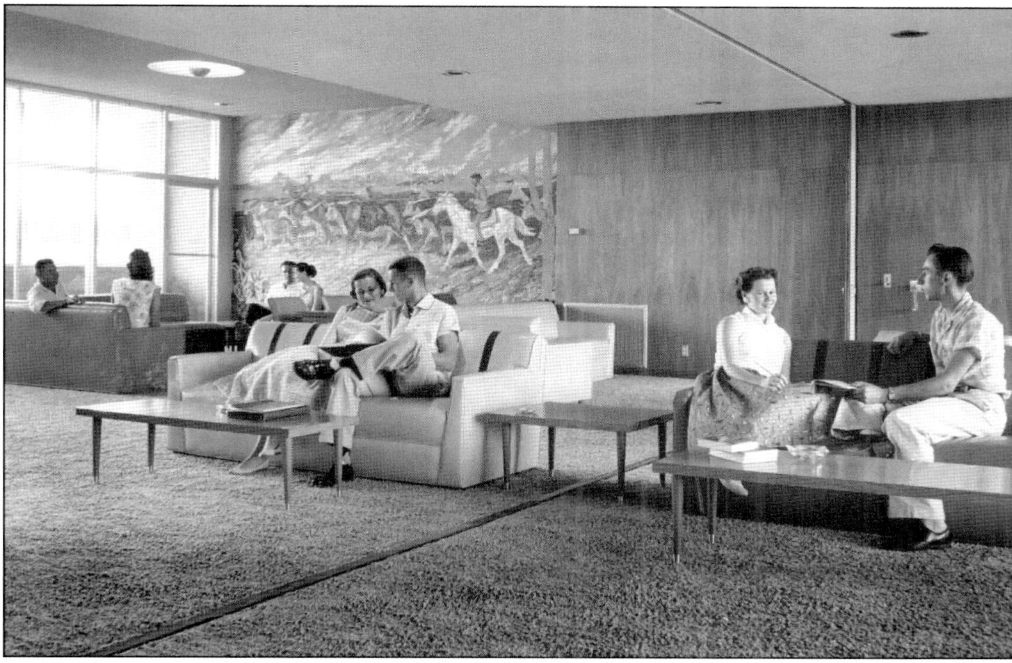

With an increase in student enrollment following World War II, it was clear that a larger facility for students to eat, study, and lounge was necessary. After taking two years to raise the money through a capital campaign and another three years to build, the Memorial Union (MU) opened its doors to welcome students on February 26, 1956. The name "Memorial Union" was chosen to honor those who served in the military. Cecelia Scoular was appointed the first director and is remembered fondly for creating a comfortable atmosphere. As a multiuse space, the MU offers a variety of services. Above is a photograph of the MU lounge just after opening. Below, the exterior of the MU appears during the 1960s, before the streets were blocked off and converted into malls. (Above, courtesy of UAASUL; below, the *State Press*.)

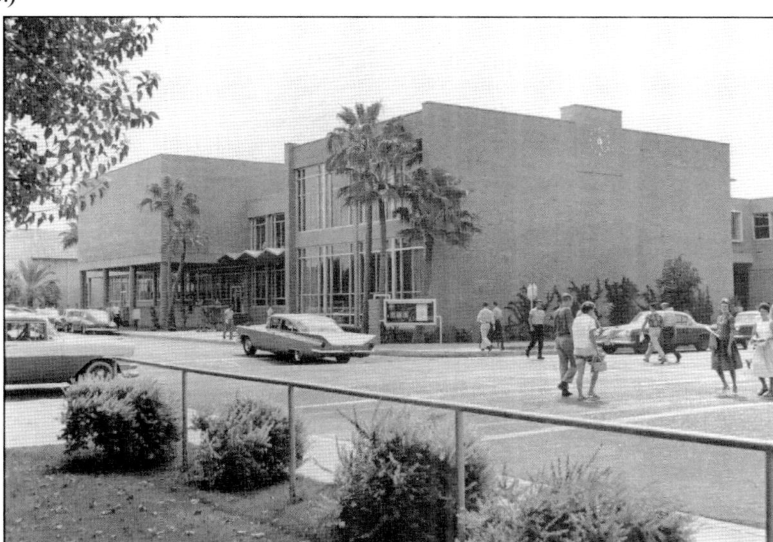

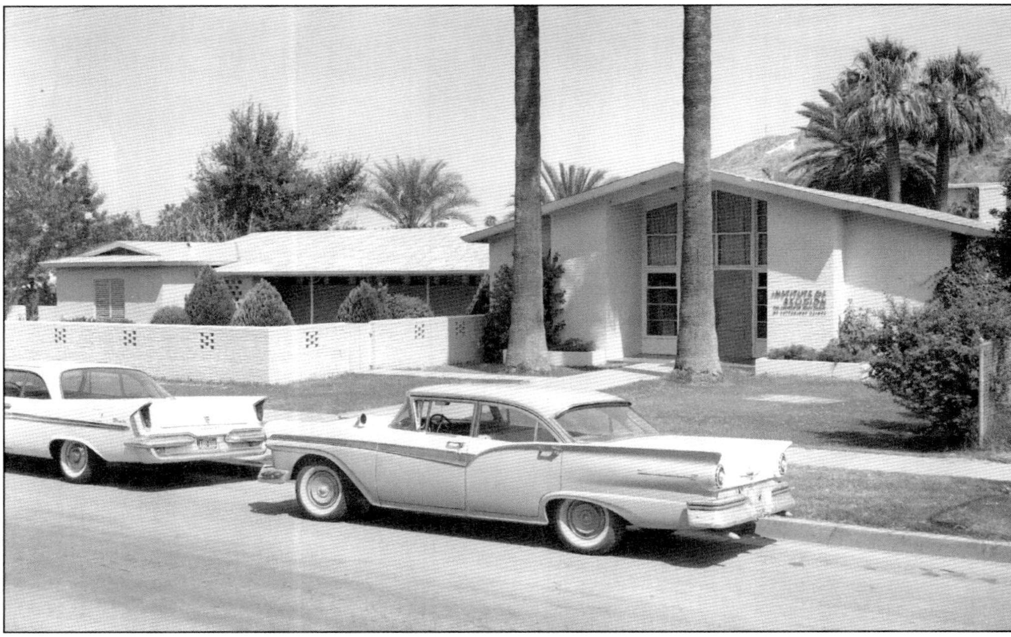

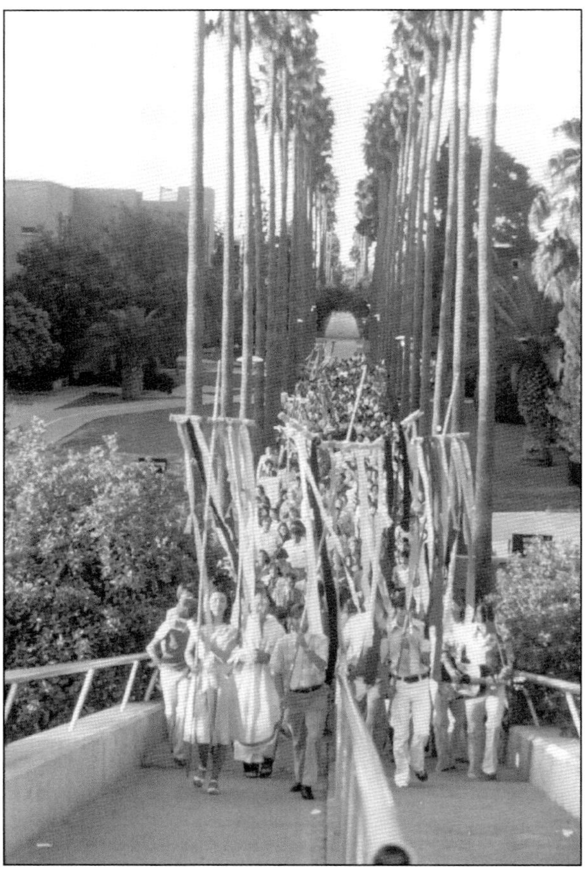

Religious groups and ministries play an important role in serving students' spiritual and social needs. The Church of Jesus Christ of Latter-day Saints (LDS), for example, has a long-standing presence on campus (17 of the original 33 normal school students were Mormon). The above building was the first LDS Institute building (1950–1961) located on 330 East Eighth Street. After multiple moves, the institute now has an impressive structure on McAllister Drive. (Courtesy of LDS Institute of Religion.)

Catholic students found comfort in their faith when they began meeting in the basement of St. Mary's Church in 1931, becoming the Newman Club soon after. By 1940, their membership reached 75, precipitating the development of the Catholic Student Center, dedicated in 1962 and later renamed the All Saints Catholic Newman Center. This 1979 image captures students participating in an Easter Vigil procession on the Palm Walk. (Courtesy of Newman Center.)

The Lutheran Church of the Good Shepherd came to Tempe in 1952, building a church a few blocks from campus at Fifteenth Street and McAllister Avenue. In response to a growing congregation, another building was funded in 1962 as a student center for Bible study sessions, group meetings, and social events, like the talent show seen here in 1966. In 1990, the congregation changed its name to University Lutheran. (Courtesy of Lutheran Campus Ministries.)

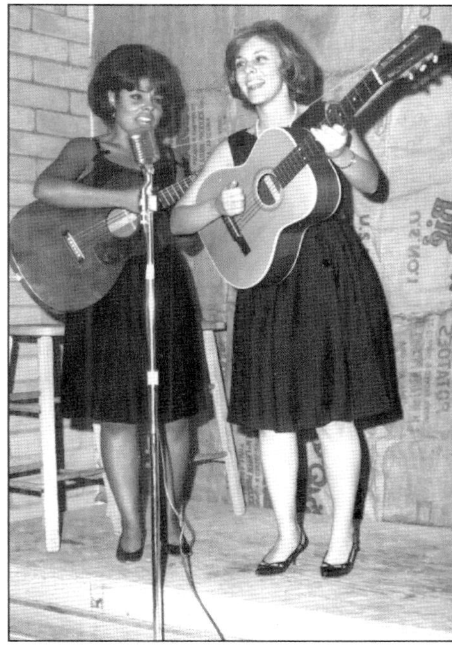

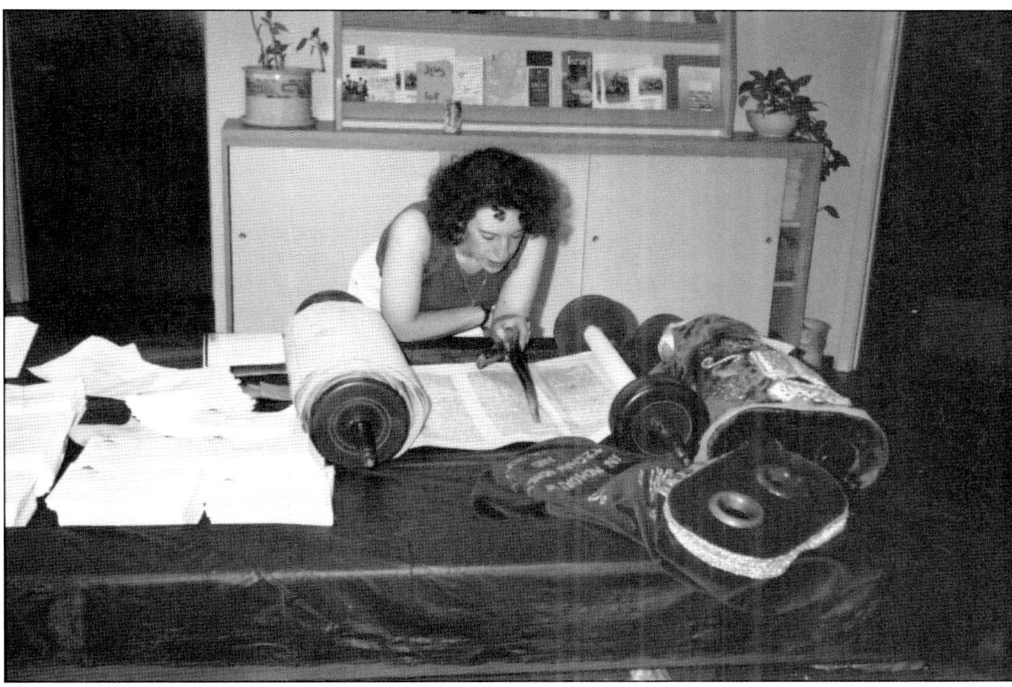

By the late 1960s, there were approximately 700 Jewish students on campus who had no synagogue, rabbi, or official meeting place. As a result, some community members supported the founding of the Hillel Advisory Council, which organized meetings, events, and Rosh Hashana services. In 1972, Rabbi Barton Lee arrived, helping to bring campus-wide recognition to Hillel. The Jewish Student Center on Mill Avenue opened in 1980. (Courtesy of Hillel Jewish Student Center.)

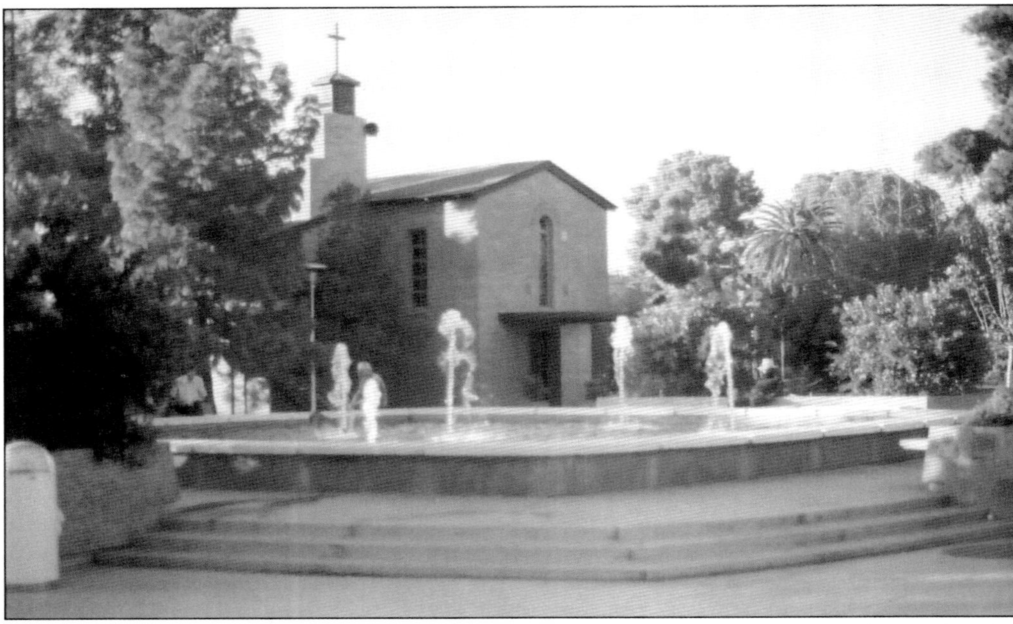

While this book only allows space to cover a few groups, there are many others who also played (and continue to play) key roles in supporting students' spiritual needs. In 1945, William Danforth, a philanthropist from Missouri, sought to help create a centralized place on campus for different groups to use for worship. He offered Arizona State College $5,000 to build a mediation chapel if students would raise the additional $10,000. The chapel served as a rallying point and promoted interfaith activities as students raised the money to have it built by 1948. Initially, services for Episcopalian, Presbyterian, and Lutheran students were held at the chapel. Catholic masses were added in the years following. Below is an interior photograph of the chapel during a Chi Alpha Christian Fellowship service. (Above, courtesy of Lutheran Campus Ministries; below, Bryan Eastin.)

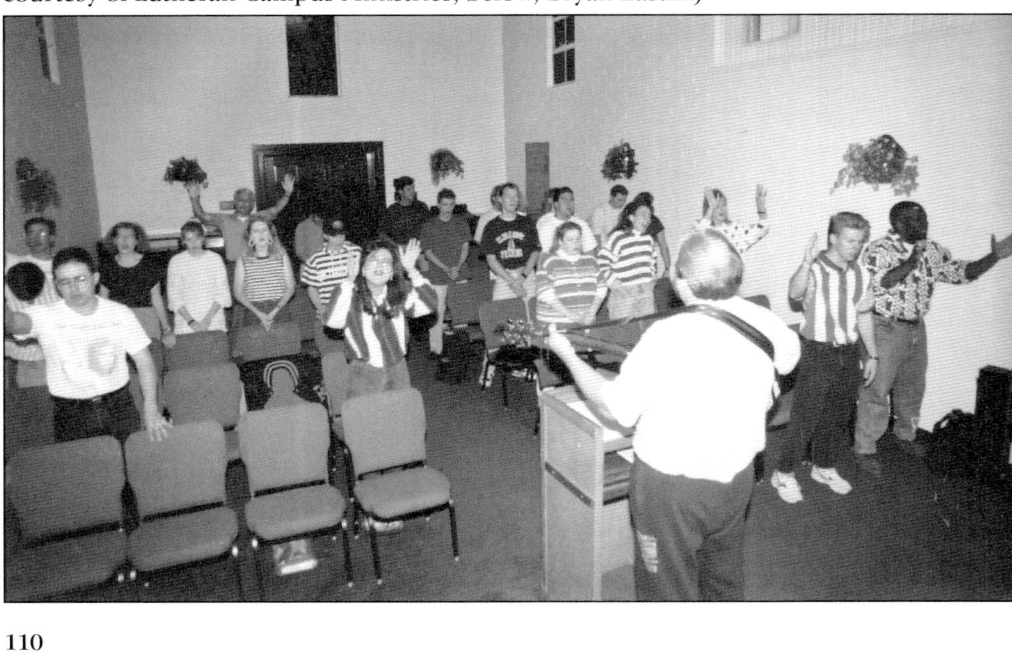

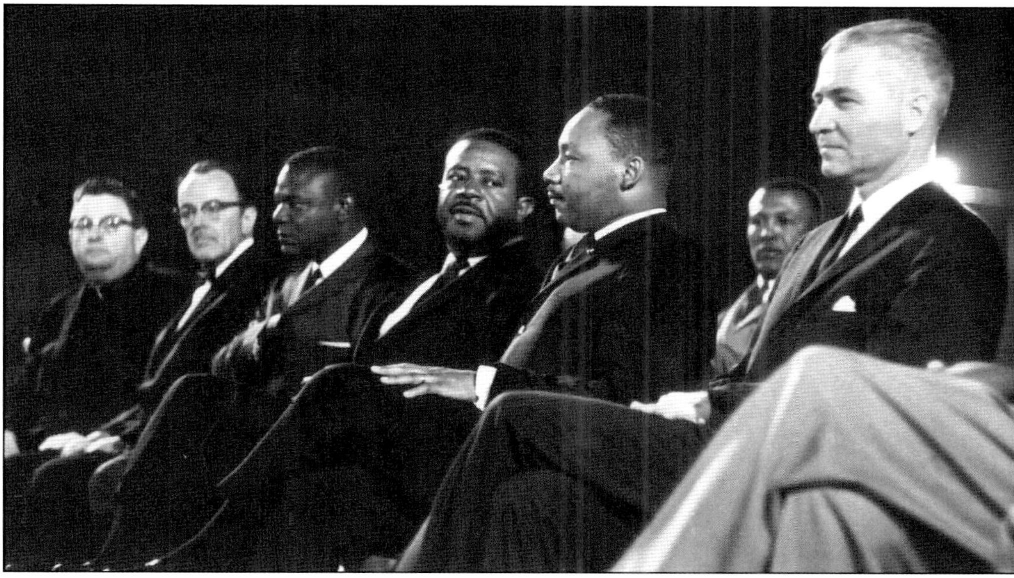

Since its inception, ASU has been a destination point for many prominent people. Students have benefitted from hearing speeches from political and religious leaders (including several presidents, the Dalai Lama, and Pope John Paul II), as well as a multitude of others important in fields that range from art to zoology. In 1964, Martin Luther King Jr., seen here, spoke to an audience of 8,000 people at ASU about human dignity. (Courtesy of Stan Gilbert, UAASUL.)

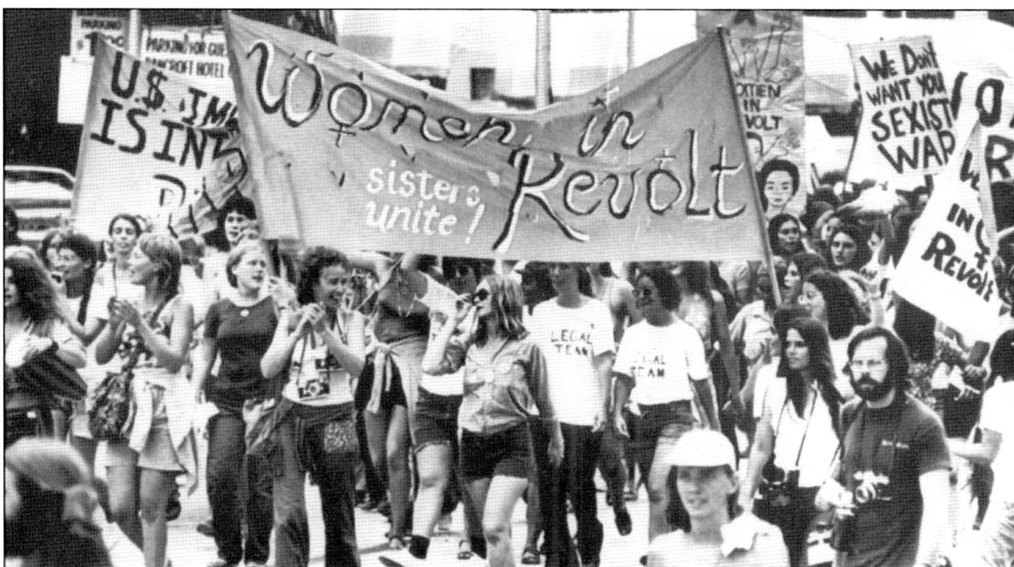

The 1960s were a tumultuous time. Anti–Vietnam War protests took place on campuses across the nation, and ASU was no exception. Despite the conservative political environment of the university, a campus antiwar effort emerged among a small group of the 23,341 students who attended ASU by 1968. They organized demonstrations and built a local peace coalition. In 1969, forty female ASU students joined protestors in Berkeley, pictured here. (Courtesy of UAASUL.)

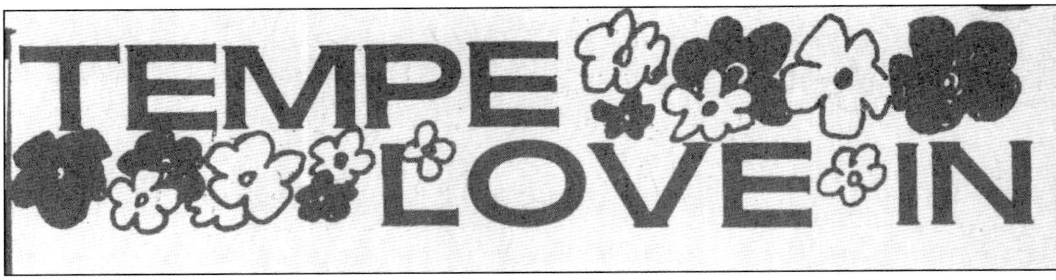

Tempe saw a hippie counterculture movement emerge in the 1960s that drew from both ASU students and local artists and musicians. Mill Avenue was the happening place, with a head shop, band performances at the Valley Art Theater, and the publication of the *Morning Sun*, an underground subversive newspaper that, among other things, featured a column called "Communist Speaks" and advertised weekly Love Ins at Tempe Town Beach. (Courtesy of Richard Mickle.)

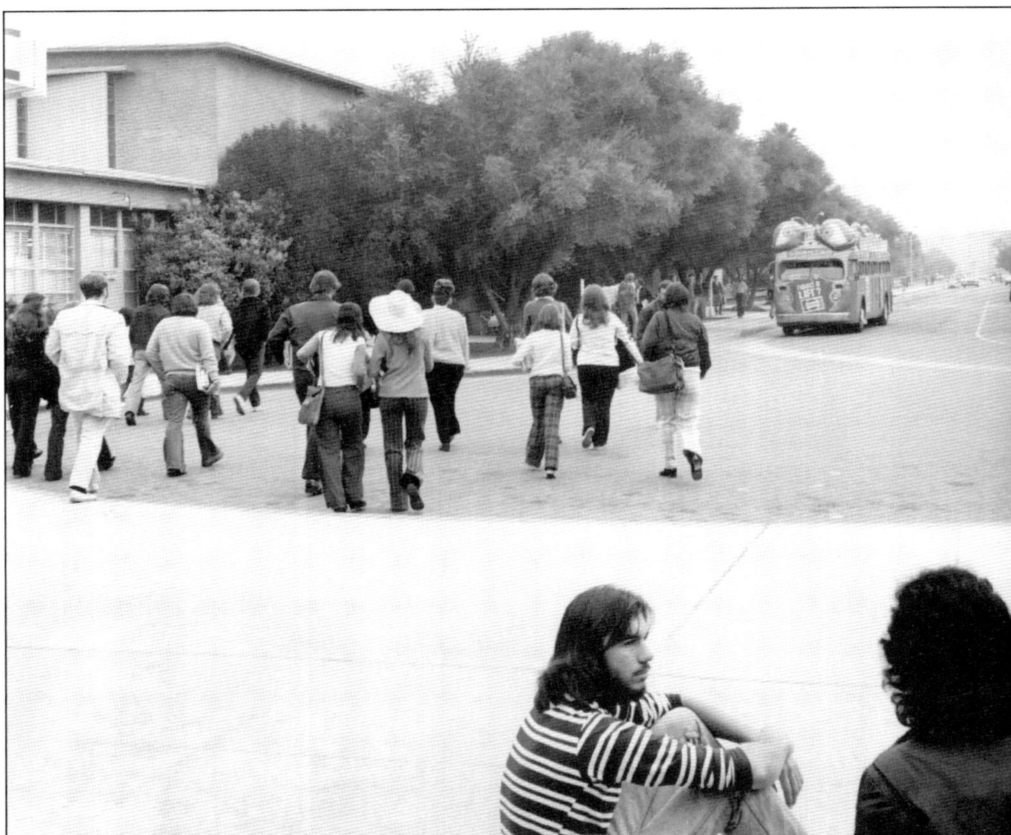

Bug-themed buses were a common sight around campus in the mid-1970s. The Bug Line, as it was fondly called, was a free bus line operated by John Balfour and some partners that traveled between the Chris-Town Mall (renamed the Spectrum Mall in the late 1990s) and ASU. It offered a convenient (and fun) form of transportation for students that was funded through advertisements from companies like Pepsi. (Courtesy of Shirley Blanton.)

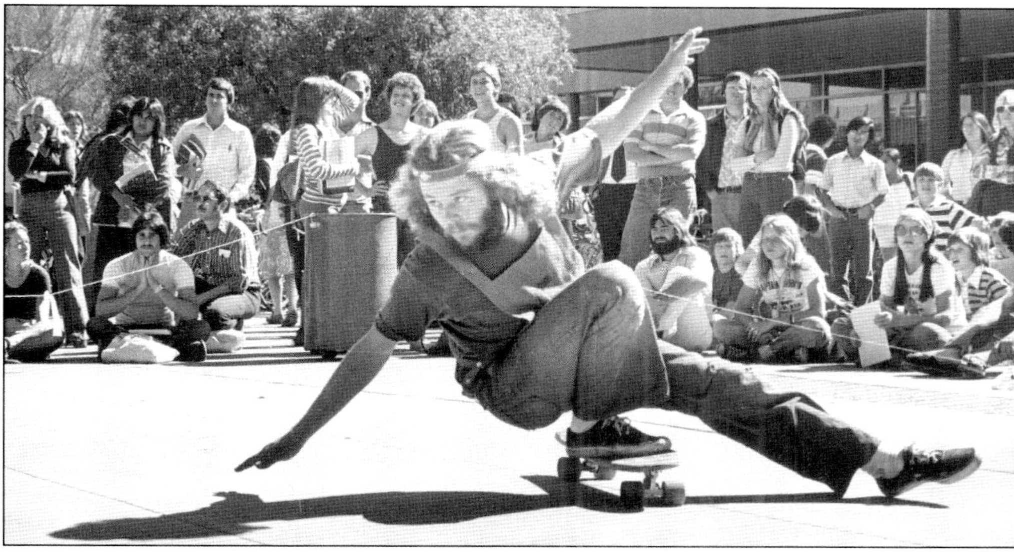

Arizona State University is an active campus. The multiple mall areas offer space for students to display their artwork, sell jewelry, hold musical performances, or show off various skills. This student draws some attention as he demonstrates his skateboarding ability in the 1970s. (Courtesy of UAASUL.)

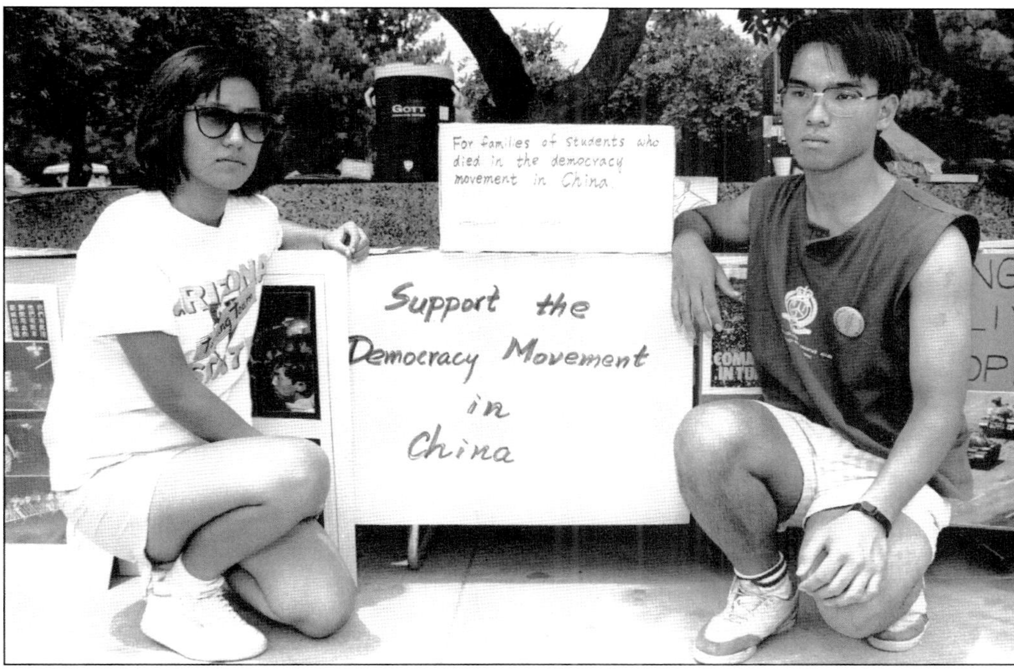

The malls around campus are also ideal for voter registration tables or for campus groups to educate students about a variety of issues from political movements to a new campus club. In this 1989 photograph, political science major Tao Wu, right, aims to share his experience of being at Tiananmen Square during the Chinese government's crackdown on protestors. Wu also spoke at a news conference in the Memorial Union. (Courtesy of Jack Beasley, the *State Press*.)

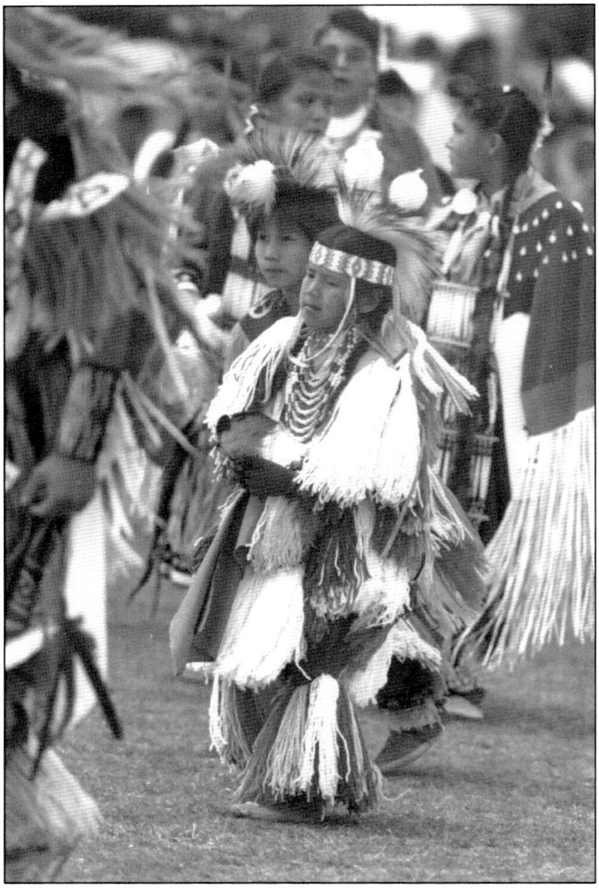

Arizona State University attracts native students from over 20 tribal communities within the state of Arizona alone, as well as from hundreds of other tribal communities across North, Central, and South America who come to study or participate in various research programs. Beginning in the 1980s, the campus began hosting annual powwows, where people of all ages turn out to socialize, drum, or enter dance competitions. (Courtesy of Irwin Daugherty, the *State Press*.)

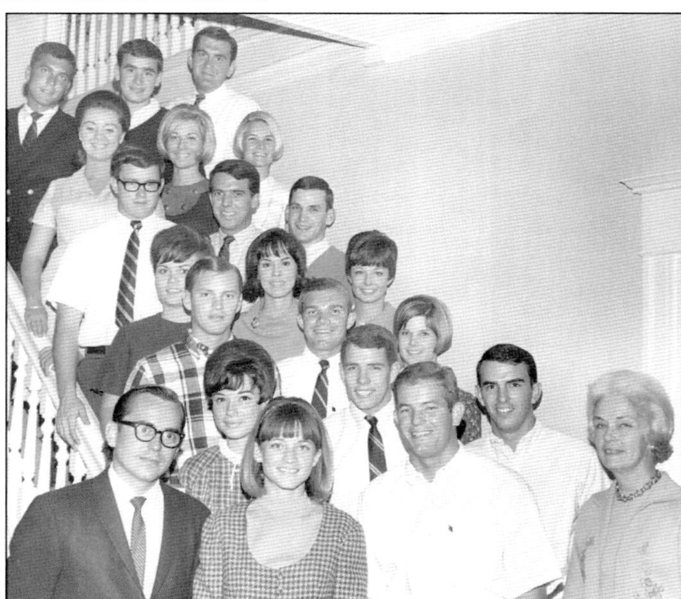

Some students choose to spend their free time helping potential students appreciate what the campus has to offer. The Devils' Advocates formed with 25 students in 1966 to work with the alumni association and the Admissions Office in recruiting high school students. The hand-selected group still exists and has grown along with the school. Members are known for their knowledge and spirit as they lead campus Sneaker Tours for students and the community. (Courtesy of Bob Francis.)

Five

BEHIND THE SCENES

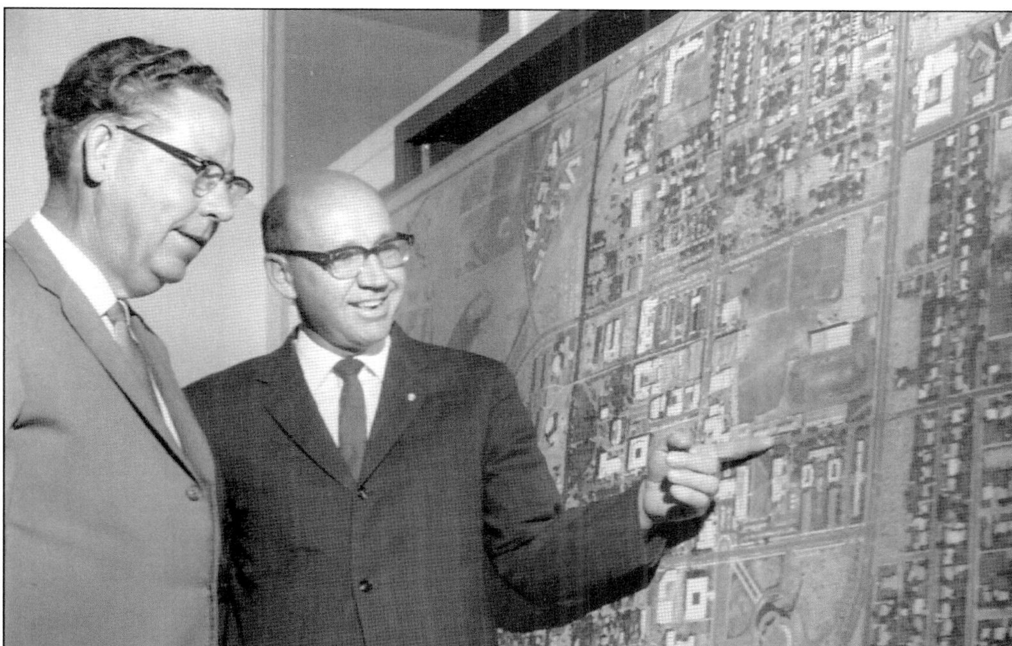

Class of 1934 alumnus Gilbert Cady (left) and Rudy Campbell exemplify thoughtful service to the university. Cady served six presidents in 41 years, becoming associate vice-president of Business Affairs. Campbell was the first voter-elected mayor of Tempe and served two terms (1974–1982 and 1992–2000) on the Arizona Board of Regents and in countless other ways. Much goes into growing and maintaining a university; the following pages offer some examples. (Courtesy of Rudy Campbell.)

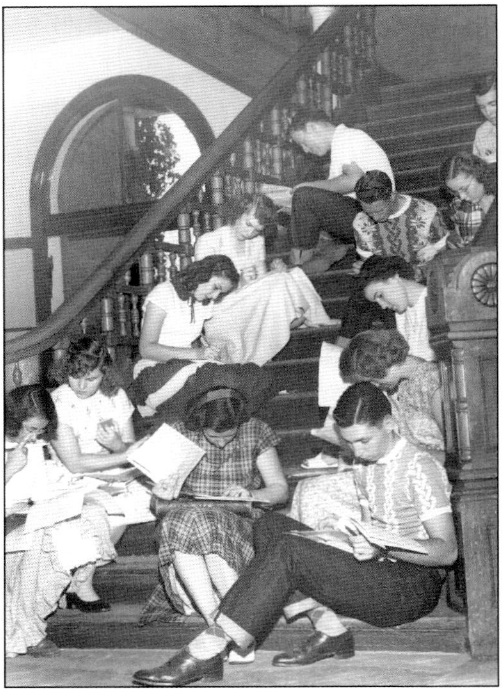

Early on, registration was a different type of experience, as evidenced by these 1940s students sitting on the steps in Old Main. Growth in enrollment led to longer lines and additional forms of all kinds. Now, a team of people in the Registrar's Office and tech support staff build on the work of the first registrar, Frederick Irish, as they coordinate processes across units to make things easier for all. (Courtesy of THM.)

The Registrar's Office is the alpha and omega of the student experience. Beyond admissions and residency classification at the start, it tracks schedules and handles program changes and withdrawals. Later, it verifies records to issue diplomas. The connection remains even after graduation, as this office supplies the transcripts students need to apply for jobs and graduate programs throughout their lifetime. Once small, below, it now has over 60 staff members. (Courtesy of UAASUL.)

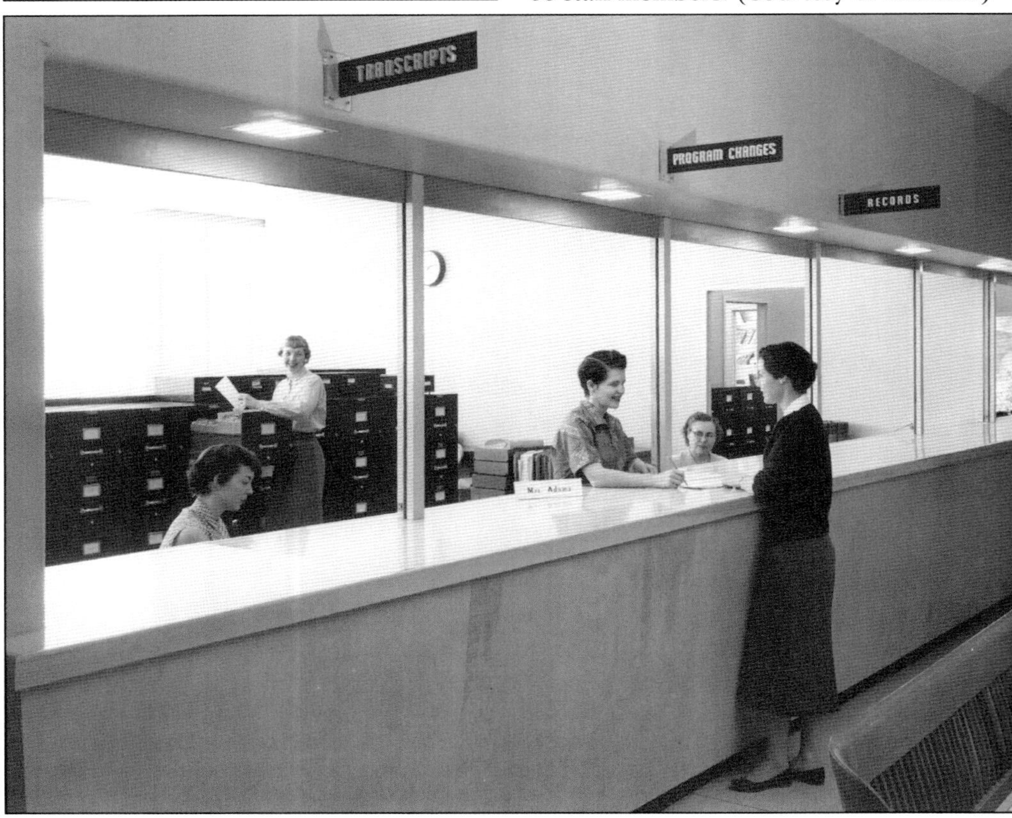

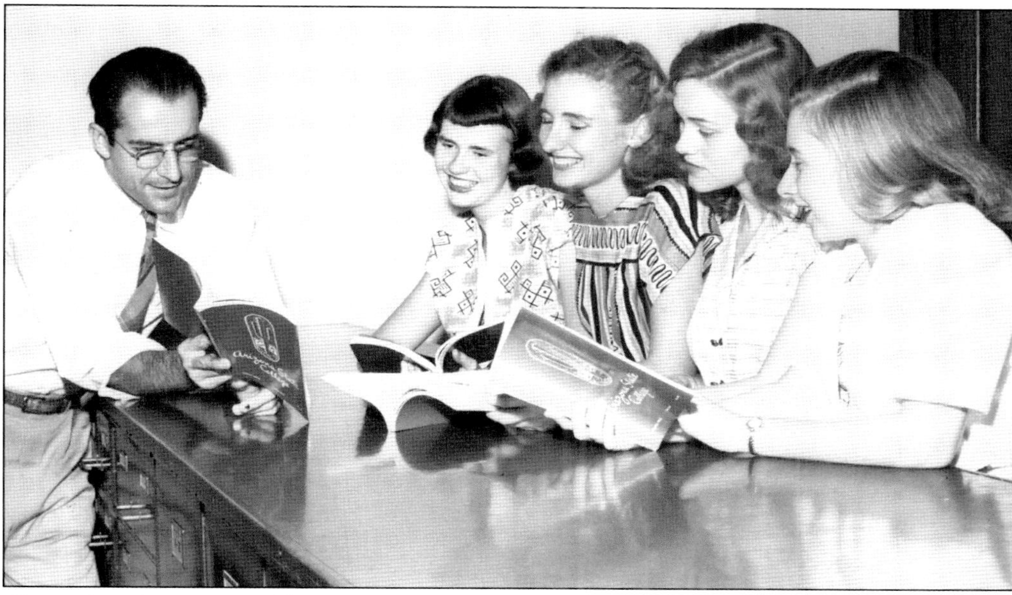

Class of 1938 alumnus Alfred Thomas Jr., registrar and director of Admissions, above, helps students choose classes from the catalog. Then, students could figure this out themselves, ask department secretaries, or consult faculty, some who still advise. Many units now, though, have professional academic advisors to help students navigate university opportunities and requirements. George Peek, a Liberal Arts dean (1967–1973), is credited with ramping up better ways to academically advise students. (Courtesy of UAASUL.)

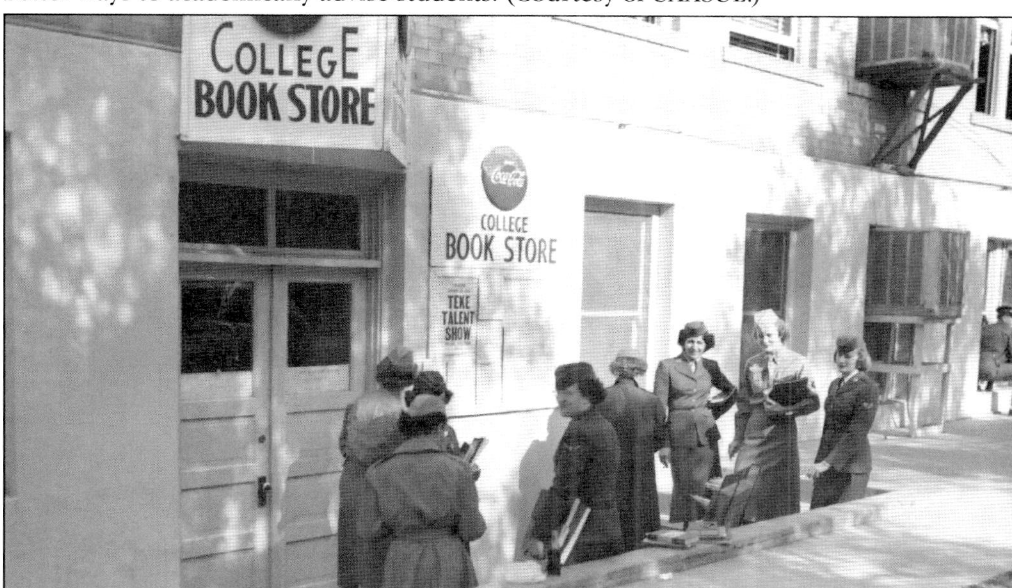

Air Force members, above, meet at an early campus bookstore in the basement of the Industrial Arts Building. Beyond the ever-changing inventory of texts, the bookstore supplies study items for classes and Sun Devil merchandise. Located in the Memorial Union for many years, early managers like Tony Bustamente rode the tide of growth. Now the freestanding bookstore sits in the heart of the campus. (Courtesy of THM.)

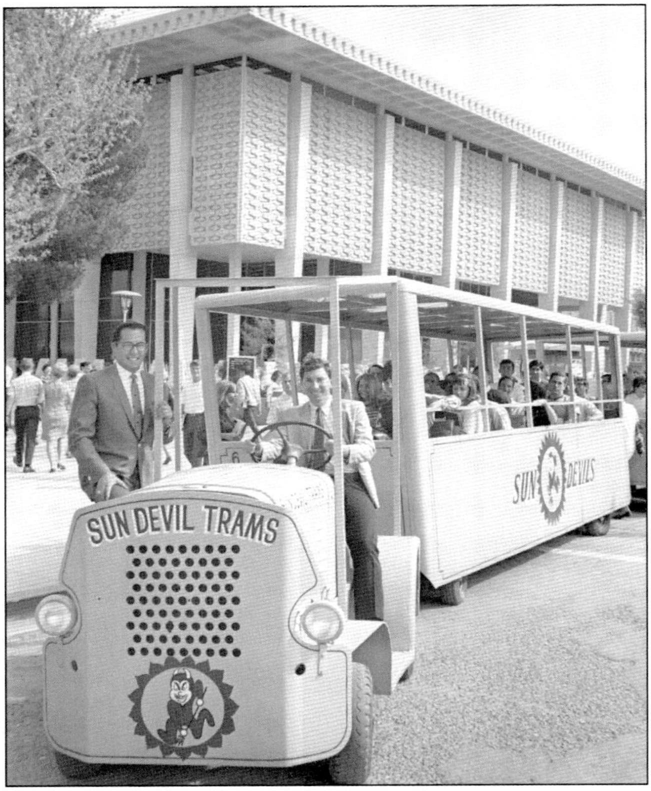

Getting around campus can be a challenge. The forerunner of buses, the Sun Devil Tram (left) is stopped in front of Hayden Library in 1968. It used to transport students from the distant Lot 59. Bicycles and skateboards are common too, and efforts are being made to reduce their use in crowded areas to keep the campus safe and pedestrian-friendly. For longer trips, light rail or shuttles run to the other campuses. (Courtesy of Shirley Blanton.)

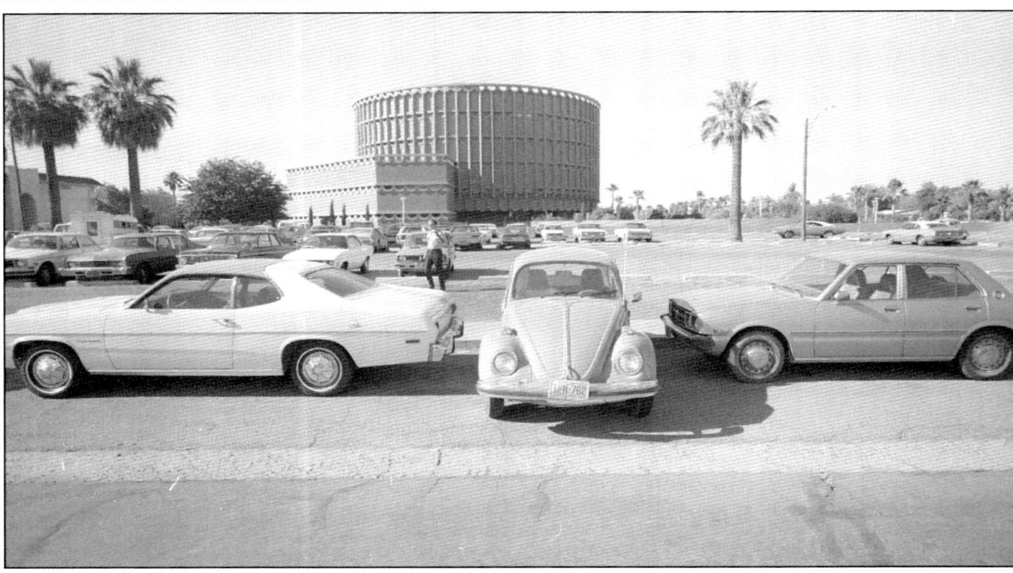

At first, the absence of hitching posts was a problem. Later, creative car parking occurred, as above, in front of the Music Building, designed to look like a marching drum. The commuter nature of campus continued, with 64 percent of students driving to campus in 1980, and now, a Center for Off-Campus and Commuter Student Services tries to help. In the 1960s, a parking decal cost $5 to park anywhere on campus. (Courtesy of Neil Miller.)

Once paired with the Campus Police, Parking and Transit seeks parking solutions and more eco-friendly solutions. The patrolman at right, in front of the old Lyceum theater in 1963, reflected the growing need to patrol for violations and keep people safe. The Arizona State College campus patrol began in 1948, comprised of students, night watchmen, and Tempe police. In 1967, the Arizona legislature approved an independent police force for ASU. (Courtesy of UAASUL.)

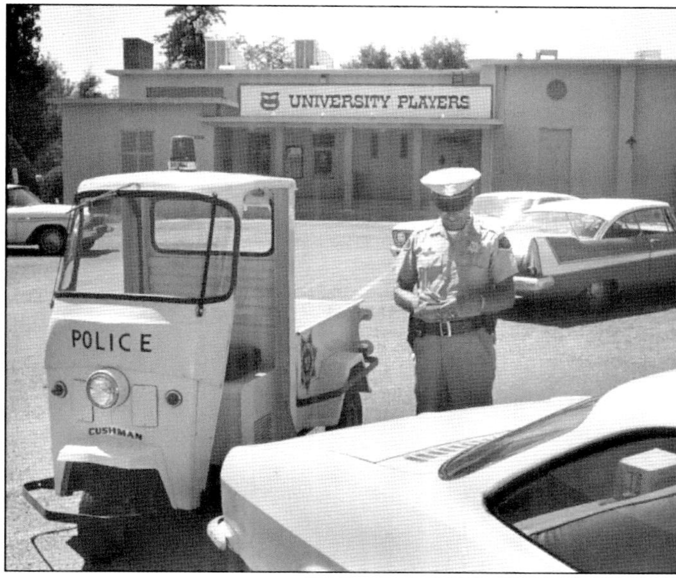

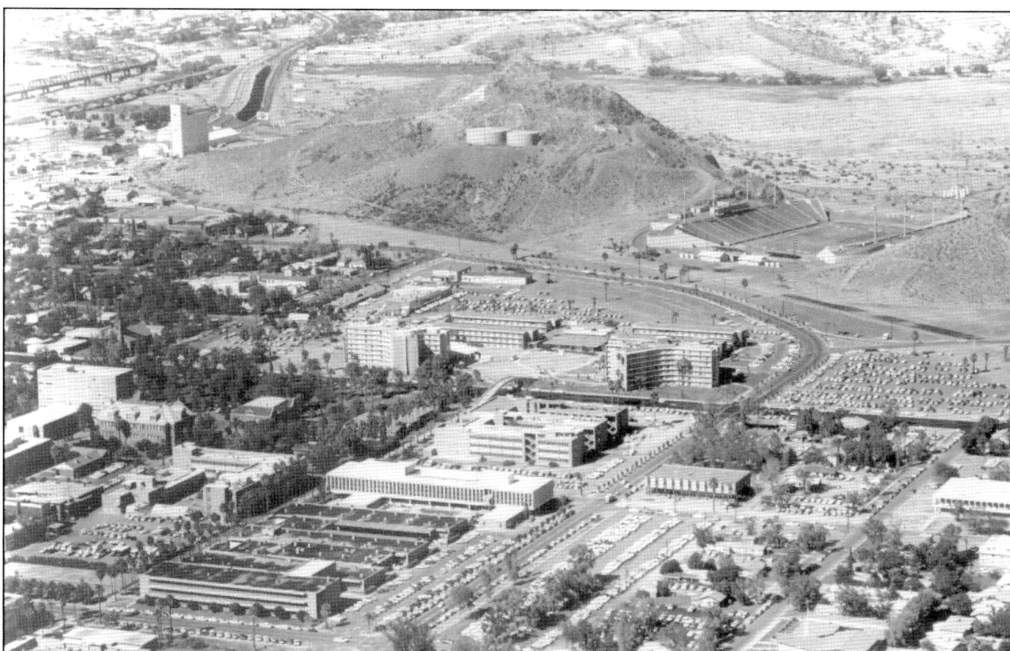

Commuter troubles are avoided by living on campus. Students once boarded with Tempe residents, then in early residence halls. Later, Greek Life–related houses and dorms were built, some shown above at center. At the time, they were considered off-campus housing. Now part of campus, Residence Life helps students succeed, as living is about more than where to sleep, it is about being in what Residence Life refers to as a "living and learning community." (Courtesy of UAASUL.)

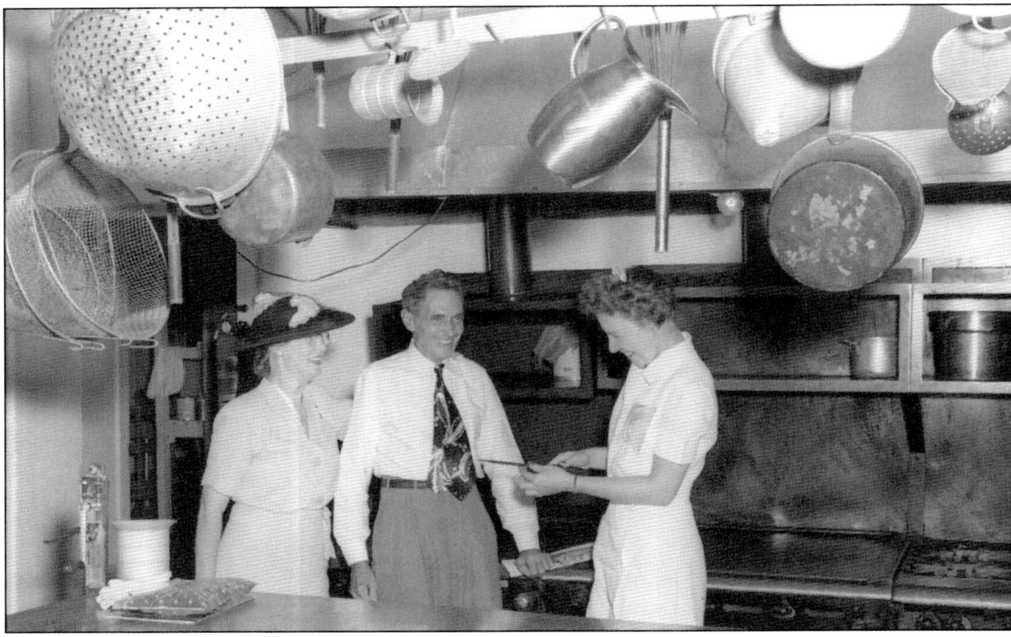

The first dining hall opened in 1905. In 1913, Martha and Robert Krause, left and center, visiting in the late 1940s, were matron and steward, preparing food and managing the hall until retiring in 1943. Students arrived to a bell, waited behind their chairs until instructed to sit, and then displayed good manners or were lovingly scolded. Martha also handled employment, as most students worked on campus. (Courtesy of THM.)

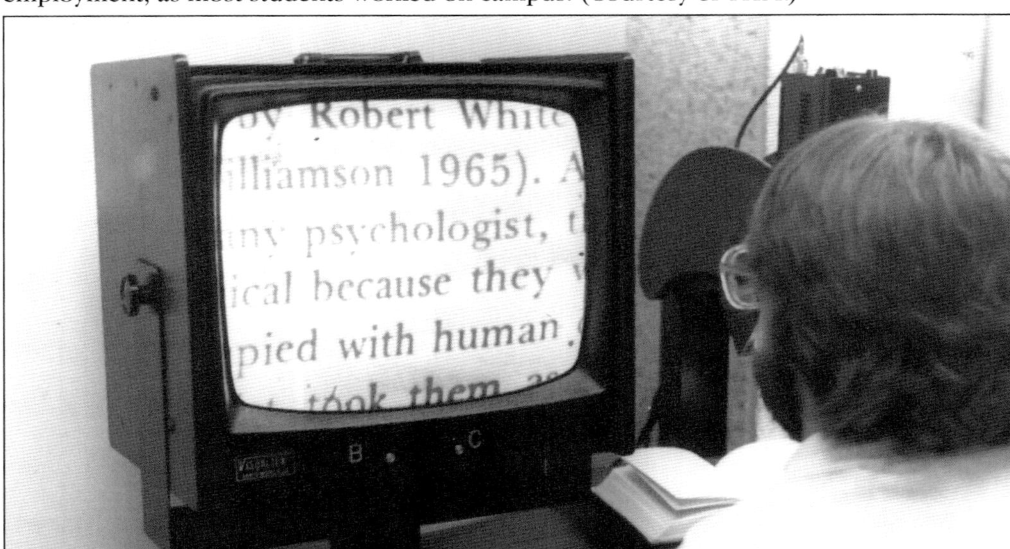

Students' needs are supported by the Disability Resource Center, which developed in response to an influx of disabled Vietnam veterans in the late 1960s who came to ASU under the GI Bill. Commitments to improve access led to ramps, transport assistance, provisions for those with sight and hearing limitations, and accommodations for those with documentable learning disabilities. (Courtesy of UAASUL.)

In normal school times, Tempe physician Benjamin Moeur handled medical needs. Eventually, there was a first aid station in 1919. By 1946, Elaine McFarland, right, was the first full-time, on-campus nurse. She served as the first Health Services director. In 1953, a 26-bed hospital and infirmary was built at the site of the 2012-remodeled facilities, which now include wellness support in addition to illness treatment. (Courtesy of THM.)

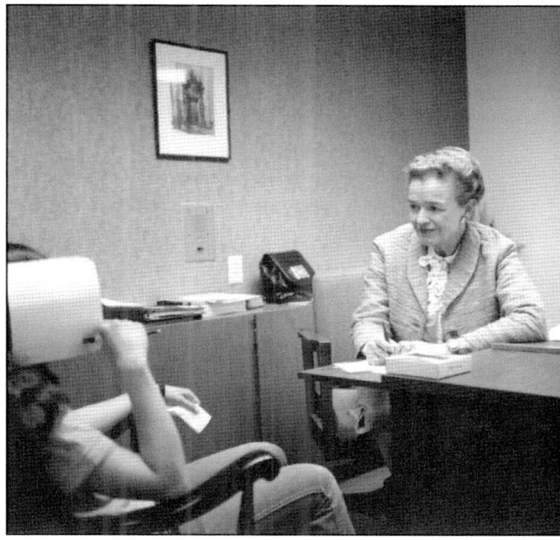

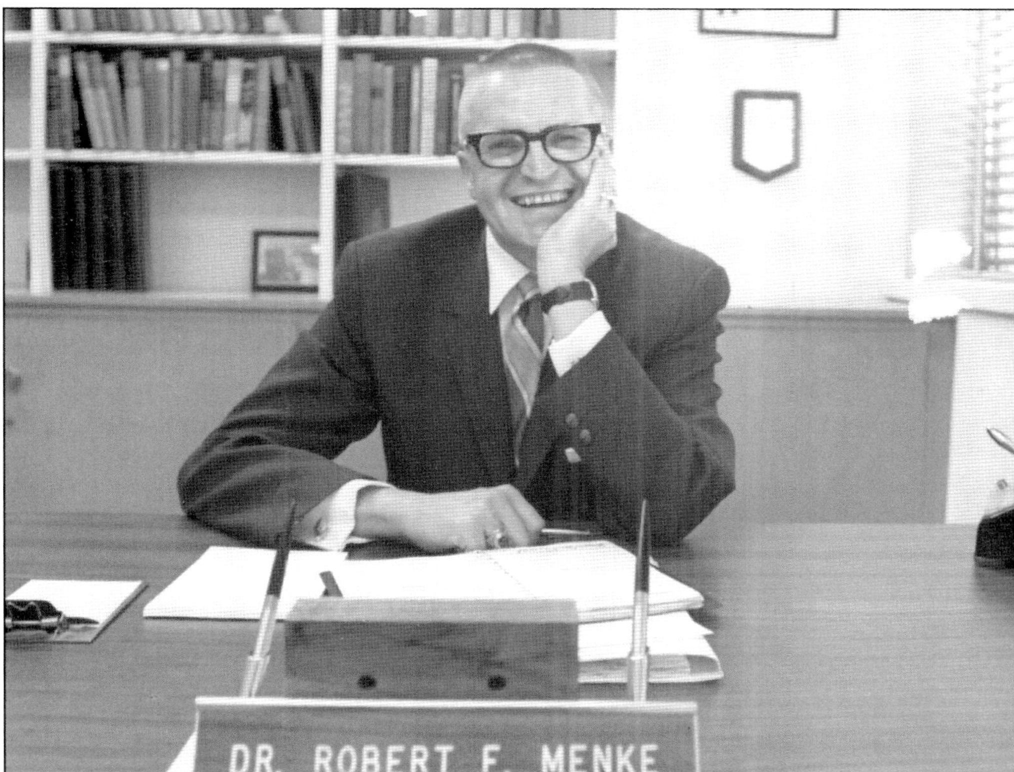

Robert Menke directed Placement (Career) Services from 1948 to 1984, continuing the work of Ira D. Payne and others. Growth inspired Menke to digitize information; as a result, he became a national leader in his field and professional organization. Career Services offers a great resource room, workshops, career fairs, and professional staff who help thousands of students and alumni find work and thousands of employers screen applicants. (Courtesy of Gary Krahenbuhl.)

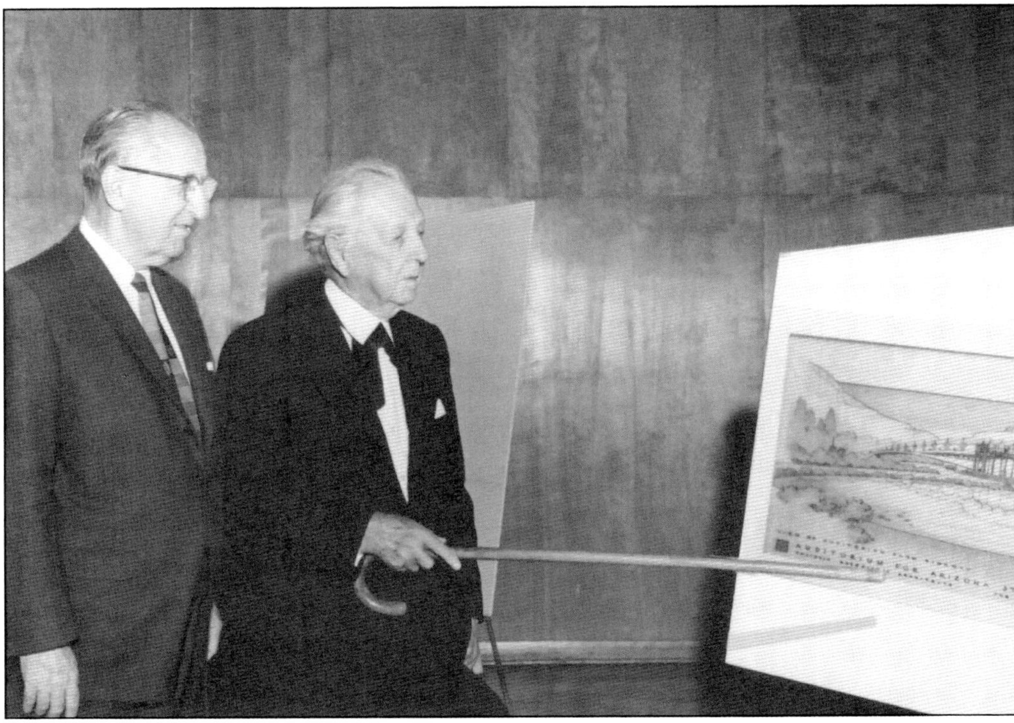

Every building was designed and built by skilled people like WPA workers, early contractor Joe E. Woods, early architect Kemper Goodwin, and countless construction workers who labored in the Arizona sun. The Office of University Architect, among others, helps coordinate these matters. Above, President Gammage (left) and architect Frank Lloyd Wright admire an illustration of the Grady Gammage Memorial Auditorium. Sadly, neither man lived to see its completion. (Courtesy of THM.)

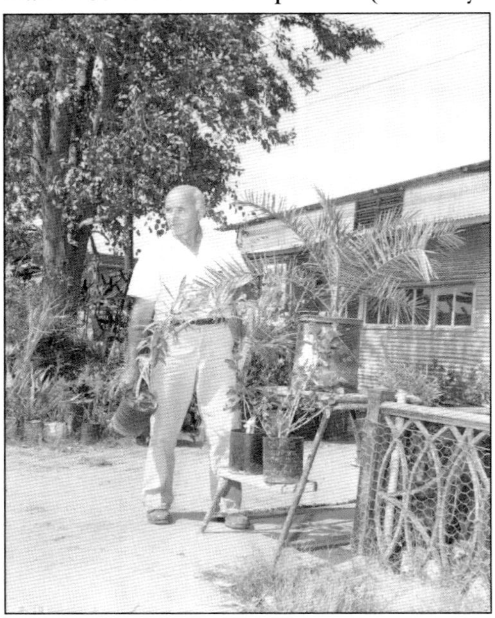

Others keep the campus maintained and beautiful. Robert Svob, left, served from 1931 to 1976, advancing from gardener to foreman of grounds construction, even directing his team in the building of the baseball diamond when coach Bobby Winkles first arrived. The Tempe campus became an arboretum in 1990 due to Victor Zafra's efforts; the "outdoor classroom" has over 300 species from different regions. (Courtesy of UAASUL.)

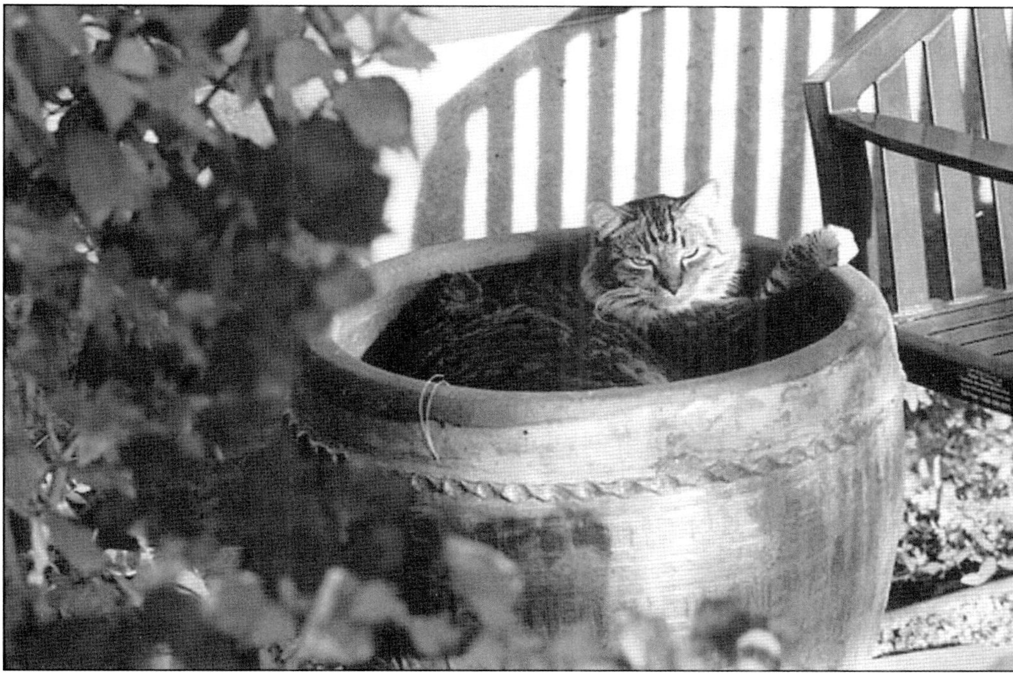

Cats also care for the campus, keeping pests under control and providing comfort to students who miss their pets. The ASU cat population is not problematic due to the Mildcats, an organization of volunteer students, faculty, and staff. They trap-and-release feral and stray cats to be spayed or neutered, marking them to prevent repeats and to help find homes for the strays. (Courtesy of Beth Easterbrook, the *State Press*.)

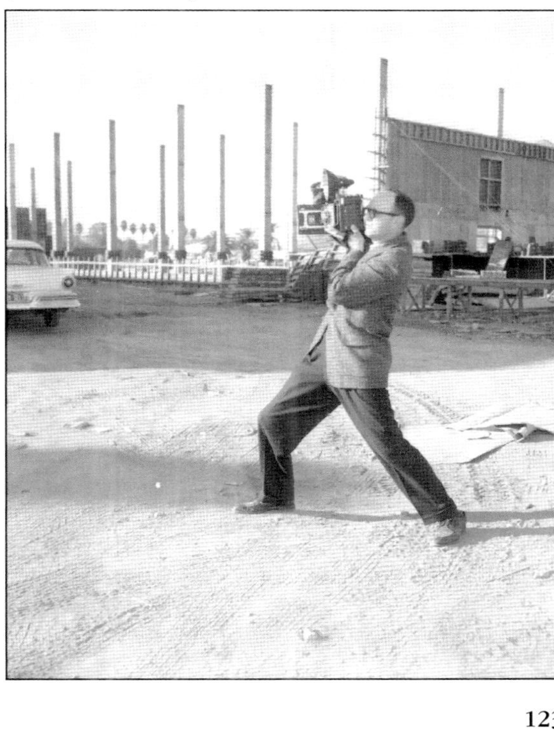

Besides student publications and faculty publishing in scholarly and creative journals, Media Relations shares ASU news with the world and helps connect writers with experts. As early as 1947, there was a news/publicity service on campus, with early directors like Joe Spring. Staff photographer from 1954 to 1998, Charles Conley (right) provided many photographs to accompany stories. These combined efforts share knowledge, spread excitement, and preserve history. (Courtesy of UAASUL.)

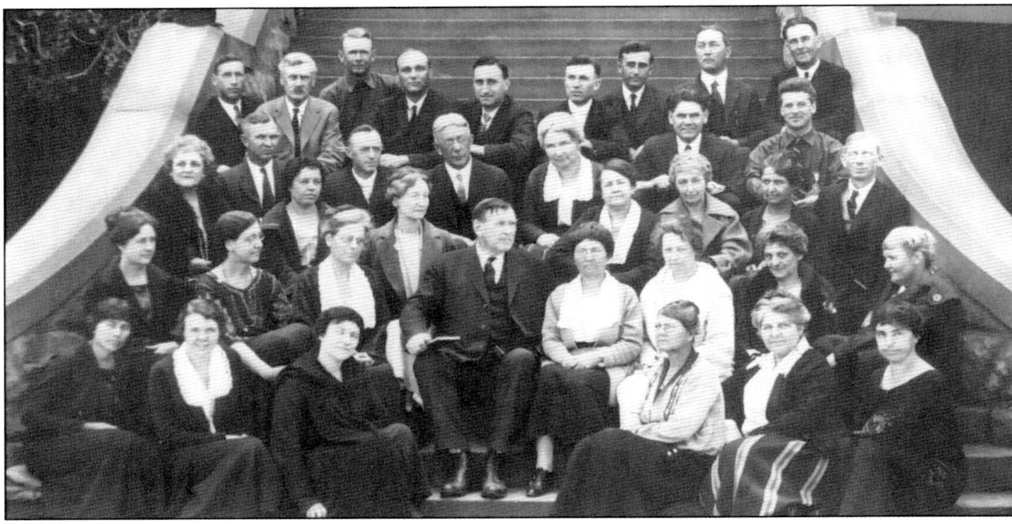

Just like the faculty in Frederick Irish's day, pictured above in 1923, or like Rufus Wyllys, who in 1949 was the first Faculty Assembly chair, faculty members still wear many hats. Beyond teaching-related tasks, which themselves take significant time, faculty activities can include mentoring, publishing, and grant writing. Also, they serve on countless committees for students, other faculty, and for those that help ASU or the community. (Courtesy of THM.)

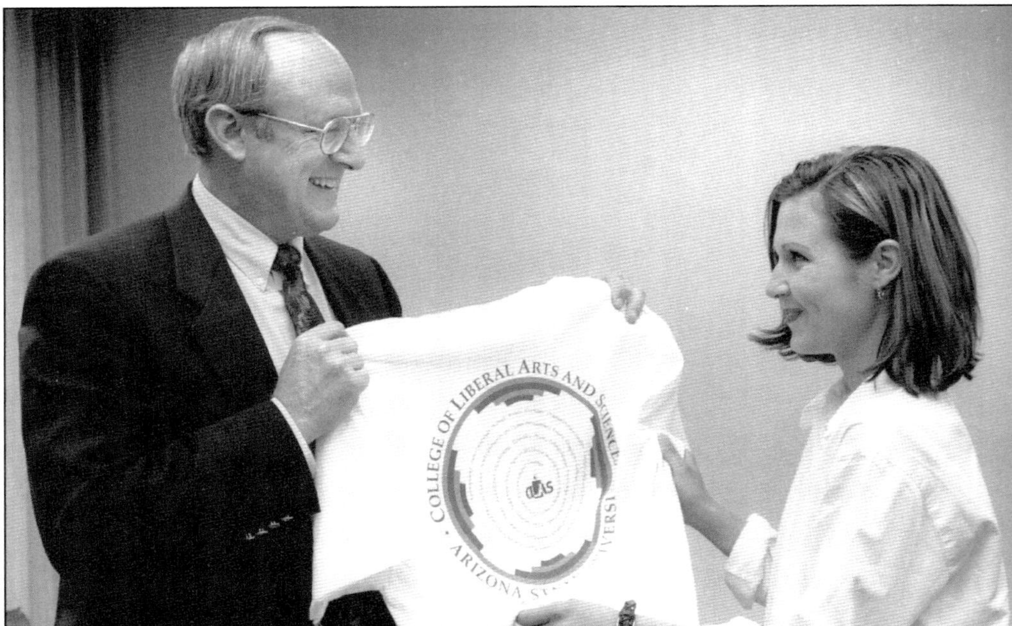

Faculty members sometimes become administrators, as did kinesiologist Gary Krahenbuhl, on the left with Julia Sommerfeld. From 1973 to 2003, he advanced from the faculty to become a dean and then senior vice president. He started many student support and recognition programs, helping them be better scholars and citizens. His "Difference Maker" Award also recognized faculty. A difference-maker himself, students surprised Krahenbuhl with an award, and faculty later endowed the award in his honor. (Courtesy of Gary Krahenbuhl.)

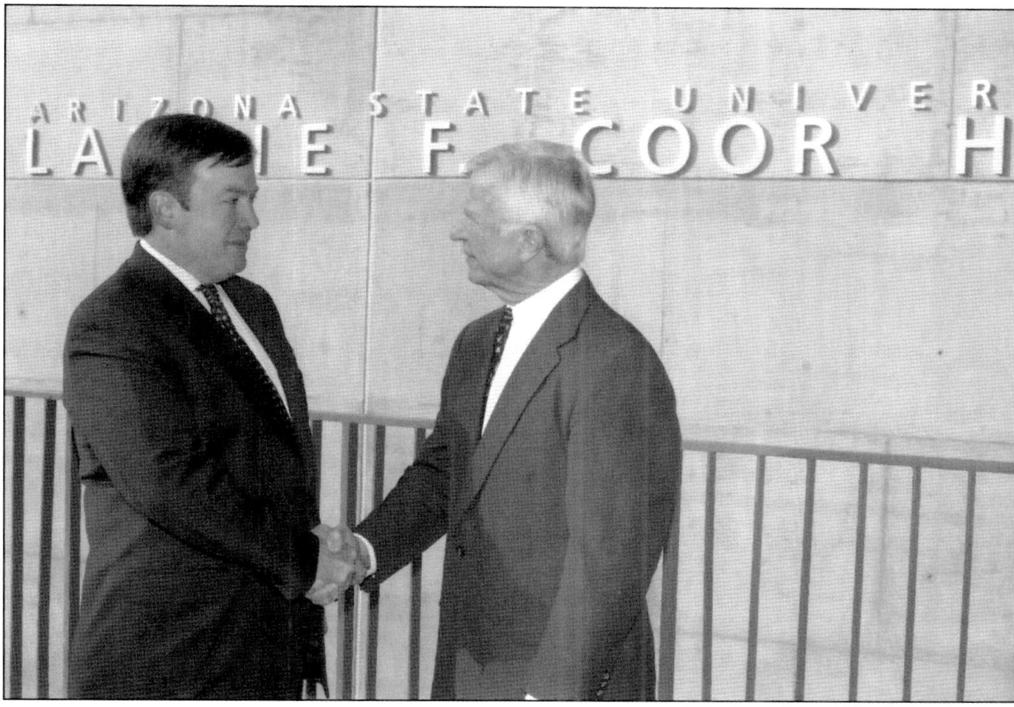

Presidents led it all, with each building on the foundation set by the others. The 15th president, Lattie Coor Jr. (at right in the photograph above), arrived with a global understanding that situated ASU within the community, state, and nation in new ways. Michael M. Crow (left), the 16th president, took office in 2002. His transformational vision of a New American University expands ASU's reach even further. (Courtesy of Thomas Story, UAASUL.)

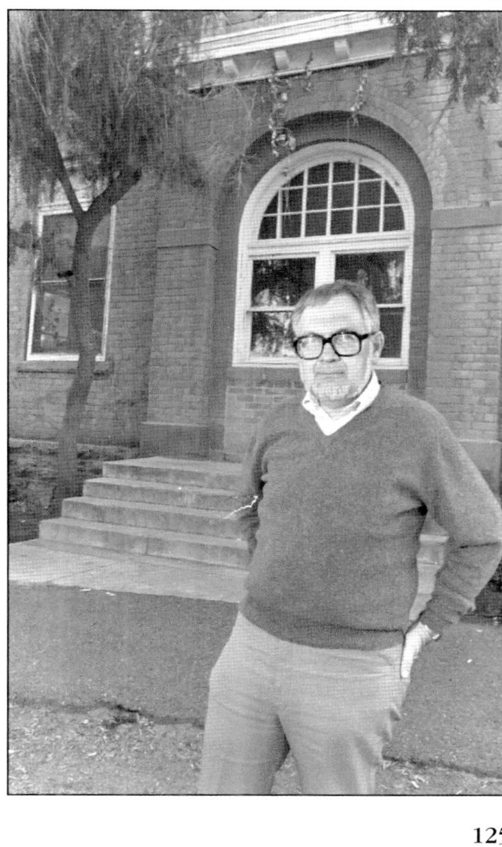

As faculty and staff retire, many stay involved, feeling as much, or more, invested in their fields and institution as alumni. After all, "you can't retire from what you are." In 1991, the ASU Retirees Association was formed, and in 2004, Richard Jacob, physics faculty from 1963 to 2001 (pictured here), helped found the Emeritus College, serving as its first dean. Together, these provide opportunities to retirees to remain part of the ASU community. (Courtesy of the *State Press*.)

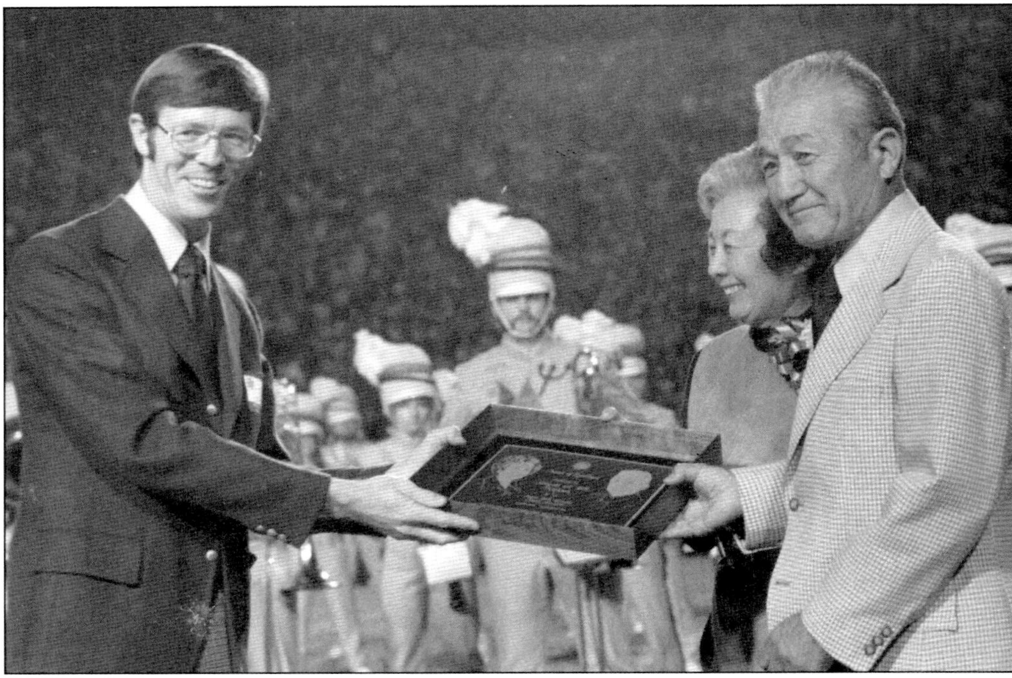

Being a Sun Devil never stops. Alumni activities are an important component of the university, as ASU is proud of its alumni. And, historically, alumni swing into action to help in numerous ways, including alumni Ed (1951) and Nadine Carson (1953), who were also Sun Angels. Above, Bill and Margaret Kajikawa, parents of current ASU alumni president and ASU senior vice president Christine Wilkinson, receive an alumni award in 1974. (Courtesy of Shirley Blanton.)

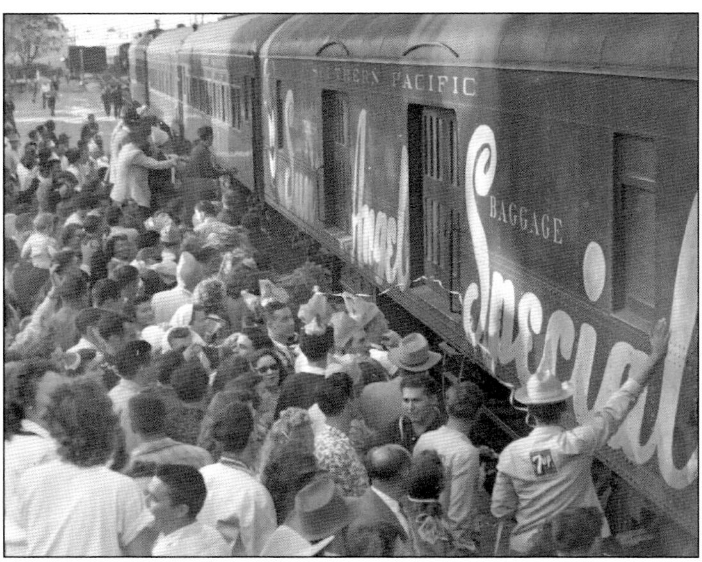

The Sun Angel Foundation, the Sun Devil club of campus supporters, began in 1946, interested "not only in sports but in the sponsorship of the future development and expansion of ASC" to meet the needs of Arizonans. Their slogan invited membership: "The cost is small, the future benefits will be great." They even sponsored a train to an away game. Their generous work continues to this day. (Courtesy of UAASUL.)

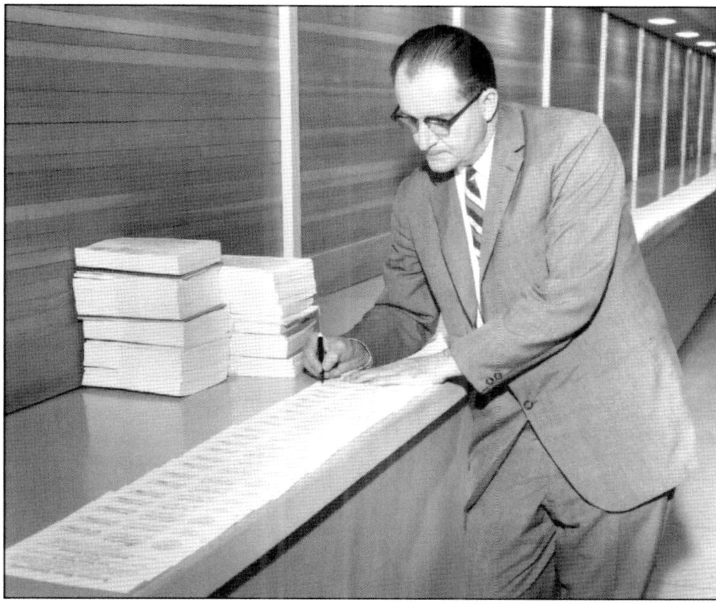

Alfred Thomas Jr., pictured here in 1960, like Cady and many others, served in several roles in his long career. When he was registrar, diplomas were signed by hand. In 2011, ASU conferred 17,090 degrees. Of that number, there were 12,194 baccalaureate degrees, 4,150 master's degrees, 545 doctoral degrees, and 201 law degrees. Students from around the globe attend ASU; in 2011, there were students from 120 countries. (Courtesy of THM.)

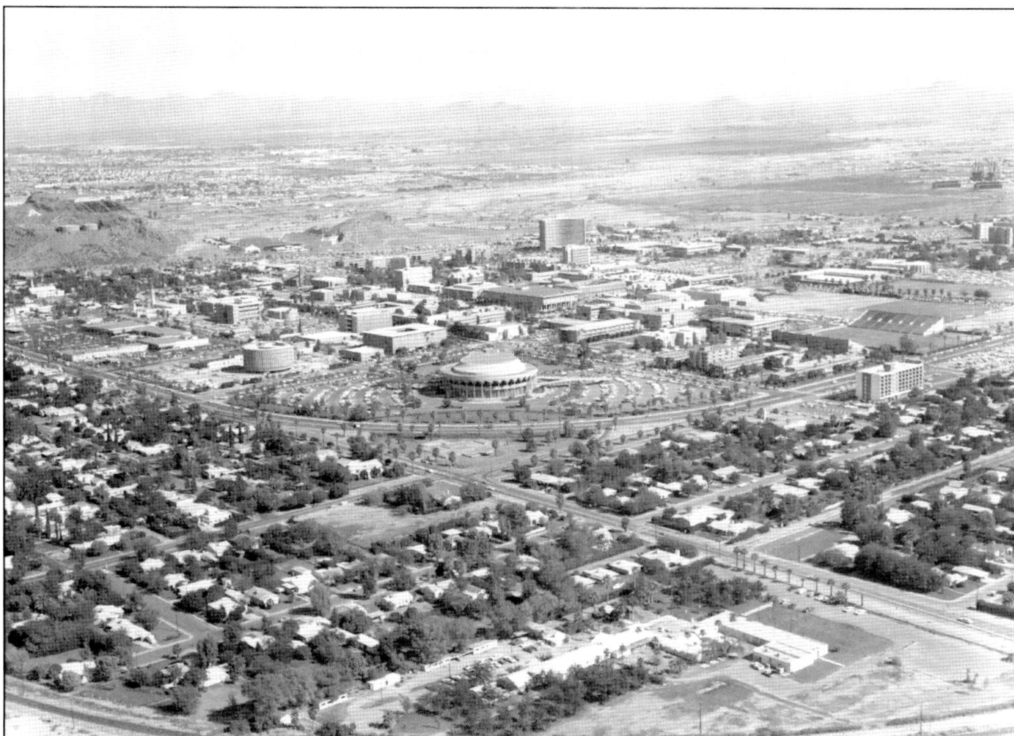

This mid-1960s aerial photograph shows part of the growth since 1895. Goodwin Stadium is visible, as is Sun Devil Stadium before its full glory. A far cry from the 20-acre start that still holds Old Main and the current University Club, the Tempe campus is over 600 acres and growing under the leadership of President Crow. Modernizing before our eyes, its pioneer heart will remain. (Courtesy of THM.)